A Canoeing and Kayaking Guide to the Streams of Kentucky

A Canoeing and Kayaking Guide to the Streams of Kentucky

by Bob Sehlinger

With an Introduction by Authur B. Lander, Jr.

Menasha Ridge Press
Birmingham, Alabama

Manufactured in the United States of America
Published by
Menasha Ridge Press
3169 Cahaba Heights Road
Birmingham, Alabama 35243

Fourth printing, 1994
ISBN 0-89732-140-5

Revision maps by RapiDesign of Waco, KY
Text revision by Tim Krasnansky
Cover photograph by Bill Millard
Cover design by Teresa Smith

This guidebook is dedicated to the incredibly talented instructors, guides, and support staff of SAGE, School of the Outdoors, Lexington and Louisville, Kentucky, and to William J. Schnute, who long ago planted the seed that came to fruition in this book.

ACKNOWLEDGEMENTS

Special thanks to my wife, Connie, to research assistants, Sherrin Scholl and Bill Conger, and to Robert A. Gunkler of the Kentucky State Department for Natural Resources and Environmental Protection. Without their efforts and unfailing belief in the value of this guidebook, the project could not have been accomplished.

Thanks also to the following advisers and contributors whose capable assistance allowed us to bring together the most current, accurate, and comprehensive data and graphics available:

David C. Bayha
Ed Benjamin
Mary Bergner
Ben Culbertson
Mickey Fulp
Bob McKenzie
Doug McKenzie
Dave Moccia
Steve Morgan
Dr. & Mrs. George A. Sehlinger
Jim & Chris Stamm
David Ross Stevens
Dr. Robert Walker
Henry Wallace

American White Water Affiliation
Canoe Magazine
Hydraulics Branches of the
Huntington, Nashville, and Louisville
Districts, U.S. Army Corps of Engineers
Kentucky Geological Survey
Rockcastle Adventures, Inc.

CONTENTS

INTRODUCTION

Wilderness-oriented recreation, canoeing and kayaking in particular, has become tremendously popular in the last decade. Millions of people, young and old alike, are rediscovering that self-confidence, determination, and appreciation of nature are as much a part of paddling as learning the basic strokes; and that drifting down a lazy, meandering river, or maneuvering a canoe or kayak through a jumble of boulders on a roller coaster of white-water, is not only great fun, but a genuine mental and physical challenge. Americans are adventuresome by character, and are quick to seek the exhilaration that only life in the outdoors can bring. Outdoor recreation has always been an integral part of our national heritage.

It is in this same spirit that we're proud to present *A Canoeing and Kayaking Guide to the Streams of Kentucky*, which we hope will serve as a point of departure for safety-conscious paddlers who wish to explore the many waterways Kentucky has to offer, but who may not have the benefit of a veteran paddler with them to point out potential hazards, or provide the pertinent information on access, running levels, river difficulty, and the like. With increasing numbers of paddlers taking to Kentucky's rivers and creeks, it is extremely important that concise and comprehensive information be available to assist canoeists and kayakers in running watercourses safely. Thus, this guidebook presents information on all of Kentucky's primary and secondary drainage systems with their paddling potential, to assist trip planners more carefully choose trips within their skill range, and at the same time not be limited to the more popular and celebrated runs.

There has been no attempt to make this book instructional or to outline the large body of material every paddler should be aware of before attempting to paddle on any moving water. The focal point and thrust of this guidebook is in geographic orientation of Kentucky's drainages, with specific attention to descriptions of individual streams. The sections on Kentucky's drainages, water quality, understanding hydrology, ecological considerations, hazards and safety, knowing your rights on the river, rating the river and the paddler, clubs and organizations, rental outlets, the bibliography, suggested reading, and a working glossary of terms are provided for background. All efforts have been made to provide the most comprehensive guidebook possible. (Should you note any inaccuracies or omissions, we would appreciate knowing about them. Please address all such information to Bob Sehlinger, c/o SAGE, School of the Outdoors, 209 East High Street, Lexington, Kentucky 40507.)

The essence of this guidebook will be the descriptions of the individual streams. Additionally, each run will be outlined in detail on one or more data sheets. Some of the rivers were divided into several sections because of their length and changing level of difficulty. The data for each section described will include: levels of difficulty (using both the International Scale of River Difficulty and a point system for matching the paddler with the river); suitable activities for each stream (day cruising or canoe camping); gradient (in feet per mile); *average* width; velocity (generally in feet per second); months normally runnable; minimum and maximum runnable water levels for both open and decked boats; monthly average water temperature; sources of additional information on water conditions; difficulties and dangers; a rescue index; portages; scouting requirements; interest highlights with a scenery rating; and an access code for identifying each put-in and take-out point.

This guidebook is the product of scouting miles of river, and hours of mapwork and research writing. It is to be understood that in no way can the basic maps that accompany the river descriptions replace topographical quadrangles in providing detailed information concerning terrain features, or county road maps for providing a better understanding of available primary and secondary access routes. Furthermore, rivers are constantly changing, not only through variation in water levels and through the natural process of erosion, but also through man's impact. At this writing, for instance, the construction of new highways is altering the Muddy Fork of the Little River, the Poor Fork of the Cumberland River, and Buck Creek. Proposals for an impoundment at Taylorsville on the Salt River, and a major recreational project for the Big South Fork of the Cumberland River, are prime examples of continuing competition for the use of Kentucky's paddling waters. With repairs completed on Wolf Creek Dam of Lake Cumberland, and the return of the lake to its normal summer pool, the lower Rockcastle Narrows will be several feet underwater, depriving paddlers of another noteworthy run.

But changes notwithstanding, the variety of runs, not only in difficulty, but in scenery encountered, is indeed astounding. Kentucky's rich water resources are a promised land to the enthusiastic paddler. Enjoy Kentucky's rivers and run them safely. Good paddling!

Arthur B. Lander, Jr.
St. Matthews, Kentucky
January, 1978

PART ONE

Red River   Photograph courtesy of the Commonwealth of Kentucky,
Department of Public Information

THE DRAINAGES OF KENTUCKY

All the major rivers in Kentucky flow in a westerly, or north-westerly, direction. From east to west, the major rivers are the Big Sandy, Licking, Kentucky, Salt, Green, Tradewater, Cumberland, and Tennessee. They all empty into the Ohio River, which forms the northern boundary of Kentucky for 664 miles from Catletts-burg on the east to the Mississippi River on the west. About 97 percent of the total area of the commonwealth drains into the Ohio River.

The claim that Kentucky has more miles of running water than any state except Alaska is not unfounded; there are approximately 54,000 miles of streams and rivers when you add up all the major tributaries to the Ohio River, plus Mayfield Creek, Obion Creek and Bayou Du Chien, which drain into the Mississippi River in the far western Jackson Purchase region. The Tennessee River, which empties into the Ohio River at Paducah, is the fifth-largest river system in the United States, with a basin of more than 40,000 square miles occupying portions of seven states (1,055 square miles are in Kentucky alone). The Ohio River at its mouth is exceeded in volume of flow only by the lower Mississippi River. On the average, the Ohio River discharges three times more water than the upper Mississippi River, and about three and one-third times more water than the Missouri River. As a point of comparison, the Ohio's volume is about the same as both the Columbia and St. Lawrence rivers, major rivers of the North American continent.

The Cumberland and Green River basins both have consider-ably more square miles than any one of Kentucky's other five major basins. The Cumberland River basin drains more than 18,000 square miles in Kentucky and Tennessee. The river's head-waters are in extreme southeastern Kentucky (Poor Fork in Letcher County and Martins Fork in Bell County) and its mouth is at Smithland, in Livingston County of western Kentucky. Between the so-called "upper and lower" Cumberland basins, the river flows through Tennessee, where at least half of its basin lies. The Green River and its many tributaries flow across central Kentucky, encompassing more than 9,000 square miles of basin. In decreasing basin size are: the Kentucky River, roughly 6,940 square miles; the Licking River, 3,670 square miles; the Salt River, 2,890 square miles; and finally the Big Sandy River basin at Kentucky's far eastern boundary with 2,280 square miles in Kentucky alone.

WATER QUALITY

The quality of streams in Kentucky is generally good although portions of several drainages are polluted by acid water and washings from coal mines, brine from oil fields, and sewage and industrial wastes.

The Levisa Fork of the Big Sandy River is basically a high-quality mountain stream. However, some mine drainage has made the water hard and high in sulfates. The upper Cumberland River also has high-quality water typical of a mountain stream, but it receives much less mine drainage and so is of better quality than Levisa Fork. The Kentucky River drains a limestone area and is typical of many of Kentucky's streams; its water is hard and of the calcium bicarbonate type. The Tradewater River is an example of a small river that contains much acid from iron, manganese, and aluminum compounds, while Mayfield Creek is an example of the excellent water in the Jackson Purchase region.

In general, the water in small creeks in Kentucky is of the highest quality, especially in the mountains, but it is also the easiest to pollute because of the limited flows. Water in the large rivers, such as the Kentucky, Green, Tennessee, and Ohio, is more or less uniform in quality (or lack thereof) because the flows of these rivers tend to decrease the differences in the quality of the water entering from the tributaries. Table 1 shows, very briefly, the variations in quality and types of water in representative streams.

KENTUCKY WILD RIVERS SYSTEM

Eight Kentucky rivers of exceptional quality and aesthetic character are protected from development by the Wild Rivers System (Kentucky Revised Statute 146.200–146.360) enacted by the Kentucky Legislature. The rivers' rights-of-way are protected from strip mining, the construction of any impoundments, new roads, and buildings, or timber cutting within 2,000 feet of the middle of the watercourses.

The eight rivers, six of which are classic paddling streams, are

TABLE 1
MINERAL QUALITY OF REPRESENTATIVE KENTUCKY STREAMS

STREAM	RANGE OF VALUES	DISSOLVED SOLIDS (PPM)	HARDNESS (PPM)	pH	PRIMARY WATER TYPE
Levisa Fork at Paintsville	High Low Average	380 75 140	175* 40 70	8.3† 6.3 7.5	Calcium, magnesium, or sodium sulfate. Contains some mine drainage.
Cumberland River at Williamsburg	High Low Average	276 59 140	105 28 65	7.1 6.4 7.3	Calcium, magnesium, or sodium bicarbonate sulfate type. Good mountain water.
Kentucky River at Frankfort	High Low Average	250 40 130	165 20 95	8.2 6.2 7.3	Calcium bicarbonate type typical of country rich in limestone.
Tradewater River at Olney	High Low Average	1,700 54 320	1,000 31 195	7.7 3.3 6.0	Calcium or magnesium sulfate type, frequently acid from mine drainage.
Mayfield Creek at Lovelaceville	High Low Average	82 50 67	33 12 22	6.9 6.0 6.5	Calcium or sodium bicarbonate type. Very good, typical of Jackson Purchase area.

*Readings above 40 are in increasing hardness, and below 40, increasing softness.
†Readings above 7.7 are alkaline, and those below 6.2 are acid.

remote and as unspoiled as any in Kentucky, and have rocky cliffs, sweeping forests and abundant fish and wildlife resources along their free-flowing paths. They are essentially untouched by the works of man, and are rich in recreational opportunity. Their protection is in the hands of Kentucky's Department for Natural Resources and Environmental Protection.

Six of Kentucky's eight wild rivers are in the upper Cumberland basin, one is in the Kentucky River drainage, and one is in the Green River system. There is one wild river in each of Kentucky's two national parks and six in Daniel Boone National Forest (including one in a national geological area in the forest). The wild rivers and their boundaries are:

Cumberland River—16.1 miles, from Summer Shoals to the backwaters of Lake Cumberland, in McCreary and Whitley counties. (1.)

Red River—9.1 miles, from the KY 746 bridge to the mouth of Swift Camp Creek, in the Red River Gorge Geological Area; in Wolfe and Powell counties of the Stanton District of Daniel Boone National Forest. (2.)

Rockcastle River—15.9 miles of whitewater, from the Old KY 80 bridge to the backwaters of Lake Cumberland, in Pulaski and Laurel counties. (3.)

Green River—26.0 miles in the confines of Mammoth Cave National Park; a classic flatwater run with camping allowed on islands or riverside sites, abundant wildlife, and rivers bubbling up from underground caverns. (4.)

Big South Fork of the Cumberland River—10.2 miles of one of the most celebrated whitewater runs in the eastern U.S., from the Tennessee border to Blue Heron, in Whitley County. (5.)

Rock Creek—18 miles of good rainbow trout stream, from the Tennessee border to the White Oak Junction bridge. (6.)

Martins Fork of the Cumberland River—3.9 miles of shallow, non-navigable water extending from the eastern boundary of Cumberland Gap National Historical Park to KY 987. The headwaters of this crystal clear, brook trout-stocked stream are in a grove of virgin hemlock trees. (7.)

Little South Fork of the Cumberland River—10.4 miles, from the KY 92 bridge in the backwaters of Lake Cumberland, in Wayne and McCreary counties. (8.)

COMPONENTS OF THE KENTUCKY WILD RIVERS SYSTEM

Rock Creek   Photograph courtesy of the Commonwealth of Kentucky, Department of Public Information

UNDERSTANDING HYDROLOGY

Understanding hydrology—how rivers are formed and how they affect man's activities—is at the very heart of paddling. To aid the paddler, brief discussions of the effects on paddling of seasonal variations of rainfall, water temperature, and volume, velocity gradient, and stream morphology will be presented.

The most basic concept about water that all paddlers must understand is, of course, the hydrologic or water cycle, which moves water from the earth to the atmosphere and back again. Water that falls to the earth is surface runoff that drains directly into rivers or their tributaries; or it is retained by the soil and used by plants; or it may be returned directly to the atmosphere through evaporation; or else it becomes groundwater by filtering down through subsoil and layers of rock. Sometimes precipitation is funnelled underground through sinkholes to underwater rivers (as in central Kentucky's cave region where a major surface basin is conspicuously absent).

Seasonal variations in the flow levels of watercourses are based on fluctuations in rainfall. Kentucky's yearly average of 46 inches of rain is equal to about 32 trillion gallons a year for all of Kentucky. About 37 percent of this, or 12 trillion gallons, runs either directly into the streams or through the ground and eventually into the streams. This much water alone would keep the Ohio River flowing for about 70 days at average flow. March and April are Kentucky's rainiest months. An average of 5.05 inches of precipitation a month falls in March, the rainiest month. October is the driest month, with an average of 2.35 inches of precipitation.

Mayfield Creek is in the Jackson Purchase region, a part of the state underlaid with thick soils, sands, and gravels. Water stored in these materials during the winter and spring later seeps out to help maintain flow in hot, dry months. In the far eastern coal field region, land slopes are steep, bedrock appears at the surface, and

9

the soil is relatively thin. There is less opportunity and capacity for water storage in the ground.

Localized soil conditions have a great deal to do with stream flow as do plantlife, terrain slope, ground cover, and air temperature. In summer, during the peak growing season, water is used more readily by plants, and higher air temperatures encourage increased evaporation. The fall and winter low water periods are caused by decreased precipitation, although since the ground is frozen and plant use of water is for the most part halted, abnormally high amounts of rain, or water from melting snow, can cause flash floods because surface runoff is high—there's no place for the water to go but into creeks and rivers. Though surface runoff is first to reach the river, it is groundwater that keeps many larger streams flowing during rainless periods. Drought can lower the water table drastically. Soil erosion is related to surface runoff—hilly land in intensive agricultural use is a prime target for loss cf topsoil and flashflooding. The Salt River basin has severe soil erosion that creates continued and increasing chances of flooding. The Barren River basin, a tributary to the Green River, is intensely farmed, but the chance of flooding is less severe since the soil is absorbent and the terrain is relatively flat.

WATER TEMPERATURE

Water temperature is another important factor to be considered by paddlers because of obvious dangers of encountering cold water when you're not prepared for it.

Surface water temperatures tend to follow air temperatures. Generally, the shallower the stream or reservoir, the closer the water temperature will be to the air temperature. Streams show a wide variation in temperature throughout the year, ranging from a low of 32°F in winter to a high of about 85°F on some days in July, August, and early September. Streams also show a daily variation; the smaller the stream, the greater the variation, with the least variation occurring in large rivers. The Ohio River may change only one to two degrees in a day, whereas changes in a small stream can be almost equal to the range in the day's air temperature.

Coal-burning steam plants and industrial users may influence the water temperature in some rivers through thermal discharges. Usually, the added heat is lost within 20 miles downstream of the entry point, but this heat loss depends upon the amount of water used, the temperature of the waste water, the size of the stream, air temperature, and other factors.

VOLUME, VELOCITY, GRADIENT, AND STREAM MORPHOLOGY

Being able to recognize potential river hazards is dependent on a practical knowledge of river hydrology—why the water flows like it does. Since river channels vary greatly in depth and width, and the composition of stream beds and their gradient also enter into the river's character, the major components of stream flow bear explanation. *Discharge* is the volume of water moving past a given point of the river at any one time. The river current or

velocity is commonly expressed as the speed of water movement in feet per second, and *stage* is the river's height in feet based on an arbitrary measurement gauge. These terms are interrelated; increased water levels mean increased volume and velocity.

Another factor in assessing stream difficulty is *gradient,* which is expressed in feet per mile. As gradient increases, so does velocity. The streams profiled in this guidebook have gradients that range from about one foot per mile to an astounding 200 feet per mile. The gradient in any stream, or section of a stream, changes with land forms, the geology, of the basin. If a river flows over rock or soil with varying resistance to erosion, ledges, waterfalls, and rapids sometimes form, dramatically affecting gradient. Velocity is also affected by the width and depth of the streambed. Rapids form where streams are shallow and swift. Large obstructions in shallow streams of high velocity cause severe rapids. Within a given channel there are likely to be rapids with different levels of difficulty. The current on straight sections of river is usually fastest in the middle. The depth of water in river bends is determined by flow rates and soil types. Water tends to cut away the land and form deep holes on the outsides of bends where the current is the swiftest.

Cumberland Falls   Photograph courtesy of the Commonwealth of Kentucky, Department of Public Information

Hazards and Safety

Hazardous situations likely to be encountered on the river must be identified and understood for safe paddling. The lure of high adventure has in part explained why there are so many more paddlers these days. Unfortunately, an alarming number were not prepared for what they encountered and lost their lives.* They didn't use good judgment or just didn't understand the potential dangers.

AMERICAN WHITE WATER
AFFILIATION SAFETY CODE

The American White Water Affiliation's safety code is perhaps the most useful overall safety guideline available.

I. PERSONAL PREPAREDNESS AND RESPONSIBILITY
   1. Be a Competent Swimmer with ability to handle yourself underwater.
   2. Wear a Lifejacket.
   3. Keep Your Craft Under Control. Control must be good enough at all times to stop or reach shore before you each any danger. Do not enter a rapid unless you are reasonably sure you can safely navigate it or swim the entire rapid in event of capsize.
   4. Be Aware of River Hazards and Avoid Them. Following are the most frequent killers.
       A. HIGH WATER: The river's power and danger, and the difficulty of rescue increase tremendously as the flow rate increases. It is often misleading to judge river level at the put-in. Look at a narrow, critical passage. Could a sudden

---

*Paddling Fatality Facts: (1) Over three-quarters of the operators in canoe/kayak accidents have had not had any formal instruction; (2) 86 percent of fatalities occurred within 90 minutes of departure on an outing; (3) approximately 74 percent of victims encountered water temperatures less than 70°F. (From a presentation by the U.S. Coast Guard at the 1976 American Canoe Association instructors' conference in Chicago.)

rise from sun on a snow pack, rain, or a dam release occur on your trip?

B. COLD: Cold quickly robs one's strength, along with one's will and ability to save oneself. Dress to protect yourself from cold water and weather extremes. When the water temperature is less than 50 degrees F., a diver's wetsuit is essential for safety in event of an upset. Next best is wool clothing under a windproof outer garment such as a splash-proof nylon shell; in this case one should also carry matches and a complete change of clothes in a waterproof package. If, after prolonged exposure, a person experiences uncontrollable shaking or has difficulty talking and moving, he must be warmed immediately by whatever means available.

C. STRAINERS: Brush, fallen trees, bridge pilings, or anything else which allows river current to sweep through but pins boat and boater against the obstacle. The water pressure on anything trapped this way is overwhelming, and there may be little or no whitewater to warn of danger.

D. WEIRS, REVERSALS, AND SOUSE HOLES: The water drops over an obstacle, then curls back on itself in a stationary wave, as is often seen at weirs and dams. The surface water is actually going UPSTREAM, and this action will trap any floating object between the drop and the wave. Once trapped, a swimmer's only hope is to dive below the surface where current is flowing downstream or try to swim out the end of the wave.

5. Boating Alone is not recommended. The preferred minimum is three craft.

6. Have a Frank Knowledge of Your Boating Ability. Don't attempt waters beyond this ability. Learn paddling skills and teamwork, if in a multiple-manned craft, to match the river you plan to boat.

7. Be in Good Physical Condition consistent with the difficulties that may be expected.

8. Be Practiced in Escape from an overturned craft, in self-rescue, and in artificial respiration. Know first aid.

9. The Eskimo Roll should be mastered by kayakers and canoers planning to run large rivers and/or rivers with continuous rapids where a swimmer would have trouble reaching shore.

10. Wear a Crash Helmet where an upset is likely. This is essential in a kayak or covered canoe.

11. Be Suitably Equipped. Wear shoes that will protect your feet during a bad swim or a walk for help, yet will not interfere with swimming (tennis shoes recommended). Carry a knife and waterproof matches. If you need eyeglasses, tie them on and carry a spare pair. Do not wear bulky clothing that will interfere with your swimming when water-logged.

II. BOAT AND EQUIPMENT PREPAREDNESS

1. Test New and Unfamiliar Equipment before relying on it for difficult runs.

2. Be Sure Craft is in Good Repair before starting a trip. Eliminate sharp projections that could cause injury during a swim.

3. Inflatable craft should have Multiple Air Chambers and should be test inflated before starting a trip.

4. Have Strong, Adequately Sized Paddles or Oars for controlling the craft and carry sufficient spares for the length of the trip.

5. Install Flotation Devices in non-inflatable craft, securely fixed, and designed to displace as much water from the craft as possible.

6. Be Certain There is Absolutely Nothing to Cause Entanglement when coming free from an upset craft; i.e., a spray skirt that won't release or tangles around the legs; life jacket buckles, or clothing that might snag; canoe seats that lock on shoe heels; foot braces that fall or allow feet to jam under them; flexible decks that collapse on boater's legs when a kayak is trapped by water pressure; baggage that dangles in an upset; loose rope in the craft, or badly secured bow/stern lines.

7. Provide Ropes to Allow You to Hold Onto Your Craft in case of upset, and so that it may be rescued. Following are the recommended methods:

   A. KAYAKS AND COVERED CANOES should have 6 inch diameter grab loops of ¼ inch rope attached to bow and stern. A stern painter 7 or 8 feet long is optional and may be used if properly secured to prevent entanglement.

   B. OPEN CANOES should have bow and stern lines (painters) securely attached consisting of 8 to 10 feet of ¼ or ⅜ inch rope. These lines must be secured in such a way that they will not come loose accidentally and entangle the boaters during a swim, yet they must be ready for immediate use during an emergency. Attached balls, floats, and knots are not recommended.

   C. RAFTS AND DORIES should have taut perimeter grab lines threaded through the loops usually provided.

8. Respect Rules for Craft Capacity and know how these capacities should be reduced for whitewater use. (Life raft ratings must generally be halved.)

9. Carry Appropriate Repair Materials: tape (heating-duct tape) for short trips, complete repair kit for wilderness trips.

10. Car Top Racks Must Be Strong and positively attached to the vehicle, and each boat must be tied to each rack. In addition, each end of each boat should be tied to car bumper. Suction cup racks are poor. The entire arrangement should be able to withstand all but the most violent accident.

III. LEADER'S PREPAREDNESS AND RESPONSIBILITY

   1. River Conditions. Have a reasonable knowledge of the difficult parts of the run, of if an exploratory trip, examine maps to estimate the feasibility of the run. Be aware of possible rapid changes in river level, and how these changes can affect the difficulty of the run. If important, determine approximate flow

rate or level. If trip involves important tidal currents, secure tide information.

2. Participants. Inform participants of expected river conditions and determine if the prospective boaters are qualified for the trip. All decisions should be based on group safety and comfort. Difficult decisions on the participation of marginal boaters must be based on group strength.

3. Equipment. Plan so that all necessary group equipment is present on the trip; 50 to 100 foot throwing rope, first aid kit with fresh and adequate supplies, extra paddles, repair materials, and survival equipment if appropriate. Check equipment as necessary at the put-in, especially: life jackets, boat flotation, and any items that could prevent complete escape from the boat in case of an upset.

4. Organization. Remind each member of individual responsibility in keeping group compact and intact between leader and sweep (capable rear boater). If group is too large, divide into smaller groups, each of appropriate boating strength, and designate group leaders and sweeps.

5. Float Plan. If trip is into a wilderness area, or for an extended period, your plans should be filed with appropriate authorities, or left with someone who will contact them after a certain time. Establishment of checkpoints along the way at which civilization could be contacted if necessary should be considered. Knowing location of possible help could speed rescue in any case.

IV. IN CASE OF UPSET

1. Evacuate Your Boat Immediately if there is imminent danger of being trapped against logs, brush, or any other form of strainer.

2. Recover With an Eskimo Roll if Possible.

3. If You Swim, Hold Onto Your Craft. It has much flotation and is easy for rescuers to spot. Get to the upstream so craft cannot crush you against obstacles.

4. Release Your Craft if This Improves Your Safety. If rescue is not imminent and water is numbing cold, or if worse rapids follow, then strike out for the nearest shore.

5. Extend Your Feet Downstream and on the surface when swimming rapids to fend against rocks. Look Ahead. Avoid possible entrapment situations: rock wedges, fissures, strainers, brush, logs, weirs, reversals, and souse holes. Watch for eddies and slackwater so that you can be ready to use these when you approach. Use every opportunity to work your way toward shore.

6. If others spill, Go After the Boaters. Rescue boats and equipment only if this can be done safely.

V. INTERNATIONAL SCALE OF RIVER DIFFICULTY
(If rapids on a river generally fit into one of the following classifications, but the water temperature is below 50 degrees F., or if the trip is an extended trip in a wilderness area, the river should be considered one class more difficult than normal.)

CLASS I	Moving water with a few riffles and small waves. Few or no obstructions.
CLASS II	Easy rapids with waves up to 3 feet, and wide, clear channels that are obvious without scouting. Some maneuvering is required.
CLASS III	Rapids with high, irregular waves often capable of swamping an open canoe. Narrow passages that often require complex maneuvering. May require scouting from shore.
CLASS IV	Long, difficult rapids with constricted passages that often require precise maneuvering in very turbulent waters. Scouting from shore is often necessary, and conditions make rescue difficult. Generally not possible for open canoes. Boaters in covered canoes and kayaks should be able to Eskimo roll.
CLASS V	Extremely difficult, long, and very violent rapids with highly congested routes which nearly always must be scouted from shore. Rescue conditions are difficult and there is significant hazard to life in event of a mishap. Ability to Eskimo roll is essential for kayaks and canoes.
CLASS VI	Difficulties of Class V carried to the extreme of navigability. Nearly impossible and very dangerous. For teams of experts only, after close study and with all precautions taken.

INJURIES AND EVACUATIONS

Even allowing for careful preparation and attention to the rules of river safety, it remains a fact of life that people and boats are somewhat more fragile than rivers and rocks. Expressed differently, accidents do occur on paddling trips, and *all* boaters should understand that it can happen to them. Although virtually any disaster is possible on the river, there seems to be a small number of specific traumas and illnesses that occur more frequently than others. These include:

1. Hypothermia
2. Dislocated shoulder (especially common among decked boaters)
3. Sprained or broken ankles (usually sustained while scouting or getting into or out of the boat)
4. Head injuries (sustained in falls on shore or during capsize)
5. Hypersensitivity to insect bite (anaphylactic shock)
6. Heat trauma (sunburn, heat stroke, heat prostration, dehydration, etc.)
7. Food poisoning (often resulting from sun spoilage of lunch foods on a hot day)
8. Badly strained muscles (particularly of the lower back, upper arm, and the trapezius)

9. Hand and wrist injuries
10. Lacerations

What happens when one of the above injuries occurs on the river? Many paddlers are well prepared to handle the first aid requirements but are unfortunately ill prepared to handle the residual problems of continued care and evacuation. The following is an excerpt from "Wilderness Emergencies and Evacuations" by Ed Benjamin, Associate Program Director, SAGE, School of the Outdoors, "When a paddler is injured during a river trip he can usually be floated out in a canoe. Unfortunately, however, circumstances do sometimes arise when the victim is non-ambulatory, or when lack of open canoes or the nature of the river preclude floating the injured party out. In such a situation the trip leader would have to choose between sending for help or performing an overland evacuation."

When sending for help, send at least two people. Dispatch with them a marked map or drawing showing your location as exactly as possible (yes, that means pencil and paper should be part of every first aid kit). Also send a note giving directions for finding you plus information on the nature of your emergency and the type of assistance you require. Have your messengers call the proper agencies, such as the local police jurisdiction, a rescue squad, the U.S. Forest Service, the State Police, plus any nonofficial parties such as professional river outfitters who could lend special expertise to the rescue. This having been done, the messengers should be instructed to report the situation simply and factually to the families of the persons involved.

Many paddlers, unfortunately, do not know where they are except in relation to the river, and all too few carry topographical maps. Rescuers need to know exactly where you are in terms of the land, roads, etc. A helicopter pilot will not make much sense of the information that your victim is on the left bank below "Lunchstop Rapid." Establish shelter for yourselves and your victim; any rescue is going to take a long time. In the time it takes your messengers to walk out, organize help, and return to you, many hours or perhaps days will pass. Psychologically prepare yourself for a long wait. To expedite the rescue attempt, build a smokey fire to help your rescuers locate you.

Many people believe that if they are ever hurt in the wilderness, a helicopter will come fly them out. This is not necessarily so. Only if you are near a military air base or a civilian air rescue service, do you have a good chance of getting a helicopter. Even if one is available, there are several serious limitations. A rescue helicopter will not fly in bad weather, over a certain altitude, or at night. A helicopter needs a clear area about 150 feet in diameter, that is reasonably level in order to land. Moreover, the pilot will probably need some sort of wind indicator on the ground such as a wind sock or a smokey fire. All helicopters are not the same; most do not have a cable on which to raise a victim, and all have limitations on where they may hover. If a helicopter is successful in landing near you, do not approach the craft until the crew signals you to do so, and then only as the crew directs. In most situations the availability or applicability of a helicopter is doubtful. More likely you will be rescued by a group of volunteers who will drive to the nearest roadhead, reach you on foot, and carry the victim out in a litter. Be advised that volunteer rescue teams are usually slow and sometimes lack adequate training (particularly for a river or climbing rescue). Occasionally you may encounter a top-notch mountain rescue team, but this is rare, especially in Kentucky.

If help cannot be obtained, or if you have a large, well-equipped group, it may be possible to carry the victim out yourself. A litter can be improvised from trees, paddles, packs, etc. Any litter used should be sufficiently strong to protect your victim from further injury. If you do attempt to evacuate the victim yourself, be advised that overland evacuations (even with the best equipment) are extremely difficult and exhausting and are best not attempted unless there are eight or more people to assist. When carrying a litter, a complement of six bearers is ideal. Not only does this spread the load, but, if one bearer looses footing, it is unlikely that the litter will be dropped. Bearers should be distributed so that there are two by the victim's head, two by the feet, and one on each side in the middle. Those carrying at the head of the victim must pay careful attention to the victim. An unconscious victim requires constant checking of vital signs. A conscious victim will be uncomfortable and frightened and will need reassurance. Bear in mind that a day warm enough to make a litter carrier perspire may be cool enough to induce hypothermia in an unmoving victim. Always have one bearer set the pace and choose the safest and easiest route. Go slow and easy and be careful. Always use a rope to belay the litter from above when ascending or descending a slope; a dropped litter can slide a long way. Paddlers should insist that their partners learn first aid. First aid gear (including pencil and paper), extra topographical maps, and rope should be carried in the sweep boat.

HYPOTHERMIA

Hypothermia, the lowering of the body's core temperature, and death from drowning or cardiac arrest after sudden immersion in cold water, are two serious hazards to the winter, early spring, and late fall paddler. Cold water robs the victim of the ability and desire to save him- or herself. When the body's temperature drops appreciably below the normal 98.6°F, sluggishness sets in, breathing is difficult, coordination is lost to even the most athletic person, pupils dilate, speech becomes slurred, and thinking irrational. Finally unconsciousness sets in, and then, death. Hypothermia can occur in a matter of minutes in water just a few degrees above freezing, but 50-degree water is unbearably cold.

To make things worse, panic can set in when the paddler is faced with a long swim through rapids. Heat loss occurs much more quickly than believed. A drop in body temperature to 96°F makes swimming and pulling yourself to safety almost impossible, and tragically, the harder you struggle, the more heat your body loses. Body temperatures below 90°F lead to unconsciousness, and a further drop to about 77°F usually results in immediate death. (But this same lowering of the body temperature slows metabolism and delays brain death in cases of drowning, therefore heroic rescue efforts have a higher chance of success.)

Paddlers subjected to spray and wetting from waves splashing into an open boat are in almost as much danger of hypothermia as a paddler completely immersed after a spill. The combination of cold air and water drain the body of precious heat at an alarming rate, although it is the wetness that causes the major losses since water conducts heat away from the body twenty times faster than air. Clothes lose their insulating properties quickly when immersed in water, and skin temperatures will rapidly drop to within a few degrees of the water temperature. The body, hard pressed to conserve heat, will then reduce blood circulation to the extremitites. This reduction in blood flowing to arms and legs makes movement and heavy work next to impossible. Muscular activity increases heat loss because blood forced to the extremities is quickly cooled by the cold water. It's a deadly, vicious cycle.

The best safeguards against cold weather hazards are recognizing the symptoms of hypothermia, preventing exposure to cold by wearing proper clothing (wool and waterproof outerwear or wet suits), understanding and respecting cold weather, knowing how the body gains, loses, and conserves body heat, and knowing how to treat hypothermia when it is detected. Actually, cold weather deaths may be attributed to a number of factors: physical exhaustion, inadequate food intake, dehydration of the body, and psychological elements such as fear, panic, and despair. Factors such as body fat, the metabolism rate of an individual, and skin thickness are variables in a particular person's reaction and endurance when immersed in cold water. Since the rate of metabolism is actually the rate at which the body produces heat from "burning" fats, carbohydrates, and proteins, one person may have a higher tolerance for cold weather than another. Stored fatty tissues also help the body resist a lowering of its core temperature. Shivering is "involuntary exercise"; the body is calling on its energy resources to produce heat. Proper food intake and sufficient water to prevent dehydration are important in any cold weather strenuous exercise, especially paddling.

The key to successfully bringing someone out of hypothermia is understanding that their body must recieve heat from an *external source*. In a field situation, strip off all wet clothes and get the victim into a sleeping bag with another person. Skin to skin transfer of body heat is by far the best method of getting the body's temperature up. By all means don't let the victim go to sleep, and feed him or her warm liquids. Build a campfire if possible. Mouth-to-mouth resuscitation or external cardiac massage may be necessary in extreme cases when breathing has stopped, but remember that a person in the grips of hypothermia has a significantly reduced metobolic rate so, the timing of artificial respiration should correspond to the victim's slowed breathing.

RATING THE RIVER— RATING THE PADDLER

For several years concerned paddlers have sought to objectively rate rivers. Central among their tools has been the International Scale of River Difficulty. While certainly a useful tool, and by no means outdated, the International Scale lacks precision and invites subjective, judgemental error. A more objective yardstick is the recently developed Difficulty Rating Chart for rivers that is based on a point system. While more cumbersome, it does succeed in describing a river more or less as it really is. Gone is the common confusion of a single rapid being described as Class II by the veteran while the novice perceives a roaring Class IV. Also eliminated is the double standard by which a river is rated Class III for open canoes but only Class II for decked boats. Instead, points are awarded as prescribed for conditions observed on the day the river is to be run. The total number of points describe the general level of difficulty.

Once the basic difficulty rating is calculated for a river, however, how is it to be matched against the skill level of a prospective paddler? The American Whitewater Affiliation relates the point system for rivers back to the International Scale and to traditional paddler classifications.

Class	Total Points	Skill Required
I	0–7	Practiced Beginner
II	8–14	Intermediate
III	15–21	Experienced
IV	22–28	Highly Skilled
V	29–35	Team of Experts
VI	36–42	Team of Experts with every precaution.

This helps, but only to the extent that the individual paddler understands the definitions of "Practiced Beginner," "Intermediate," "Experienced," and so on. If, like most of us, the paddler

23

finds these traditional titles ambiguous and hard to differentiate, he or she will probably classify himself or herself according to self-image. When this occurs, we are back to where we started.

Correctly observing the need for increased objectivity in rating paddlers as well as in rating rivers, several paddling clubs have developed self-evaluation systems where points are awarded to paddlers that correspond to the points scale of the river rating chart (Table 2). Thus an individual can determine a point total through self-evaluation and compare his or her skill, in quantified terms, to any river rated through use of the chart. The individual paddler, for instance, may compile 18 points through self-evaluation and note that this rating compares favorably with the difficulty rating of 17 points and unfavorably with a difficulty rating of 23 points. It should be reiterated here, however, that river ratings via the River Difficulty Chart pertain to a river only on a given day and at a specific water level. Generalized ratings, when given, represent the difficulty of the river under ideal weather and water conditions.

The most widely publicized of the paddler self-evaluations was created by the Keel-Haulers Canoe Club of Ohio. This system brings the problem of matching paddlers with rivers into perspective but seems to overemphasize nonpaddling skills. One of our canoe clinic students who is athletically inclined but almost totally without paddling skill achieved a rating of 15 points using the Keel-Haulers system. His rating, based almost exclusively on general fitness and strength, incorrectly implied that he was capable of handling many Class-II and Class-III rivers. A second problem evident in the system is lack of depth in skill category descriptions. Finally, confusion exists in several rating areas as to whether the evaluation applies to open canoes, decked boats, or both.

To remedy these perceived shortcomings and to bring added objectivity to paddler self-evaluation, I have attempted to refine the paddler rating system. Admittedly the refined system is more complex and exhaustive, but I hope not more so than warranted by the situation. Heavy emphasis is placed on paddling skills with description adopted from several different evaluation formats including a non-numerical system proposed by Dick Schwind.*

Instructions: All items, except the first, carry points that may be added to obtain an overall rating. All items except "Rolling Ability" apply to both open and decked boats. Rate open and decked boat skills separately.

*Schwind, Dick; "Rating System for Boating Difficulty," American Whitewater Journal, Volume 20, Number 3, May/June 1975.

1. **Prerequisite Skills:** Before paddling on moving current, the paddler should:
   a. Have some swimming ability.
   b. Be able to paddle instinctively on nonmoving water (lake). (This presumes knowledge of basic strokes.)
   c. Be able to guide and control the canoe from either side without changing paddling sides.
   d. Be able to guide and control the canoe (or kayak) while paddling backwards.
   e. Be able to move the canoe (or kayak) laterally.
   f. Understand the limitations of the boat.
   g. Be practiced in "wet exit" if in a decked boat.

2. **Equipment:** Award points on the suitablity of your equipment to whitewater. Whether you own, borrow, or rent the equipment makes no difference. *Do not* award points for both *Open Canoe* and *Decked Boat.*

   Open Canoe

0 Points:	Any canoe less than 16 ft. for tandem; any canoe less than 15 ft. for solo.
1 Point:	Canoe with moderate rocker, full depth, and recurved bow; should be 16 ft. or more in length for tandem and 15 ft. or more in length for solo and have bow and stern painters.
2 Points:	Whitewater canoe: Strong rocker design, full bow with recurve, full depth amidships, no keel; meets or exceeds minimum length requirements as described under "1 Point"; made of hand-laid fiberglass, Kevlar, Marlex, or ABS *Royalex; bow and stern painters.* Canoe as described under "1 Point" but with extra flotation.
3 Points:	Canoe as described under "2 Points" but with extra flotation.

   Decked Boat (K-1, K-2, C-1, C-2)

0 Points:	Any decked boat lacking full flotation, spray skirt, or foot braces.
1 Point:	Any fully equipped decked boat with a wooden frame.
2 Points:	Decked boat with full flotation, spray skirt and foot braces; has grab loops; made of hand-laid fiberglass, Marlex, or Kevlar.
3 Points:	Decked boat with foam wall reinforcement and split flotation; Neoprene spray skirt; boat has knee braces, foot braces, and grab loops; made of hand-laid fiberglass or Kevlar only.

3. **Experience:** Compute the following to determine *preliminary points,* then convert the preliminary points to *final* points according to the conversion table.

TABLE 2
RATING THE RIVER

	Factors Related Primarily To Success in Negotiating SECONDARY FACTORS			Factors Affecting Both Success & Safety PRIMARY FACTORS					Factors Related Primarily To Safe Rescue SECONDARY FACTORS		
PTS	Bends	Length (feet)	Gradient (ft./mile)	Obstacles (rocks and trees)	Waves	Turbulence	Resting or rescue spots	Water Velocity	Width and depth	Temp. (F)	Accessibility
0	Few, very gradual	<100 feet	Less than >5 ft. regular slope	None	Few inches high, avoidable	None	Almost anywhere	<3 mph.	Narrow (<75 feet); and shallow (<3 feet)	>65°	Road along river
1	Many, gradual	100–700 ft.	5–15 ft., regular slope	Few. Passage almost straight through	Low (up to 1 ft.), regular, avoidable	Minor eddies		3–6 mph	Wide (>75 feet) (<3 feet)	55°–65°	<1 hour travel by foot or water
2	Few, sharp blind. Scouting necessary	700–5,000 ft.	15–40 ft., ledges or steep drops	Courses easily recognizable	Low to med. (up to 3 ft.), regular, avoidable	Medium eddies		6–10 mph	<75 feet >3 feet	45°–55°	1 hour to 1 day travel foot or water
3		>5,000 ft.	>40 steep drops, small falls	Maneuvering. Course not easily recognizable	Med. to large (up to 5 ft.), mostly regular, avoidable	Strong eddies and cross currents	A good one below every danger spot	>10 mph or flood	>75 feet >3 feet	<45°	>1 day travel by foot or water

TABLE 2—Continued

4	Intricate maneuvering; course hard to recognize	Large irregular, avoidable or, med. to large, unavoidable	Very strong eddies, strong currents
5	Course tortuous; frequent scouting	Large, irregular, unavoidable	Large scale eddies and cross currents some up and down
6	Very tortuous; always scout from shore	Very large, >5 ft. irregular, unavoidable, spec. equipment required	Almost none

SOURCE: Prepared by Guidebook Committee—AWWA (From "American White Water," Winter, 1957)

NOTE: RATING	APPROXIMATE DIFFICULTY	TOTAL POINTS (from above)	APPROXIMATE SKILL REQUIRED
I	Easy	0–7	Practiced Beginner
II	Requires Care	8–14	Intermediate
III	Difficult	15–21	Experienced
IV	Very Difficult	22–28	Highly Skilled (Several years with organized group)
V	Exceedingly Difficult	29–35	Team of Experts
VI	Utmost Difficulty-Near Limit of Navigability		

Conversion Table

Preliminary Points	Final Points
0–20	0
21–60	1
61–100	2
101–200	3
201–300	4
301–up	5

Note: This is the only evaluation item where it is possible to accrue more than 3 points.

Number of days spent each year paddling Class-I rivers   × 1 = _____
Number of days spent each year paddling Class-II rivers   × 2 = _____
Number of days spent each year paddling Class-III rivers   × 3 = _____
Number of days spent each year paddling Class-IV rivers   × 4 = _____
Number of days spent each year paddling Class-V rivers   × 5 = _____

Preliminary Points Subtotal   _____

Number of years paddling experience _____ × subtotal =

Total Preliminary Points ⋅   _____

4. **Swimming:**
   - 0 Points: Cannot swim
   - 1 Point: Weak swimmer
   - 2 Points: Average swimmer
   - 3 Points: Strong swimmer (competition level or skin diver)

5. **Stamina:**
   - 0 Points: Cannot run mile in less than 10 minutes
   - 1 Point: Can run the mile in 7 to 10 minutes
   - 2 Points: Can run the mile in less than 7 minutes

6. **Upper Body Strength:**
   - 0 Points: Cannot do 15 push-ups
   - 1 Point: Can do 16 to 25 push-ups
   - 2 Points: Can do more than 25 push-ups

7. **Boat Control:**
   - 0 Points: Can keep boat fairly straight
   - 1 Point: Can manuever in moving water; can avoid big obstacles
   - 2 Points: Can manuever in heavy water; knows how to work with the current
   - 3 Points: Finesse in boat placement in all types of water, using current to maximum advantage

8. **Aggressiveness:**
   - 0 Points: Does not play or work river at all
   - 1 Point: Timid; plays a little on familiar streams
   - 2 Points: Plays a lot; works most rivers hard
   - 3 Points: Plays in heavy water with grace and confidence

9. **Eddy Turns:**
   - 0 Points: Has difficulty making eddy turns from moderate current
   - 1 Point: Can make eddy turns in either direction from

moderate current; can enter moderate current from eddy

2 Points: Can catch medium eddies in either direction from heavy current; can enter very swift current from eddy

3 Points: Can catch small eddies in heavy current

10. **Ferrying:**
0 Points: Cannot ferry

1 Point: Can ferry upstream and downstream in moderate current

2 Points: Can ferry upstream in heavy current; can ferry downstream in moderate current

3 Points: Can ferry upstream and downstream in heavy current

11. **Water Reading:**
0 Points: Often in error

1 Point: Can plan route in short rapid with several well-spaced obstacles

2 Points: Can confidently run lead in continuous Class II; can predict the effects of waves and holes on boat

3 Points: Can confidently run lead in continuous Class III; has knowledge to predict and handle the effects of reversals, side currents, and turning drops

12. **Judgement:**
0 Points: Often in error

1 Point: Has average ability to analyze difficulty of rapids

2 Points: Has good ability to analyze difficulty of rapids and make independent judgements as to which should not be run

3 Points: Has the ability to assist fellow paddlers in evaluating the difficulty of rapids; can explain subtleties to paddlers with less experience

13. **Bracing:**
0 Points: Has difficulty bracing in Class-II rivers

1 Point: Can correctly execute bracing strokes in Class-II water

2 Points: Can correctly brace in intermittent whitewater with medium waves and vertical drops of 3 ft. or less

3 Points: Can brace effectively in continuous whitewater with large waves and large vertical drops (4 ft. and up)

14. **Rescue Ability:**
0 Points: Self-rescue in flatwater

1 Point: Self-rescue in mild whitewater

2 Points: Self-rescue in Class III; can assist others in mild whitewater

3 Points: Can assist others in heavy whitewater

15. Rolling Ability:

0 Points:	Can only roll in pool
1 Point:	Can roll 3 out of 4 times in moving current
2 Points:	Can roll 3 out of 4 times in Class-II whitewater
3 Points:	Can roll 4 out of 5 times in Class-III and -IV whitewater

ECOLOGICAL CONSIDERATIONS

Presenting a set of ecological guidelines for all paddlers sounds like preaching, but with the number of persons using our creeks and rivers today, it is indeed a valid point. Many of the streams listed in this guide flow through national parks and forests, state-owned forests and wildlife management areas, and privately owned lands that in some cases are superior in quality and aesthetics to lands under public ownership. It is the paddling community's responsibility to uphold the integrity of these lands and their rivers by exercising ecologically sound guidelines. Litter, fire scars, pollution from human excrement and cutting live trees is unsightly and affects the land in a way that threatens to ruin the outdoor experience for everyone.

Paddlers should pack out everything they packed in: all paper litter and such nonbiodegradable items as cartons, foil, plastic jugs, and cans. Help keep our waterways clean for those who follow. If you are canoe camping, leave your campsite in better shape than you found it. If you must build a fire, build it at an established site, and when you leave, dismantle rock fireplaces, thoroughly drown all flames and hot coals, and scatter the ashes. Never cut live trees for firewood (in addition to destroying a part of the environment, they don't burn well). Dump all dishwater in the woods away from watercourses. Emulate the cat, bury all excrement.

Kentucky River at Frankfort   Photograph courtesy of the Commonwealth of Kentucky, Department of Public Information

KNOWING YOUR RIGHTS
ON THE RIVER

The definition of a "navigable" stream is open to discussion. The term is not clear and its interpretation has sparked controversy all across the country. In Kentucky, a navigable stream is one that can support either commerical or recreational boating. That covers a lot of water—the commercial classification meaning specifically barge traffic, the recreational aspect connoting power-boats, canoes, kayaks, rafts, houseboats, and so on. It's a broad, debatable term especially in the eyes of the mining industry, which cannot pollute navigable waters without being fined. Attempts have been made in the past to protect all waterways from flagrant pollution, but the measure met with defeat in the state legislature due to heavy opposition from mining lobbyists.

The paddler's right to run rivers, all of which are "in the public domain," is guaranteed in Kentucky statutes. Landowners' rights to prohibit trespassing on their land along creeks, if they so desire, are also guaranteed. Therefore, access to rivers must be secured at highway rights-of-way or on publicly owned lands if permission to cross privately owned lands cannot be secured. In granting you access to a river, landowners are extending a privilege to you as they extend such to hunters who stop by their doors and seek permission to shoot doves in their cornfields. Don't betray landowners' trust if they extend to you the privilege to camp or launch canoes or kayaks from their riverbanks. Don't litter, drive through newly planted fields, or forget to close gates. Tenure of land, landholding, and the right to do with it what you want, is serious business to landowners. Some farmers can't accept the concept of "land stewardship" ascribed to by many city paddlers today. They don't feel any compulsion or responsibility towards the paddling community and their pursuit of legal rights. In some cases they might even resent people driving hundreds of miles for the pleasure of floating down a river. They may even feel that they "own" the river you want to paddle.

On the other hand, it may be that the landowner you seek permission from is intrigued with paddling and will be quite friendly and approachable. Value this friendship and don't give cause to deny you access to the river at some time in the future.

Paddlers are trespassing when they portage, camp, or even stop for a lunch break, if they disembark from their boats on the water. If you are approached by a landowner when trespassing, by all means be cordial and understanding and explain your predicament (in the case of a portage or lunch break). Never knowingly camp on private land without permission. If you do encounter a perturbed landowner, don't panic. Keep cool and be respectful.

Landowners certainly have the right to keep you off their land, and the law will side with them unless they inflict harm upon you, in which case they may be both civilly or criminally liable. If you threaten a landowner verbally, and physically move towards him or her with apparent will to do harm, he or she has all the rights of self-defense and can protect him- or herself in accordance with the perceived danger that you impose. Likewise, if the landowner points a gun at you, fires warning shots, assaults, injures, or wounds you or a boater in your group, you are certainly in the right to protect yourself. The landowner has no right to detain you as if holding you for the sheriff. If you fear for your own life at the hands of the landowner, you do have the right to protect yourself.

The confrontations between belligerent paddlers and cantankerous landowners are to be avoided, that's for sure. Although the happenstance of such a meeting may be rare, paddlers nonetheless should know their rights, and the rights of landowners. Judges don't like trespassers any more than they like landowners who shoot trespassers.

How to Use Stream Information

For each stream in this guide there are a description, a data sheet, and at least one map. (Although both the Big Sandy and Ohio rivers are within Kentucky's borders, they have not been included in this guidebook because they are commercial, wide and nonscenic, and have numerous, obvious access points.)

DESCRIPTIONS

These are intended to give you a feel for the stream and its surroundings, and are presented in general, nontechnical terms.

DATA SHEETS

Each data sheet provides the necessary technical and quantative information for each of the streams listed, as well as some additional descriptive data. Occasionally certain facts will be treated in both the verbal description and the data sheet for added emphasis. Listed below are fuller explanations of many of the categories found on the data sheets.

LEVEL OF DIFFICULTY. The level of difficulty is given according to the International Scale of River Difficulty and according to the River Evaluation Chart on page 26. Both ratings are relative and pertain to the stream described under more or less ideal water levels and weather conditions. For streams with two International Scale ratings, the first represents the average level of difficulty of the entire run and the second (expressed parenthetically) represents the level of difficulty of the most difficult section or rapids on the run. Paddlers are cautioned that changes in water levels or weather conditions can alter *stated average* difficulty rating appreciably.

APPROPRIATE FOR. This item was included strictly for convenience. For a better indicator of whether or not a listed stream is for you, evaluate yourself according to the paddler self-evaluation format on pages 25–30, and match your numerical score with the numerical point rating of the river. For definitional purposes, "families" connotes adults of varying skill levels who want to take possibly nonswimming adults or children in the canoe with them. (We always assume that personal flotation devices, PFD's, e.g., life-jackets) will be worn by all parties on moving water. We also assume that no passengers will be carried in whitewater). "Beginners" are paddlers with knowledge of strokes and self-rescue who can manuever their boat more or less intuitively on still water (lakes and ponds). True "intermediates" meet all "beginner" qualifications, have a working knowledge of river dynamics, have some ability in rescuing others, and (for this guidebook) are competent and at home on Class-II whitewater. "Advanced paddlers" (not "experts") are paddlers who possess all the foregoing qualifications in addition to specialized rescue skills, and who are competent and at home on Class-III and -IV whitewater. Needless to say, these definitions could be refined or elaborated ad infinitum. They are not intended to be all-inclusive but rather to give the reader a reasonable idea of how to classify him- or herself and how experienced practitioners of the sport may tend to class him or her.

GRADIENT. Gradient is expressed in feet per mile and refers to the steepness of the stream bed over a certain distance. It is important to remember that gradient (or "drop" as paddlers refer to it) is an average figure and does not tell the paddler when or how the drop occurs. A stream that has a listed gradient of 25 feet per mile may drop gradually in one- or two-inch increments (like a long, rocky slide) for the course of a mile or it may drop only slightly over the first 0.9 of a mile and then suddenly drop 24 feet at one waterfall. As a general rule, gradient can be used as a rough indicator of level of difficulty for a given stream (i.e., the greater the gradient, the more difficult the stream). In practice, gradient is almost always considered in conjunction with other information.

VELOCITY. This figure represents the speed of the current, on the average, in nonflood conditions. Velocity can vary incredibly from section to section on a given stream depending on the stream's width, volume, and gradient at any point along its length. Velocity is a partial indicator of how much reaction time you might have on a certain river. Paddlers are known to describe a high velocity stream as "coming at them pretty fast," meaning that the speed of the current does not allow them much time for decision and action.

MONTHS RUNNABLE. The months given are based on the average rainfall for a year.

RUNNABLE WATER LEVEL: *MINIMUM.* This represents the lowest water level at which a given stream is navigable. For purposes of continuity and because of disagreement in many instances between depth markers on the same stream, all water levels are expressed in terms of volume as cubic feet per second (cfs). Use of cfs is doubly informative in that knowledge of volume at a gauge on one stream is often a prime indicator of the water levels of ungauged runnable streams in the same watershed, or for other sections of the gauged stream, either up- or downstream. *MAXIMUM.* In this guidebook, "runnable" does not mean the same thing as "possible." The maximum runnable water level refers to the highest water level at which the stream can be safely run (this may vary for open and decked boats). With one or two exceptions (which can only be run when flooded), this categorically excludes rivers in flood.

WATER TEMPERATURE. This is the average water temperature for each month of the year computed over a ten-year period. It represents an average. Actual water temperatures on a given day may vary considerably from the stated average. The statistic was included to help paddlers determine the need for special warm or cold weather clothing or equipment.

SOURCE OF ADDITIONAL INFORMATION ON WATER CONDITIONS. Various sources of additional information on water conditions are listed. Professional outfitters can provide both technical and descriptive information and relate the two in a paddling context. T.V.A. and the various hydraulics branches of the respective district Corps of Engineers' offices can provide flow data in cfs but will not be able to interpret the data for you in terms of paddling. Other sources listed (forest rangers, police departments, etc.) will normally provide only descriptive information, e.g., "The creek's up pretty good today," or even "The river doesn't have enough water in it for boating."

PORTAGES. This guidebook adheres to the rule that dams should be portaged. Additionally, portages are recommended for certain rapids and other dangers. The fact, however, that this guidebook does not specify a portage at a certain spot or rapid does not necessarily mean that you should not portage. It is the mark of good paddler to be able make safe and independent decisions concerning his or her own ability for a given river or rapid.

SCOUTING REQUIRED. This guidebook attempts to list spots on specific rivers where scouting is *required*, i.e., recommended for the continuation of life and good health. This guidebook also subscribes to the rule of thumb that you should scout any time you cannot see what is ahead (whitewater or flatwater and even on familiar rivers). That small, turning drop that you have run a thousand times may have a big log wedged across it today.

SCENERY RATING. Taste is relative and in the absolute sense mine is no better or worse than anyone else's. My preference is that you form your own conclusions about the comparative beauty of the streams listed in this guide. Knowing, however, that it takes a long time to run all of the state's major drainages, I was presumptuous enough to include a comparative scenery rating based strictly on my own perceptions. It.runs from "unattractive" to "spectacular." To indicate how capricious my taste is, I have rated below some popular canoe streams in surrounding states using the same scale.

Little Miami (Ohio) . . . . Pretty to pretty in spots
Whitewater River (Indiana) . . . . Pretty to pretty in spots
Nantahala River (North Carolina) . . . . Pretty to beautiful in spots
New River (West Virginia) . . . . . . Beautiful to beautiful in spots
Current River (Missouri) . . . . Beautiful to beautiful in spots
Hiwasse River (Tennessee) . . Beautiful to exceptionally beautiful
Tellico River (Tennessee . . . . Exceptionally beautiful
Chattooga III–IV (Georgia) . Exceptionally beautiful to spectacular

ACCESS CODE. Access codes correspond to the letter-denoted access points on accompanying maps. The code is usually four digits, but it may be more or less. Each digit relates to description of the actual access point on the river. For example, the access code 1357 indicates that: (1) a paved road goes to the river; (3) it is a short carry from your vehicle to the water's edge; (5) you don't have to carry down a steep hill or embankment; and (7) there is a clear trail, road, or path to the river. The number 9 means that the access is on private land and permission must be secured to put in or take out a boat. Absence of the number 9 *does not necessarily* mean that the access is public, it could mean that the landowner has historically granted access and that it is not essential that each boater secure permission individually. It could also mean that the landowner is nonresident or extremely difficult to locate. The rule of thumb is to be respectful of the property regardless.

MAPS

As stated in the introduction, maps in this guide are not intended to replace topographical quadrangles for terrain features. Rather, they are intended to illustrate the general configuration of the stream, access points, and surrounding shuttle networks. (Some of the maps are congested to the point that access letters may not be exactly where they should, but are only in the general vicinity. You may have to scout the area before launching.)

PART TWO

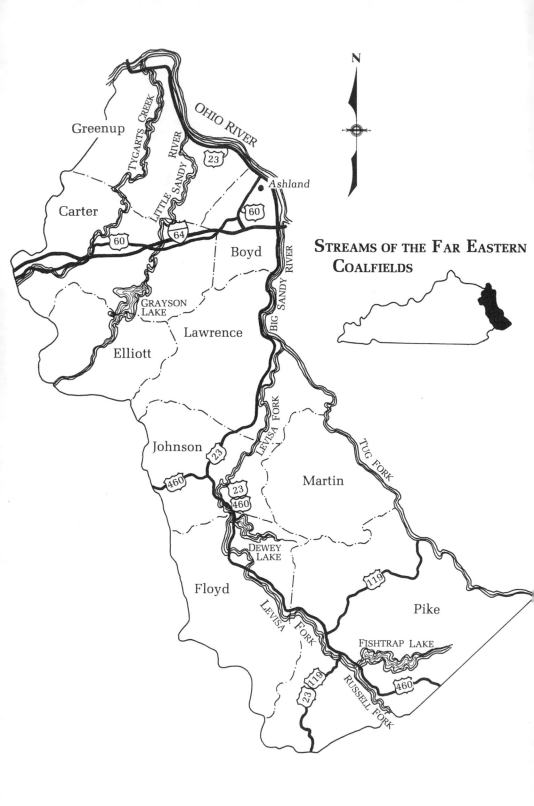

N

Greenup

OHIO RIVER

TYGARTS CREEK

LITTLE SANDY RIVER

23

Ashland

60

Carter

60

64

Boyd

BIG SANDY RIVER

STREAMS OF THE FAR EASTERN COALFIELDS

GRAYSON LAKE

Lawrence

Elliott

Johnson

23

460

LEVISA FORK

TUG FORK

Martin

23
460

DEWEY LAKE

119

Floyd

LEVISA FORK

Pike

FISHTRAP LAKE

119

460

23 119

RUSSELL FORK

1
STREAMS OF THE FAR EASTERN COAL FIELDS

RUSSELL FORK OF THE LEVISA FORK
OF THE BIG SANDY RIVER

Seldom run (for good reason) and almost unknown except to a handful of expert decked-boat paddlers, the Russell Fork is rated Class IV through Class VI by those who have attempted it (including the late Randy Carter who gave up and walked).

Flowing out of Virginia and joined by the Pound River, the Russell Fork cuts a 1600-foot gorge in the lonely Pine Ridge Mountains forming what is referred to as the "Great Breaks of the Pine Ridge." This incredible chasm with its giant vertical walls and pounding whitewater, bisects the Kentucky–Virginia border for several miles before plunging out of the mountains near Elkhorn City, Kentucky.

The put-in is in Virginia on the Pound River below the dam with easy Class-II water on down to the confluence with the Russell Fork. Below the confluence, the gradient begins to increase and the river broadens slightly to accommodate the additional volume. As canyon walls begin to rise on both sides, a jeep trail can be seen winding to near the river's edge on the right. For anyone beginning to feel a little overwhelmed, this is the last chance to stop before the bottom falls out. With the drop increasing markedly and steep sandstone walls rising on both sides, the Russell Fork now pounds its way along a giant semicircular loop at the base of the mountain. Here, hidden by the shadows of the gorge, is a hellish continuum of thundering vertical drops and foam-blasted boulder gardens where the river gradient reaches an amazing 160 feet per mile.

Many of the rapids in this section, including the consecutive 5-,

8-, and 9-foot vertical drops of "Triple Drop," the awesome "El Horrendo" with drops of 10 and 15 feet spaced only a boat length apart, and the boulder strewn S-turn at Red Cliff, had never been run before October of 1976. And, in the opinion of this writer, the fact that these truly dangerous rapids have been run does not justify downgrading their difficulty rating to Class V. In every sense of the definition, these rapids (and several others) are Class VI: "Class VI carried to the extremes of navigability. . . . For teams of experts only with every precaution taken . . . nearly impossible and very dangerous." In the case of the Russell Fork, taking every precaution includes having exceptional rescue support available, scouting all the major rapids, and making arrangements with the Corps of Engineers for a water release calculated to provide an optimal flow (about 1300 cfs). Optimal flow here is essential; 200 cfs more or less can make the Russell Fork dangerous beyond belief. Needless to say, this section is for experts in top condition with bulletproof rolls.

Beyond the loop, as the river turns due north and heads toward Elkhorn City, there is a trail approaching the river off KY 80. This point can serve as a take-out for the difficult upper run or as a put-in for a Class-II run down to Elkhorn City or beyond.

Although scouting is not difficult and portage routes around the major rapids are available, the Russell Fork should never be attempted by open boaters or by any but *expert decked boaters.* The rapids are intensely complex, technical, violent, and continuous. An upset in one of the milder rapids (Class III–IV) could lead to a nightmare swim through a Class-VI run.

Dangers on this run, other than the obvious, include two long railroad tunnels on the left ridge that some paddlers risk walking through to facilitate scouting.

LEVISA FORK OF THE BIG SANDY RIVER

The Levisa Fork flows out of Virginia into Pike County in southeastern Kentucky where it is impounded to form Fishtrap Lake. Below the lake, the Levisa Fork comprises one of the major drainages of Eastern Kentucky as it flows through Floyd, Johnson, and Lawrence counties before coming together with the Tug Fork to form the Big Sandy River. Runnable almost all year below the dam at Fishtrap Lake to its confluence with the Tug Fork, the Levisa Fork is a big river, averaging 80 to 110 feet in width. Civilization is continuous along the Levisa Fork with a highway paralleling the stream on one side and a railroad on the other. Additionally, the Levisa Fork runs through the sizable communities of Pikeville, Paintsville, Prestonsburg, and Louisa. Amazingly, despite man's overwhelming presence, the Levisa Fork is not a total loss as a canoeing stream. Sunk between deep banks that hide the bustle of civilization above, the stream itself is tree-lined and not at all unpleasant. Access is plentiful along its entire length and the river is free of powerboat traffic except for a small stretch in Lawrence County. Tall hills and bluffs (some man made) make for pleasant viewing. The Levisa Fork's level of difficulty is Class I with occasional small shoals and rapids (Class I+). Dangers to navigation are limited to deadfalls (which are easily avoided), a man-made rapid below Louisa, and several low-water bridges. Difficulties include a mud bottom and banks of soft sand that can easily swallow a paddler up to the waist if he or she steps in the wrong place when putting in or taking out.

JOHN'S CREEK

John's Creek flows northwest out of Pike County into Dewey Lake and from there through Floyd County to empty into the Levisa Fork of the Big Sandy River south of Paintsville. The upper section from KY 194 to Dewey Lake can be run all year. The section running from below the dam to the Levisa Fork can be run whenever water is being released from the dam. The upper section is almost devoid of current as a rule, but is a passable canoe-camping run when combined with portions of Dewey Lake. Below the dam the creek is only 15 to 25 feet wide, clogged with dead-falls, logjams, and various forms of debris, and is only safe to run at moderate water levels. Scenery on both sections consists of wooded hillsides and sandy banks with dense scrub vegetation. Access to the upper section is plentiful and good. Access to the lower section is nonexistent beyond the put-in, with the nearest take-out being four miles beyond the mouth on the Levisa Fork in Paintsville.

(NOTE: John's Creek is included with the maps of the Levisa Fork of the Big Sandy River.)

LITTLE SANDY RIVER

The Little Sandy River is born in southern Elliott County and flows northeast to the Ohio River through Carter and Greenup counties. From Sandy Hook to the Dehart Road bridge above Grayson Lake, the stream is runnable from January through April and following heavy rains at any time of year. This section is beautiful beyond belief with exposed rock bluffs and overhangs and a luxurious forest of both evergreens and hardwoods. Interspaced along the river are flat terraces carpeted with lush bluegrass perfect for camping. The Little Sandy flows over a bed of gravel and mud in this upper gorge section with frequent sandbars and small Class-I+ rapids to make paddling interesting. The river's width is from 20 to 35 feet on the average. Navigational hazards are primarily deadfalls washed into the gorge from above Sandy Hook.

From the Dehart Road bridge downstream into Grayson Lake, the Little Sandy can be run all year thanks to the water backup from the lake pool. This section also runs through a gorge and is extremely scenic with small waterfalls visible at adjoining feeder streams. Obviously, due to the backwash, the stream is wider here (75 to 80 feet) and there is no current. Access is good and many take-outs are available according to how far into the lake you wish to paddle. This section is excellent for canoe camping and there are no navigational hazards.

The Little Sandy continues to be extraordinary from the tailwater of the dam (off KY 7 in Carter County) to the intersection of the new KY 7 bridge near Leon. Small and intimate, once again the river averages 25 to 40 feet in width and flows beneath steep rock walls and overhangs on the west, and forest (with some cultivated land) on the east. This section can be combined with a loop of the Jenny Wiley Trail that runs along the river starting at the base of the dam. The run ends with a small Class-II rapid at the new KY 7 bridge. Access is good and navigational dangers are limited to an occasional deadfall. Runnable most of the year, the water level is dependent on releases from the dam.

Downstream of the new KY 7 bridge towards Grayson, the river flows through a wide valley, pastoral in setting but with increased human habitation. While not nearly as scenic as the upstream sections, the river here continues to make for pleasant paddling. Departing the Grayson Plain, the Little Sandy River proceeds northeast through gently rolling farmland toward the Ohio River. Increasing to 40 to 50 feet in width, and running over a mud bottom with 9- to 16-foot mud banks, the river stays substantially the same through northern Carter County and all of Greenup County. Access is good. Navigational dangers are minimal and are once again limited primarily to deadfalls. A special point of interest in Greenup County is a historic covered bridge spanning the stream near Oldtown.

TYGARTS CREEK

Originating in southwestern Carter County, Tygarts Creek flows northeast through Carter and Greenup counties to empty into the

Ohio River across the river from Portsmouth, Ohio. From Olive Hill to the KY 182 bridge near Carter Caves State Resort Park, the creek flows through a deep, secluded gorge with evergreen- and hardwood-topped bluffs and some borderline Class-II rapids. Runnable in late winter through early spring and after heavy rains, this section abounds in wildlife. Throughout the gorge, Tygarts Creek is extremely narrow (15 to 25 feet) and swiftly flows over a rock, sand, and gravel bottom. Navigational dangers include deadfalls and logjams and an undercut rock on the left shortly after passing under the I-64 bridge.

From the KY 182 bridge downstream, Tygarts Creek continues to flow through a gorge for an additional five miles before descending into the valley south of Iron Hill. While the beginning of this section is very scenic, the final several miles are rather lackluster (as is the remainder of the creek as it flows northeast towards the Ohio) and therefore have not been included in the accompanying data sheets. Between Iron Hill and its mouth, Tygarts Creek can be run from November to mid-June, but it is not particularly appealing. The river's width here is 30 to 45 feet with steep banks of mud. Vegetation at riverside is essentially scrub weeds, and trees are conspicuously absent. Surrounding terrain is rolling farmland with some cultivation of the flattened floodplains adjoining the stream. Deadfalls and logjams are common as are some of the less aesthetic effects of lateral erosion. One bright spot in this section, however, is a covered bridge one-half mile south of the Plum Fork church in Greenup County. Access from Iron Hill to the Ohio River is poor.

RUSSELL FORK OF THE LEVISA FORK OF THE BIG SANDY RIVER

SECTION: Pound River Dam to Elkhorn City (Dickenson Co., VA, Pike Co., KY)

USGS QUADS: Elkhorn City

LEVEL OF DIFFICULTY International Class IV-VI Numerical Points 37

SUITABLE FOR: Cruising   **GRADIENT** (feet per mile): 4.6-180+

APPROPRIATE FOR: Experts

VELOCITY (mph): 2.6-5.0+   **AVERAGE WIDTH** (ft): 35-60

MONTHS RUNNABLE: Only with special arrangements for dam release

RUNNABLE WATER LEVEL (cfs) Minimum 1300
Maximum   Open: Cannot be run   Decked: 1500

MEAN WATER TEMPERATURE (°F)

Jan. 41	Feb. 42	Mar. 48	Apr. 55	May 65	Jun. 76
Jul. 78	Aug. 78	Sep. 73	Oct. 65	Nov. 46	Dec. 40

SOURCE OF ADDITIONAL INFORMATION ON WATER CONDITIONS

Corps of Engineers (703) 835-1438

HAZARDS: Undercut rocks, keeper hydraulics, difficult rapids, scarcity of eddy

RESCUE INDEX: B-C
A Extremely remote; evacuation only with expert help—6 hours to secure assistance
B Remote; 3-6 hours to secure assistance
C Accessible but difficult; up to 3 hours to secure assistance—evacuation difficult
D Accessible; up to 1 hour to secure assistance, evacuation not difficult

PORTAGES: Routes around most rapids are available at 1300 cfs.

SCOUTING: Entire run on foot prior to running

INTEREST HIGHLIGHTS: Scenery, history, geology, whitewater

SCENERY: Spectacular to exceptionally beautiful

ACCESS POINT	ACCESS CODE	KEY
A	1 3 6 7	1 Paved Road
B*	2 3 6 7	2 Unpaved Road
C†	2 3 6 7	3 Short Carry
D	1 3 6 7	4 Long Carry
		5 Easy Grade
		6 Steep Grade
		7 Clear Trail
		8 Brush and Trees
		9 Private Property, Permission Needed
		10 Launching Fee Charged
		11 No Access—For Reference Only

*Four-wheel drive recommended
†A Class II-III run can be had by running from points C-D

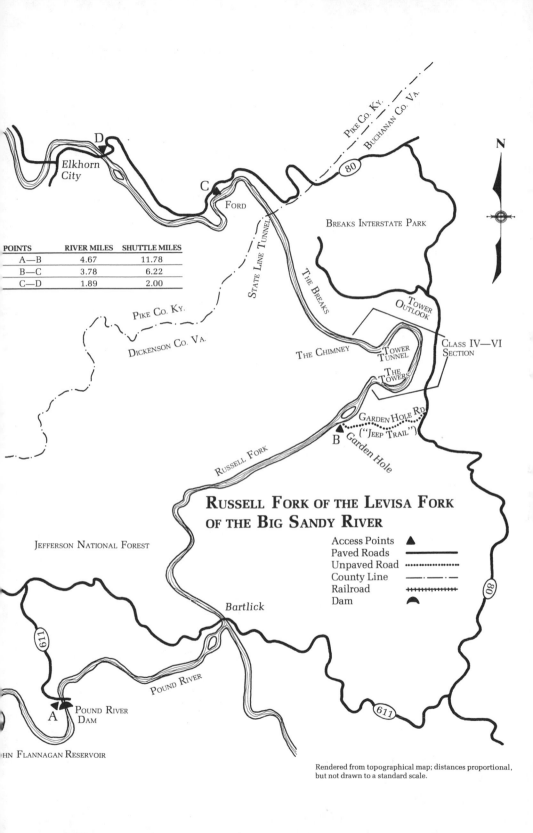

N

D

Elkhorn
City

C

Ford

PIKE CO. KY.
BUCHANAN CO. VA.

80

BREAKS INTERSTATE PARK

POINTS	RIVER MILES	SHUTTLE MILES
A—B	4.67	11.78
B—C	3.78	6.22
C—D	1.89	2.00

STATE LINE TUNNEL

THE BREAKS

TOWER
OUTLOOK

PIKE CO. KY.

DICKENSON CO. VA.

THE CHIMNEY

TOWER
TUNNEL

CLASS IV—VI
SECTION

THE
TOWERS

GARDEN HOLE RD.
("JEEP TRAIL")

B   Garden Hole

RUSSELL FORK

RUSSELL FORK OF THE LEVISA FORK
OF THE BIG SANDY RIVER

JEFFERSON NATIONAL FOREST

Access Points   ▲
Paved Roads   ——————
Unpaved Road   ·················
County Line   —·—·—·—
Railroad   +++++++++
Dam   ◠

Bartlick

80

611

POUND RIVER

611

A   POUND RIVER
     DAM

HN FLANNAGAN RESERVOIR

Rendered from topographical map; distances proportional,
but not drawn to a standard scale.

SECTION: Fishtrap Dam to KY 1426 (Pike Co., Floyd Co.)

USGS QUADS: Millard, Pikeville, Broadbottom, Harold, Lancer

LEVEL OF DIFFICULTY International Class I (II)   Numerical Points 5

SUITABLE FOR: Cruising   **GRADIENT** (feet per mile): 1.46

APPROPRIATE FOR: Families, Beginners, Intermediates, Advanced

VELOCITY (mph): 2.6-5.0   **AVERAGE WIDTH** (ft): 70-90

MONTHS RUNNABLE: All

RUNNABLE WATER LEVEL (cfs) Minimum 400
  Maximum Up to flood stage

MEAN WATER TEMPERATURE (°F)

Jan. 43	Feb. 44	Mar. 49	Apr. 55	May 67	Jun. 77
Jul. 80	Aug. 79	Sep. 73	Oct. 65	Nov. 46	Dec. 41

SOURCE OF ADDITIONAL INFORMATION ON WATER CONDITIONS

  Corps of Engineers (703) 835-1438
  Fishtrap Lake Dam (606) 437-7496

HAZARDS: None

RESCUE INDEX: D
  A Extremely remote; evacuation only with expert help—6 hours to secure assistance
  B Remote; 3-6 hours to secure assistance
  C Accessible but difficult; up to 3 hours to secure assistance—evacuation difficult
  D Accessible; up to 1 hour to secure assistance, evacuation not difficult

PORTAGES: None

SCOUTING: None required

INTEREST HIGHLIGHTS: Scenery, local culture and industry

SCENERY: Pleasant to pretty

ACCESS POINT	ACCESS CODE	KEY
A	1 3 5 7	1 Paved Road
B	1 3 6 7	2 Unpaved Road
C*	1 3 6 8	3 Short Carry
D	1 3 6 7	4 Long Carry
E	1 3 6 7	5 Easy Grade
F†	1 3 5 7	6 Steep Grade
G‡	1 3 6 7	7 Clear Trail
		8 Brush and Trees
		9 Private Property, Permission Needed
		10 Launching Fee Charged
		11 No Access—For Reference Only

*At Shelbiana Rd. bridge at the mouth of Shelby Creek
†In Betsy Layne on School St. at the mouth of Betsy Layne Branch
‡In Banner at the mouth of Akers Branch

Levisa Fork of the Big Sandy River—1

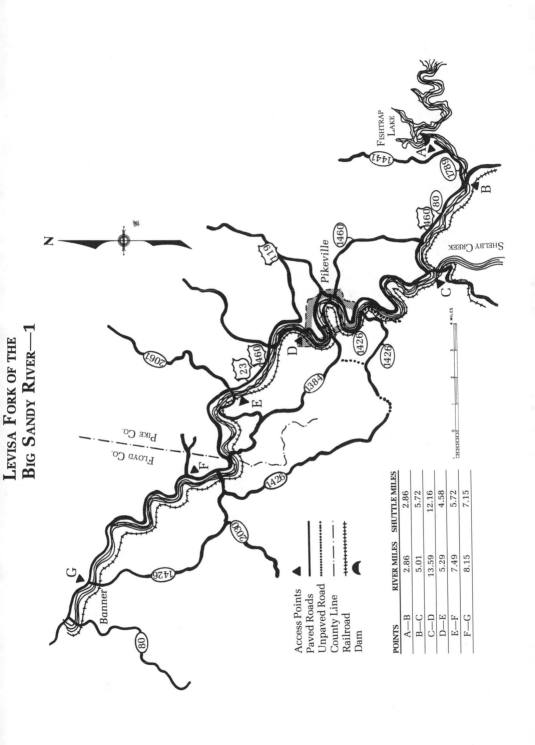

N

Fishtrap Lake

1441

1789

A

80

460

B

Shelby Creek

1460

Pikeville

119

2061

23

460

D

1384

1426

1426

E

1426

Floyd Co.

Pike Co.

F

2030

1426

Banner

G

80

4 MILES

Access Points
Paved Roads
Unpaved Road
County Line
Railroad
Dam

POINTS	RIVER MILES	SHUTTLE MILES
A—B	2.86	2.86
B—C	5.01	5.72
C—D	13.59	12.16
D—E	5.29	4.58
E—F	7.49	5.72
F—G	8.15	7.15

SECTION: KY 1426 to Paintsville (Floyd Co., Johnson Co.)

USGS QUADS: Lancer, Prestonburg, Paintsville

LEVEL OF DIFFICULTY International Class I (II)   Numerical Points   5

SUITABLE FOR: Cruising   **GRADIENT** (feet per mile):   1.25

APPROPRIATE FOR: Families, Beginners, Intermediates, Advanced

VELOCITY (mph): 2.6-5.0   **AVERAGE WIDTH** (ft): 80-100

MONTHS RUNNABLE: All

RUNNABLE WATER LEVEL (cfs) Minimum **400**
   Maximum Up to flood stage

MEAN WATER TEMPERATURE (°F)

Jan. 43	Feb. 44	Mar. 49	Apr. 55	May 67	Jun. 77
Jul. 80	Aug. 79	Sep. 73	Oct. 65	Nov. 46	Dec. 41

SOURCE OF ADDITIONAL INFORMATION ON WATER CONDITIONS
   Corps of Engineers (703) 835-1438
   Dewey Lake Dam (606) 886-6398

HAZARDS: None

RESCUE INDEX: D
   A Extremely remote; evacuation only with expert help—6 hours to secure assistance
   B Remote; 3-6 hours to secure assistance
   C Accessible but difficult; up to 3 hours to secure assistance—evacuation difficult
   D Accessible; up to 1 hour to secure assistance, evacuation not difficult

PORTAGES: None

SCOUTING: None required

INTEREST HIGHLIGHTS: Scenery, local culture and industry

SCENERY: Pleasant to pretty

ACCESS POINT	ACCESS CODE	KEY
G*	1 3 6 7	1 Paved Road
H	1 3 6 8	2 Unpaved Road
I	1 3 6 7	3 Short Carry
J†	1 3 6 8	4 Long Carry
		5 Easy Grade
		6 Steep Grade
		7 Clear Trail
		8 Brush and Trees
		9 Private Property, Permission Needed
		10 Launching Fee Charged
		11 No Access—For Reference Only

*In Banner at the mouth of Akers Branch
†Mouth of Paint Creek at KY 1428 bridge

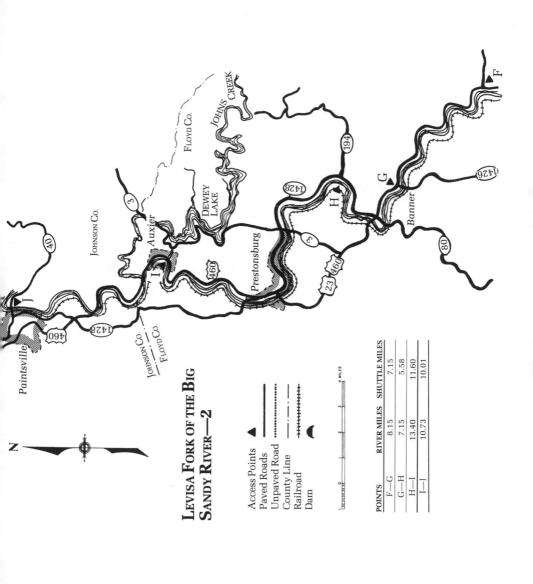

Levisa Fork of the Big Sandy River—2

	Access Points
	Paved Roads
	Unpaved Road
	County Line
	Railroad
	Dam

0   1   2   3   4 MILES

POINTS	RIVER MILES	SHUTTLE MILES
F—G	8.15	7.15
G—H	7.15	5.58
H—I	13.40	11.60
I—J	10.73	10.01

SECTION: Auxier to Louisa (Floyd Co., Johnson Co., Lawrence Co.)

USGS QUADS: Prestonsburg, Paintsville, Offutt, Richardson, Milo, Louisa

LEVEL OF DIFFICULTY International Class I (II) Numerical Points 5

SUITABLE FOR: Cruising   **GRADIENT** (feet per mile): 1.03

APPROPRIATE FOR: Families, Beginners, Intermediates, Advanced

VELOCITY (mph): 2.6-5.0   **AVERAGE WIDTH** (ft): 80-110

MONTHS RUNNABLE: All

RUNNABLE WATER LEVEL (cfs) Minimum 400
Maximum Up to flood stage

MEAN WATER TEMPERATURE ($^{\circ}$F)

Jan. 43	Feb. 44	Mar. 49	Apr. 55	May 67	Jun. 77
Jul. 80	Aug. 79	Sep. 73	Oct. 65	Nov. 46	Dec. 41

SOURCE OF ADDITIONAL INFORMATION ON WATER CONDITIONS
Corps of Engineers (703) 835-1438

HAZARDS: Louisa, deadfalls, low bridges

RESCUE INDEX: D
  A Extremely remote; evacuation only with expert help—6 hours to secure assistance
  B Remote; 3-6 hours to secure assistance
  C Accessible but difficult; up to 3 hours to secure assistance—evacuation difficult
  D Accessible; up to 1 hour to secure assistance, evacuation not difficult

PORTAGES: Around man-made rapid at Louisa

SCOUTING: None required

INTEREST HIGHLIGHTS: Scenery, local culture and industry

SCENERY: Pleasant to pretty

ACCESS POINT	ACCESS CODE	KEY
I	1 3 6 7	1 Paved Road
J*	1 3 6 8	2 Unpaved Road
K†	1 3 6 8	3 Short Carry
L‡	2 3 6 7	4 Long Carry
M§	1 3 6 8	5 Easy Grade
N//	2 3 6 8	6 Steep Grade
O	1 3 6 8	7 Clear Trail
P#	1 3 6 7	8 Brush and Trees
		9 Private Property, Permission Needed
		10 Launching Fee Charged
		11 No Access—For Reference Only

 * Mouth of Paint Creek at KY 1428 bridge
† KY 581 bridge at the mouth of Wiley Creek
‡ KY 581 at the mouth of Childers Branch
§ KY 581 at the mouth of Georges Creek
// KY 2038 at the mouth of House Branch
Toll bridge off U.S. 23

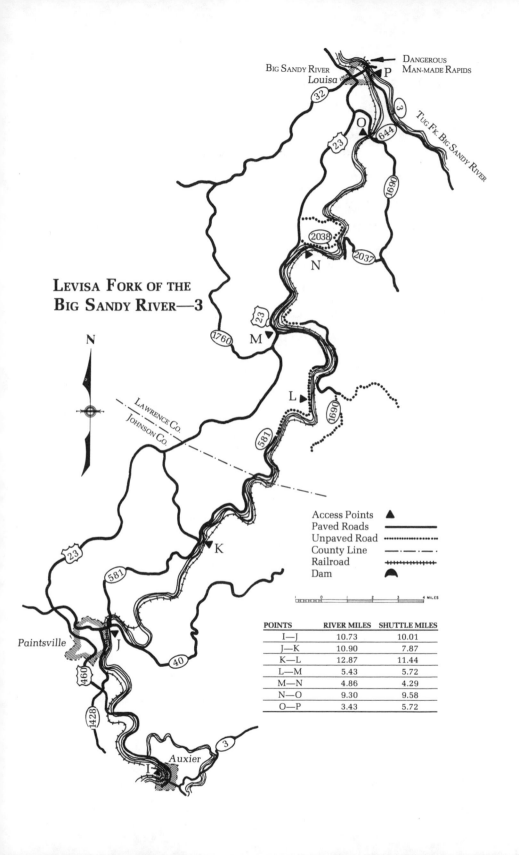

DANGEROUS
MAN-MADE RAPIDS

BIG SANDY RIVER
Louisa

TUG FK. BIG SANDY RIVER

LEVISA FORK OF THE
BIG SANDY RIVER—3

N

LAWRENCE CO.
JOHNSON CO.

Access Points ▲
Paved Roads ――――
Unpaved Road ••••••••
County Line ―・―・―
Railroad +++++++
Dam

Paintsville

Auxier

POINTS	RIVER MILES	SHUTTLE MILES
I—J	10.73	10.01
J—K	10.90	7.87
K—L	12.87	11.44
L—M	5.43	5.72
M—N	4.86	4.29
N—O	9.30	9.58
O—P	3.43	5.72

SECTION: Sandy Hook to Grayson Lake (Elliott Co., Carter Co.)

USGS QUADS: Sandy Hook, Isonville, Bruin, Willard

LEVEL OF DIFFICULTY International Class I-II   Numerical Points **8**

SUITABLE FOR: Cruising, camping **GRADIENT** (feet per mile): **4.65**

APPROPRIATE FOR: Above lake pool: Beginners, Intermediates, Advanced
Lake pool: Families, Beginners, Intermediates, Advanced
VELOCITY (mph): 2.6-5.0   **AVERAGE WIDTH** (ft): **20-35**

MONTHS RUNNABLE: January to April above lake pool (Dehart Road bridge)

RUNNABLE WATER LEVEL (cfs) Minimum **140**
Maximum   Up to flood stage

MEAN WATER TEMPERATURE ($^\circ$F)

Jan. 39	Feb. 40	Mar. 42	Apr. 53	May 64	Jun. 74
Jul. 76	Aug. 75	Sep. 66	Oct. 60	Nov. 44	Dec. 38

SOURCE OF ADDITIONAL INFORMATION ON WATER CONDITIONS
Corps of Engineers (606) 474-5107

HAZARDS: Deadfalls, low trees, flash floods

RESCUE INDEX: C
A Extremely remote; evacuation only with expert help—6 hours to secure assistance
B Remote; 3-6 hours to secure assistance
C Accessible but difficult; up to 3 hours to secure assistance—evacuation difficult
D Accessible; up to 1 hour to secure assistance, evacuation not difficult

PORTAGES: None required

SCOUTING: Blind curves above lake pool

INTEREST HIGHLIGHTS: Scenery, wildlife, local culture and industry

SCENERY: Beautiful to exceptionally beautiful

ACCESS POINT	ACCESS CODE	KEY
A	1 3 6 8	1 Paved Road
B	1 3 5 7	2 Unpaved Road
C	1 3 5 7	3 Short Carry
D	1 3 5 7	4 Long Carry
E	1 3 5 7	5 Easy Grade
F	1 3 5 7	6 Steep Grade
		7 Clear Trail
		8 Brush and Trees
		9 Private Property, Permission Needed
		10 Launching Fee Charged
		11 No Access—For Reference Only

Little Sandy River—1

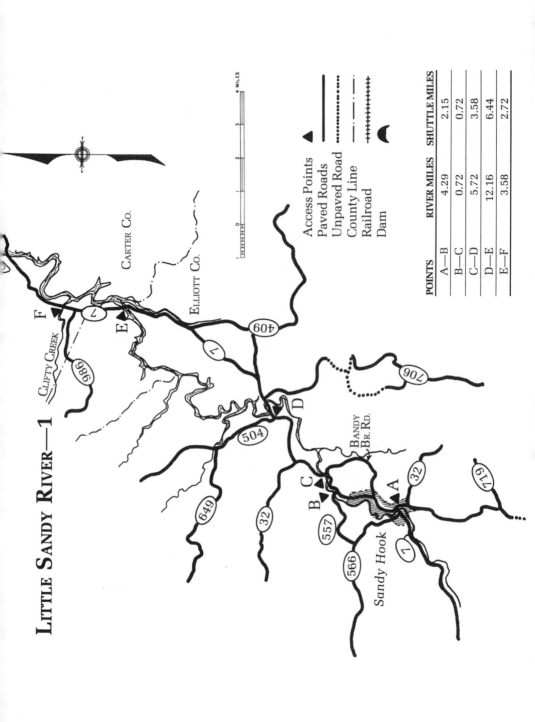

Carter Co.

Elliott Co.

Sandy Hook

Clifty Creek

Bandy Br. Rd.

Access Points	◄
Paved Roads	
Unpaved Road	
County Line	
Railroad	
Dam	◖

POINTS	RIVER MILES	SHUTTLE MILES
A—B	4.29	2.15
B—C	0.72	0.72
C—D	5.72	3.58
D—E	12.16	6.44
E—F	3.58	2.72

0 1 2 3 4 MILES

SECTION: Grayson Dam to the Ohio River (Carter Co., Greenup Co.)

USGS QUADS: Willard, Grayson, Oldtown, Argillite, Greenup

LEVEL OF DIFFICULTY International Class I   Numerical Points 5

SUITABLE FOR: Cruising   **GRADIENT** (feet per mile): 1.66

APPROPRIATE FOR: Families, Beginners, Intermediates, Advanced

VELOCITY (mph): 2.6-5.0   **AVERAGE WIDTH** (ft): 30-45

MONTHS RUNNABLE: Most of the year, subject to dam releases

RUNNABLE WATER LEVEL (cfs) Minimum 150
Maximum   Up to flood stage

MEAN WATER TEMPERATURE (°F)

Jan. 39	Feb. 40	Mar. 42	Apr. 53	May 64	Jun. 74
Jul. 76	Aug. 75	Sep. 66	Oct. 60	Nov. 44	Dec. 38

SOURCE OF ADDITIONAL INFORMATION ON WATER CONDITIONS
Corps of Engineers (606) 474-5107

HAZARDS: Deadfalls*

RESCUE INDEX: C-D
A Extremely remote; evacuation only with expert help—6 hours to secure assistance
B Remote; 3-6 hours to secure assistance
C Accessible but difficult; up to 3 hours to secure assistance—evacuation difficult
D Accessible; up to 1 hour to secure assistance, evacuation not difficult

PORTAGES: None required

SCOUTING: Blind curves for strainers

INTEREST HIGHLIGHTS: Scenery, history, wildlife, local culture and industry

SCENERY: Dam to KY 7: Beautiful to exceptionally beautiful;
KY 7 to the Ohio River: Pleasant to pretty in spots

ACCESS POINT	ACCESS CODE	KEY
G	1 4 5 7	1 Paved Road
H	1 3 5 7	2 Unpaved Road
I	1 3 5 8 9	3 Short Carry
J	1 3 6 8	4 Long Carry
K	2 3 6 7	5 Easy Grade
L	1 3 6 7	6 Steep Grade
M	1 3 6 8	7 Clear Trail
N	1 3 6 8	8 Brush and Trees
O	1 3 5 7	9 Private Property, Permission Needed
		10 Launching Fee Charged
		11 No Access—For Reference Only

*Man-made rapid (Class II) at new KY 7 bridge

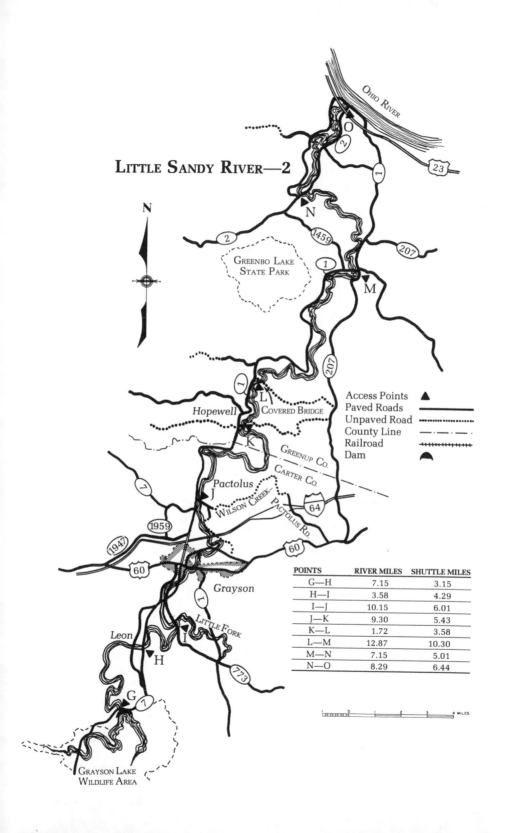

LITTLE SANDY RIVER—2

N

OHIO RIVER

GREENBO LAKE
STATE PARK

Hopewell COVERED BRIDGE

Access Points ▲
Paved Roads ────────
Unpaved Road ·············
County Line ─·─·─·─
Railroad ┼┼┼┼┼┼
Dam ◣

GREENUP CO.
CARTER CO.

Pactolus
WILSON CREEK–
PACTOLUS RD.

Grayson

Leon
LITTLE FORK

GRAYSON LAKE
WILDLIFE AREA

POINTS	RIVER MILES	SHUTTLE MILES
G—H	7.15	3.15
H—I	3.58	4.29
I—J	10.15	6.01
J—K	9.30	5.43
K—L	1.72	3.58
L—M	12.87	10.30
M—N	7.15	5.01
N—O	8.29	6.44

4 MILES

SECTION: Olive Hill to KY 182 (Carter Co.)

USGS QUADS: Olive Hill, Grahn, Tygarts Valley

LEVEL OF DIFFICULTY International Class I-II   Numerical Points 7

SUITABLE FOR: Cruising   **GRADIENT** (feet per mile): 2.01

APPROPRIATE FOR: Beginners, Intermediates, Advanced

VELOCITY (mph): 2.6-5.0   **AVERAGE WIDTH** (ft): 20-40

MONTHS RUNNABLE: December to mid-April and after heavy rains

RUNNABLE WATER LEVEL (cfs) Minimum   140
   Maximum   Up to flood stage

MEAN WATER TEMPERATURE (°F)

Jan. 39	Feb. 40	Mar. 43	Apr. 53	May 65	Jun. 73
Jul. 75	Aug. 73	Sep. 66	Oct. 59	Nov. 44	Dec. 39

SOURCE OF ADDITIONAL INFORMATION ON WATER CONDITIONS
   Olive Hill Police Dept. (606) 286-2551

HAZARDS: Deadfalls, undercut rocks, flash floods

RESCUE INDEX: B-C
   A Extremely remote; evacuation only with expert help—6 hours to secure assistance
   B Remote; 3-6 hours to secure assistance
   C Accessible but difficult; up to 3 hours to secure assistance—evacuation difficult
   D Accessible; up to 1 hour to secure assistance, evacuation not difficult

PORTAGES: None required

SCOUTING: At blind curves

INTEREST HIGHLIGHTS: Scenery, wildlife, geology, local culture and
                                                         industry

SCENERY: Beautiful to beautiful in spots

ACCESS POINT	ACCESS CODE	KEY
A	1 4 6 7 9	1 Paved Road
B	1 3 5 7	2 Unpaved Road
		3 Short Carry
		4 Long Carry
		5 Easy Grade
		6 Steep Grade
		7 Clear Trail
		8 Brush and Trees
		9 Private Property, Permission Needed
		10 Launching Fee Charged
		11 No Access—For Reference Only

TYGARTS CREEK

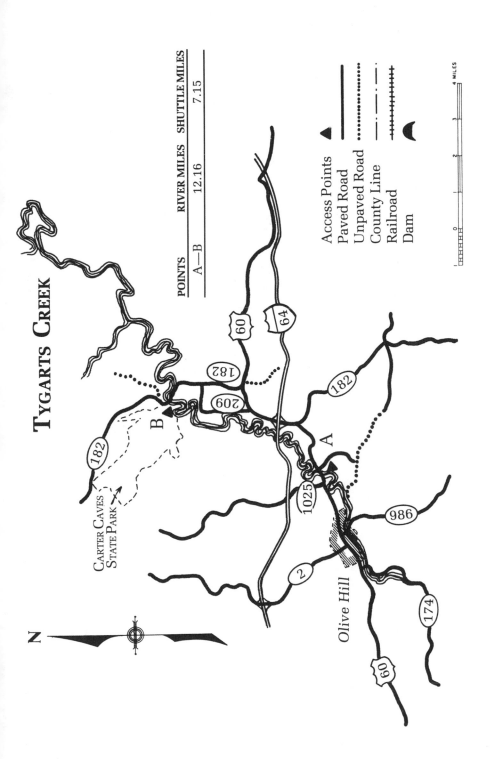

POINTS	RIVER MILES	SHUTTLE MILES
A—B	12.16	7.15

Access Points
Paved Road
Unpaved Road
County Line
Railroad
Dam

4 MILES

0   1   2   3

N

CARTER CAVES
STATE PARK

B

A

Olive Hill

182

60
64

182

209

182

1025

2

986

60

174

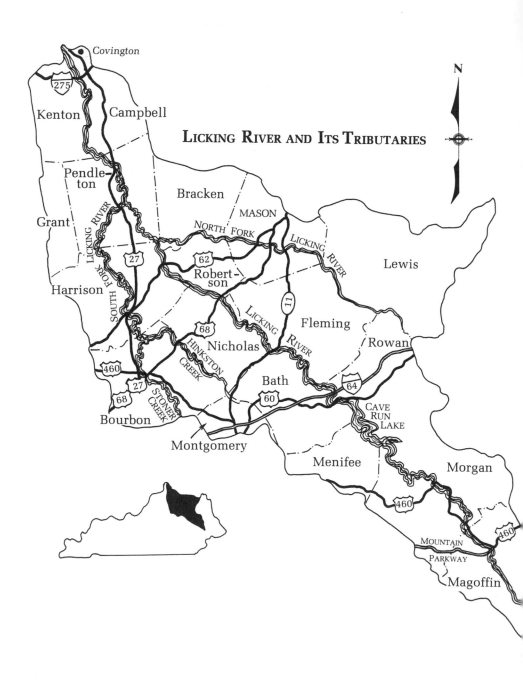

LICKING RIVER AND ITS TRIBUTARIES

N

Covington

275

Kenton   Campbell

Pendle-
ton
                    Bracken

Grant   MASON

            NORTH FORK   LICKING RIVER   Lewis

LICKING RIVER   27   62
                          Robert-
                          son

Harrison   11

SOUTH FORK   LICKING RIVER   Fleming

            68   Rowan
                    Nicholas
HINKSTON CREEK

460   Bath   64

    27   60   CAVE
68   RUN
STONER CREEK   LAKE

Bourbon

        Montgomery   Menifee   Morgan

                                            460

                                    MOUNTAIN   460
                                    PARKWAY

                                            Magoffin

2
The Licking River
and Its Tributaries

NORTH FORK OF THE LICKING RIVER

Flowing from east to west, the North Fork of the Licking River drains portions of Lewis, Fleming, Mason, Bracken, and Robertson counties before joining the Middle Fork of the Licking River southeast of Falmouth. Running over a mud bottom through hilly grazing land, the North Fork is often clogged with logjams and diverted around small islands of scrub vegetation. The North Fork can be canoed west of Lewisburg in Mason County from November through early June but is not particularly appealing. Often there seem to be as many trees in the river as along the banks. Access, however, is good for those who wish to make the effort.

The entire North Fork is a Class-I stream with deadfalls and logjams posing the major hazards to navigation.

MIDDLE FORK OF THE LICKING RIVER

The Middle Fork of the Licking River originates in southern Magoffin County and flows northwest draining portions of Morgan (where the river empties into Cave Run Lake), Menifee, Rowan, Bath, Fleming, Nicholas, Robertson, Harrison, and Pendleton counties. From its origin to Cave Run Lake, the Middle Fork is littered, jammed, and generally too small to canoe. From the tailwater of the dam downstream to the KY 32 bridge near Myers, the Middle Fork is runnable from mid-October to early June, subject to water releases from the dam. From the KY 32 bridge to its confluence with the North and South Forks, the river is runnable all year long. the Middle Fork of the Licking River runs through hilly farmland and woodlands. Flowing over a bottom of sand and mud with mud banks of varying steepness, the stream is generally lined with hardwood and scrub vegetation. Sandbars and islands of grass and scrub vegetation are common all along its length (even at relatively high water) and deadfalls are common. Many access points are on private property where permission must be obtained to put-in or take-out. All runs from the dam to the confluence with North Fork are Class I, but the current can be extremely swift and forceful in the spring. Canoe camping is recommended only in the area of the Blue Licks Battlefield State Park where the river forms the western boundary of the park. As it flows north, the Middle Fork broadens from 25 feet at the tailwater of the dam to 60 feet in the Blue Licks area to 95 to 110 feet at its confluence with the South Fork in Falmouth.

HINKSTON CREEK

A major tributary of the South Fork of the Licking River, Hinkston Creek originates in western Bath County and flows northwest along the Bourbon–Nicholas county line before joining Stoner Creek near Ruddels Mills. Flowing over a mud and gravel bottom between 12 to 15 foot mud banks, Hinkston Creek winds through gently rolling farmland. Much of the streamside is treelined and several varieties of tall grasses can also be found. Runnable from November to early June downstream of Millersburg, the creek is Class I with some sandbars and frequent midstream islands covered with scrub vegetation. Surrounding countryside is historically interesting with numerous stone fences, many old homes, and a covered bridge. Average stream width is from 30 to 40 feet, and access is fair to good. Logjams and deadfalls are the primary hazards to navigation (you must put in below a five-foot dam if starting in Millersburg).

STONER CREEK

Stoner Creek drains central Bourbon County and runs north through Paris to its confluence with Hinkston Creek. Runnable from November to mid-June north of Paris and December through April south of Paris, Stoner Creek flows through some of the world's most famous thoroughbred horse farms. The creek itself is primarily Class I. It has numerous grass islands and flows over a mud and rock bottom between steep, 15-foot banks. Access is good north of Paris, but in the upper sections of the stream, to the south of Paris, access is difficult, with most put-ins and take-outs located on private property. It is here, unfortunately, that the most interesting scenery occurs. Deadfalls are the primary hazards to navigation.

SOUTH FORK OF THE LICKING RIVER

The South Fork of the Licking River originates at the confluence of Hinkston and Stoner Creeks near Ruddels Mills, south of Cynthiana, and flows north over a mud and sand bottom and joins the North and Middle Forks of the Licking River near Falmouth. Running in steep mud banks lined with water maple and sycamore, the South Fork is Class I throughout with grass islands and numerous sandbars. Its average width is from 40 feet at its origin to 80 to 90 feet at its confluence with the other forks. Surrounding terrain is generally hilly farms and wooded land. The South Fork flows through the town of Cynthiana. Access to the river is generally good. Hazards to navigation include numerous dams (some of which exceed five feet in height) that *must* be portaged, and deadfalls.

LICKING RIVER FROM FALMOUTH
TO THE OHIO RIVER

The Licking River below the confluence of its three forks is a big river and is runnable all year. Its scenery is pleasant with the river winding in lengthy curves through broad valleys bordered by tall hills and ridges. The banks are steep and muddy as a rule although flat terraces occur frequently about five feet up from the waterline. Its average width is 190 to 220 feet. Trees, mostly hardwoods, line the banks. For a large, navigable river, there is a conspicuous absence of powerboat traffic, due probably to the scarcity of access points. Through Kenton County, north to Newport where the Licking River empties into the Ohio River, the railroad effectively monopolizes the west bank. Beyond the sprawling switchyards, steep ridges make it almost impossible to reach the water. Along the east bank in Campbell County, large farms and other types of private property buffer the stream. Comparatively long distances between access points, then, limit this section's attractiveness to paddlers. The level of difficulty is Class I throughout and occasional floating debris represents the only hazard to navigation. Access, as mentioned, is scarce, but it is reasonably good where it exists.

SECTION: Lewisburg to the confluence of the Middle Fork (Mason Co., Bracken Co.)

USGS QUADS: Orangeburg, Mays Lick, Sardis, Mount Olivet, Claysville

LEVEL OF DIFFICULTY International Class I   Numerical Points 3

SUITABLE FOR: Cruising   **GRADIENT** (feet per mile): 2.65

APPROPRIATE FOR: Beginners, Intermediates, Advanced

VELOCITY (mph): 2.6-5.0   **AVERAGE WIDTH** (ft): 30-50

MONTHS RUNNABLE: November to early June

RUNNABLE WATER LEVEL (cfs) Minimum 200
   Maximum   Up to flood stage

MEAN WATER TEMPERATURE ($^\circ$F)

Jan. 42	Feb. 41	Mar. 43	Apr. 51	May 65	Jun. 74
Jul. 76	Aug. 75	Sep. 68	Oct. 61	Nov. 45	Dec. 41

SOURCE OF ADDITIONAL INFORMATION ON WATER CONDITIONS
   None available

HAZARDS: Deadfalls

RESCUE INDEX: C
   A Extremely remote; evacuation only with expert help—6 hours to secure assistance
   B Remote; 3-6 hours to secure assistance
   C Accessible but difficult; up to 3 hours to secure assistance—evacuation difficult
   D Accessible; up to 1 hour to secure assistance, evacuation not difficult

PORTAGES: None required

SCOUTING: None required

INTEREST HIGHLIGHTS: Scenery, local culture and industry

SCENERY: Uninspiring to pretty in spots

ACCESS POINT	ACCESS CODE	KEY
A	1 3 5 7	1 Paved Road
B	1 3 5 8	2 Unpaved Road
C	1 3 6 8	3 Short Carry
D	1 3 6 7	4 Long Carry
E	1 3 5 7	5 Easy Grade
F	1 3 6 8	6 Steep Grade
G	1 3 5 7	7 Clear Trail
H	1 3 5 7	8 Brush and Trees
I	1 3 6 8	9 Private Property, Permission Needed
J	1 3 5 8	10 Launching Fee Charged
K	1 3 5 8	11 No Access—For Reference Only

NORTH FORK OF THE LICKING RIVER

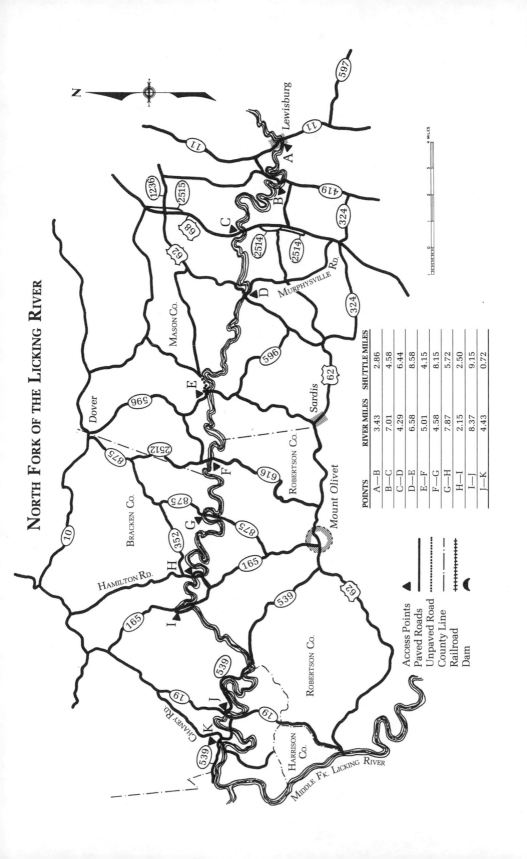

POINTS	RIVER MILES	SHUTTLE MILES
A—B	3.43	2.86
B—C	7.01	4.58
C—D	4.29	6.44
D—E	6.58	8.58
E—F	5.01	4.15
F—G	4.58	8.15
G—H	7.87	5.72
H—I	2.15	2.50
I—J	8.37	9.15
J—K	4.43	0.72

Access Points
Paved Roads
Unpaved Road
County Line
Railroad
Dam

SECTION: Tailwater of Cave Run Dam to KY 32 (Bath Co., Nicholas Co.)

USGS QUADS: Bangor, Salt Lick, Farmers, Colfax, Hillsboro, Sherburne, Moorefield, Cowan

LEVEL OF DIFFICULTY International Class I   Numerical Points 3

SUITABLE FOR: Cruising   **GRADIENT** (feet per mile): 1.22

APPROPRIATE FOR: Families, Beginners, Intermediates, Advanced

VELOCITY (mph): 2.6-5.0   **AVERAGE WIDTH** (ft): 30-65

MONTHS RUNNABLE: Mid-October to early June and subject to release from dam

RUNNABLE WATER LEVEL (cfs) Minimum   170
   Maximum   Up to flood stage

MEAN WATER TEMPERATURE (°F)

Jan. 42	Feb. 42	Mar. 46	Apr. 54	May 68	Jun. 76
Jul. 79	Aug. 77	Sep. 69	Oct. 60	Nov. 45	Dec. 40

SOURCE OF ADDITIONAL INFORMATION ON WATER CONDITIONS
   Corps of Engineers (606) 783-7001

HAZARDS: Deadfalls

RESCUE INDEX: B-C
   A Extremely remote; evacuation only with expert help—6 hours to secure assistance
   B Remote; 3-6 hours to secure assistance
   C Accessible but difficult; up to 3 hours to secure assistance—evacuation difficult
   D Accessible; up to 1 hour to secure assistance, evacuation not difficult

PORTAGES: Around deadfalls

SCOUTING: None

INTEREST HIGHLIGHTS: Scenery

SCENERY: Pretty to pretty in spots

ACCESS POINT	ACCESS CODE	KEY
A	1 3 5 7	1 Paved Road
B	1 3 5 7	2 Unpaved Road
C	2 3 5 7	3 Short Carry
D	1 3 6 7	4 Long Carry
E	1 3 6 7	5 Easy Grade
F*	1 3 6 7	6 Steep Grade
		7 Clear Trail
		8 Brush and Trees
		9 Private Property, Permission Needed
		10 Launching Fee Charged
		11 No Access—For Reference Only

*Side road off KY 32 at mouth of Cassidy Creek

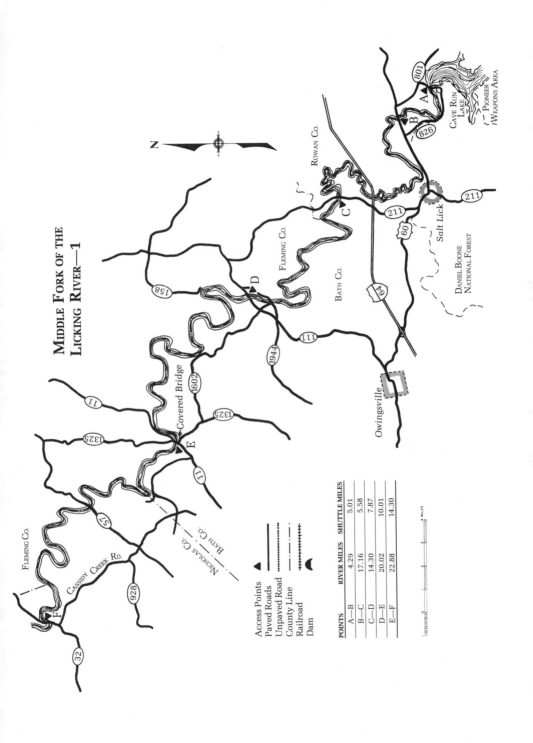

MIDDLE FORK OF THE LICKING RIVER—1

POINTS	RIVER MILES	SHUTTLE MILES
A—B	4.29	5.01
B—C	17.16	5.58
C—D	14.30	7.87
D—E	20.02	10.01
E—F	22.88	14.30

Access Points ▲
Paved Roads
Unpaved Road
County Line
Railroad
Dam ◖

SECTION: KY 32 to Claysville (Fleming Co., Nicholas Co., Robertson Co., Harrison Co.)

USGS QUADS: Cowan, Piqua, Shady Nook

LEVEL OF DIFFICULTY International Class I   **Numerical Points** 4

SUITABLE FOR: Cruising, camping§ **GRADIENT** (feet per mile): 1.15

APPROPRIATE FOR: Families, Beginners, Intermediates, Advanced

VELOCITY (mph): 2.6-5.0   **AVERAGE WIDTH** (ft): 60-80

MONTHS RUNNABLE: All

RUNNABLE WATER LEVEL (cfs) Minimum 280
Maximum Up to flood stage

MEAN WATER TEMPERATURE (°F)

Jan. 42	Feb. 42	Mar. 46	Apr. 54	May 68	Jun. 76
Jul. 79	Aug. 77	Sep. 69	Oct. 60	Nov. 45	Dec. 40

SOURCE OF ADDITIONAL INFORMATION ON WATER CONDITIONS
Corps of Engineers (606) 783-7001

HAZARDS: Deadfalls

RESCUE INDEX: C
 A Extremely remote; evacuation only with expert help—6 hours to secure assistance
 B Remote; 3-6 hours to secure assistance
 C Accessible but difficult; up to 3 hours to secure assistance—evacuation difficult
 D Accessible; up to 1 hour to secure assistance, evacuation not difficult

PORTAGES: None required

SCOUTING: None required

INTEREST HIGHLIGHTS: Scenery, local culture and industry

SCENERY: Pretty to pretty in spots

ACCESS POINT	ACCESS CODE	KEY
F*	1 3 6 7	1 Paved Road
G	1 4 6 7 9	2 Unpaved Road
H†	2 3 6 7	3 Short Carry
		4 Long Carry
		5 Easy Grade
		6 Steep Grade
		7 Clear Trail
		8 Brush and Trees
		9 Private Property, Permission Needed
		10 Launching Fee Charged
		11 No Access—For Reference Only

*Side road off of KY 32 at the mouth of Cassidy Creek
†Side road off of U.S. 62 at the mouth of Greasy Creek
§Overnight trip camping at Blue Licks Battlefield State Park

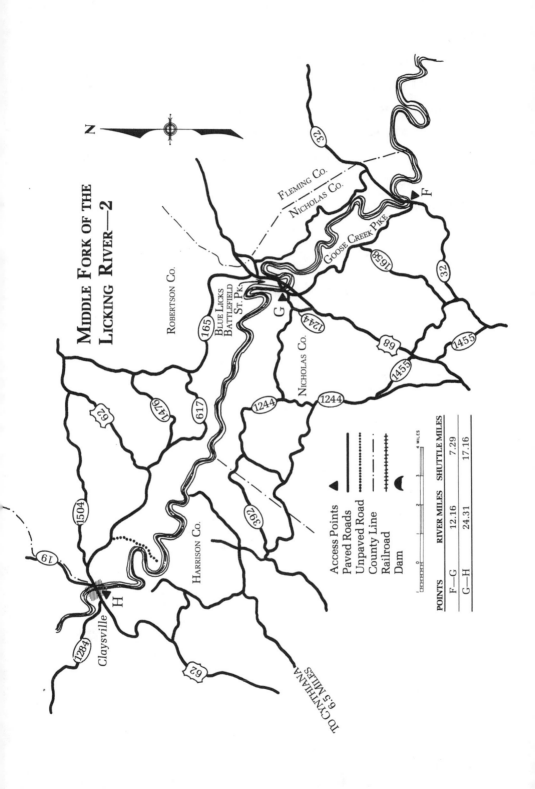

MIDDLE FORK OF THE LICKING RIVER—2

N

ROBERTSON CO.

FLEMING CO.
NICHOLAS CO.

GOOSE CREEK PIKE

BLUE LICKS
BATTLEFIELD
ST. PK.

NICHOLAS CO.

HARRISON CO.

Claysville

TO CYNTHIANA
6.5 MILES

Access Points	▲
Paved Roads	
Unpaved Road	
County Line	
Railroad	
Dam	◗

0 1 2 3 4 MILES

POINTS	RIVER MILES	SHUTTLE MILES
F—G	12.16	7.29
G—H	24.31	17.16

SECTION: Claysville to Falmouth (Harrison Co., Bracken Co., Pendleton Co.)

USGS QUADS: Shady Nook, Claysville, Berlin, Faimouth

LEVEL OF DIFFICULTY International Class I   Numerical Points 4

SUITABLE FOR: Cruising   **GRADIENT** (feet per mile): 1.02

APPROPRIATE FOR: Families, Beginners, Intermediates, Advanced

VELOCITY (mph): 2.6-5.0   **AVERAGE WIDTH** (ft): 70-90

MONTHS RUNNABLE: All

RUNNABLE WATER LEVEL (cfs) Minimum 280
    Maximum Up to flood stage

MEAN WATER TEMPERATURE (°F)

Jan. 42	Feb. 42	Mar. 46	Apr. 54	May 68	Jun. 76
Jul. 79	Aug. 77	Sep. 69	Oct. 60	Nov. 45	Dec. 40

SOURCE OF ADDITIONAL INFORMATION ON WATER CONDITIONS
    Corps of Engineers (606) 783-7001

HAZARDS: Deadfalls

RESCUE INDEX: C
    A Extremely remote; evacuation only with expert help—6 hours to secure assistance
    B Remote; 3-6 hours to secure assistance
    C Accessible but difficult; up to 3 hours to secure assistance—evacuation difficult
    D Accessible; up to 1 hour to secure assistance, evacuation not difficult

PORTAGES: None required

SCOUTING: None required

INTEREST HIGHLIGHTS: Scenery, local culture and industry

SCENERY: Pretty to pretty in spots

ACCESS POINT	ACCESS CODE	KEY
H†	2 3 6 7	1 Paved Road
I	1 3 6 7	2 Unpaved Road
J	1 3 6 8	3 Short Carry
		4 Long Carry
		5 Easy Grade
		6 Steep Grade
		7 Clear Trail
		8 Brush and Trees
		9 Private Property, Permission Needed
		10 Launching Fee Charged
		11 No Access—For Reference Only

†Side road off of U.S. 62 at the mouth of Greasy Creek

72

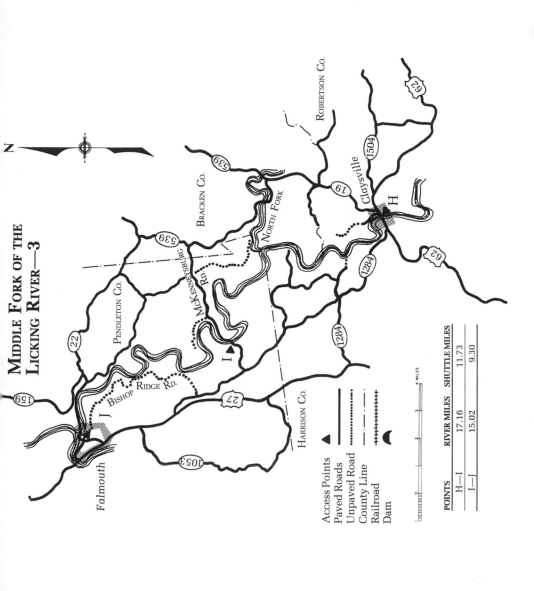

Middle Fork of the Licking River—3

N

Falmouth

Pendleton Co.

Bishop Ridge Rd.

McKennysburg Rd.

Bracken Co.

North Fork

Claysville

Robertson Co.

Harrison Co.

159

22

539

539

27

1053

1284

1284

19

1504

62

62

J

I

H

Access Points
Paved Roads
Unpaved Road
County Line
Railroad
Dam

0   1   2   3   4 MILES

POINTS	RIVER MILES	SHUTTLE MILES
H–I	17.16	11.73
I–J	15.02	9.30

SECTION: Millersburg to Ruddels Mills (Bourbon Co.)

USGS QUADS: Carlisle, Millersburg, Shawhan

LEVEL OF DIFFICULTY International Class I   Numerical Points   4

SUITABLE FOR: Cruising   **GRADIENT** (feet per mile): 1.57

APPROPRIATE FOR: Families, Beginners, Intermediates, Advanced

VELOCITY (mph): 2.6-5.0   **AVERAGE WIDTH** (ft): 30-40

MONTHS RUNNABLE: November to early June

RUNNABLE WATER LEVEL (cfs) Minimum   150
  Maximum   Up to flood stage

MEAN WATER TEMPERATURE ($^\circ$F)

Jan. 42	Feb. 42	Mar. 45	Apr. 52	May 66	Jun. 77
Jul. 79	Aug. 78	Sep. 68	Oct. 61	Nov. 46	Dec. 41

SOURCE OF ADDITIONAL INFORMATION ON WATER CONDITIONS
  None available

HAZARDS: Deadfalls

RESCUE INDEX: D
  A Extremely remote; evacuation only with expert help—6 hours to secure assistance
  B Remote; 3-6 hours to secure assistance
  C Accessible but difficult; up to 3 hours to secure assistance—evacuation difficult
  D Accessible; up to 1 hour to secure assistance, evacuation not difficult

PORTAGES: None required

SCOUTING: None required

INTEREST HIGHLIGHTS: Scenery, history, local culture and industry

SCENERY: Pretty

ACCESS POINT	ACCESS CODE	KEY
A	1 3 6 7	1 Paved Road
B	1 3 5 7	2 Unpaved Road
C	1 3 6 7	3 Short Carry
D	1 3 5 8 9	4 Long Carry
E	1 3 5 7	5 Easy Grade
		6 Steep Grade
		7 Clear Trail
		8 Brush and Trees
		9 Private Property, Permission Needed
		10 Launching Fee Charged
		11 No Access—For Reference Only

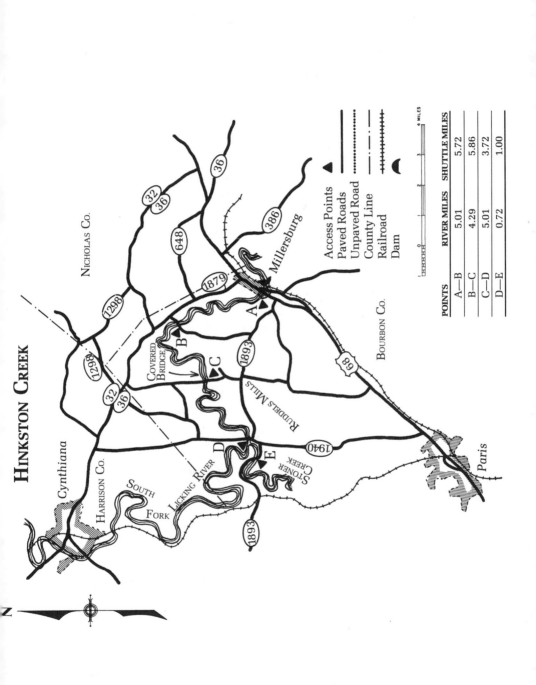

HINKSTON CREEK

POINTS	RIVER MILES	SHUTTLE MILES
A—B	5.01	5.72
B—C	4.29	5.86
C—D	5.01	3.72
D—E	0.72	1.00

Access Points
Paved Roads
Unpaved Road
County Line
Railroad
Dam

0   1   2   3   4 MILES

SECTION: Thomas Road bridge to Ruddels Mills (Bourbon Co.)

USGS QUADS: Paris East, Paris West, Shawhan

LEVEL OF DIFFICULTY International Class I   Numerical Points **4**

SUITABLE FOR: Cruising   **GRADIENT** (feet per mile): **2.36**

APPROPRIATE FOR: Families, Beginners, Intermediates, Advanced

VELOCITY (mph): 0-5.0   **AVERAGE WIDTH** (ft): 30-40

MONTHS RUNNABLE: November to early June

RUNNABLE WATER LEVEL (cfs) Minimum   160
    Maximum   Up to flood stage

MEAN WATER TEMPERATURE ($^\circ$F)

Jan. 42	Feb. 43	Mar. 45	Apr. 53	May 66	Jun. 76
Jul. 77	Aug. 77	Sep. 68	Oct. 62	Nov. 45	Dec. 41

SOURCE OF ADDITIONAL INFORMATION ON WATER CONDITIONS
    Paris Police Dept. (606) 987-2100

HAZARDS: Deadfalls, low bridges

RESCUE INDEX: D
    A Extremely remote; evacuation only with expert help—6 hours to secure assistance
    B Remote; 3-6 hours to secure assistance
    C Accessible but difficult; up to 3 hours to secure assistance—evacuation difficult
    D Accessible; up to 1 hour to secure assistance, evacuation not difficult

PORTAGES: None required

SCOUTING: None required

INTEREST HIGHLIGHTS: Scenery, history, local culture and industry

SCENERY: Pretty to beautiful in spots

ACCESS POINT	ACCESS CODE	KEY
A	1 3 6 7 9	1 Paved Road
B	1 3 6 7 9	2 Unpaved Road
C*	1 3 6 7*	3 Short Carry
D	1 3 5 8	4 Long Carry
E	1 3 5 7	5 Easy Grade
F	1 3 5 7 9	6 Steep Grade
G	1 3 5 7	7 Clear Trail
		8 Brush and Trees
		9 Private Property, Permission Needed
		10 Launching Fee Charged
		11 No Access—For Reference Only

*One-quarter mile upstream on Hutchins Creek

STONER CREEK

Access Points
Paved Roads
Unpaved Road
County Line
Railroad
Dam

N

Bourbon Co.

North Middleton

South Fork of the Licking River

Hinkston Creek

Coulthard Rd.

Peacock Rd.

Spears Mills Rd.

Thomas Rd.

Stony Point Rd.

Paris

POINTS	RIVER MILES	SHUTTLE MILES
A—B	2.72	2.00
B—C	14.16	8.15
C—D	1.72	1.43
D—E	3.00	1.29
E—F	6.44	4.58
F—G	5.72	5.15

SECTION: Ruddels Mills to Berry (Bourbon Co., Harrison Co.)

USGS QUADS: Shawhan, Cynthiana, Breckinridge, Berry

LEVEL OF DIFFICULTY International Class I   Numerical Points 3

SUITABLE FOR: Cruising   **GRADIENT** (feet per mile): 3.46

APPROPRIATE FOR: Families, Beginners, Intermediates, Advanced

VELOCITY (mph): 0-2.5   **AVERAGE WIDTH** (ft): 45-65

MONTHS RUNNABLE: All

RUNNABLE WATER LEVEL (cfs) Minimum 200
Maximum Up to flood stage

MEAN WATER TEMPERATURE (°F)

Jan. 43	Feb. 42	Mar. 46	Apr. 54	May 68	Jun. 77
Jul. 79	Aug. 77	Sep. 69	Oct. 61	Nov. 45	Dec. 42

SOURCE OF ADDITIONAL INFORMATION ON WATER CONDITIONS
Cynthiana Police Dept. (606) 234-4242

HAZARDS: Dams, deadfalls

RESCUE INDEX: C-D
  A Extremely remote; evacuation only with expert help—6 hours to secure assistance
  B Remote; 3-6 hours to secure assistance
  C Accessible but difficult; up to 3 hours to secure assistance—evacuation difficult
  D Accessible; up to 1 hour to secure assistance, evacuation not difficult

PORTAGES: Around dams at Cynthiana, Poindexter, Robinson, and Berry

SCOUTING: As required to portage around dams

INTEREST HIGHLIGHTS: Scenery, history, local culture and industry

SCENERY: Pretty to pretty in spots

ACCESS POINT	ACCESS CODE	KEY
A*	1 3 5 7	1 Paved Road
B	1 3 6 7	2 Unpaved Road
C	1 3 6 7	3 Short Carry
D	1 3 6 8	4 Long Carry
E	1 3 5 7	5 Easy Grade
F	1 3 5 8	6 Steep Grade
		7 Clear Trail
		8 Brush and Trees
		9 Private Property, Permission Needed
		10 Launching Fee Charged
		11 No Access—For Reference Only

*On Stoner Creek

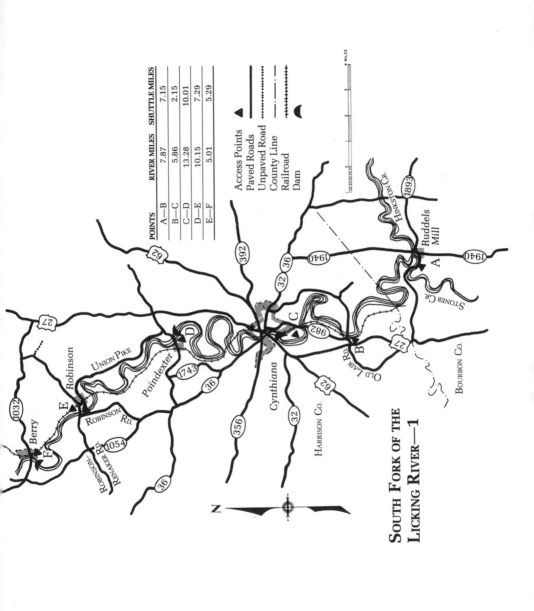

POINTS	RIVER MILES	SHUTTLE MILES
A—B	7.87	7.15
B—C	5.86	2.15
C—D	13.28	10.01
D—E	10.15	7.29
E—F	5.01	5.29

Access Points
Paved Roads
Unpaved Road
County Line
Railroad
Dam

MILES

SOUTH FORK OF THE
LICKING RIVER—1

SECTION: Berry to Falmouth (Harrison Co., Pendleton Co.)

USGS QUADS: Berry, Goforth, Falmouth

LEVEL OF DIFFICULTY International Class I   Numerical Points 3

SUITABLE FOR: Cruising   **GRADIENT** (feet per mile): 3.23

APPROPRIATE FOR: Families, Beginners, Intermediates, Advanced

VELOCITY (mph): 0-2.5   **AVERAGE WIDTH** (ft): 45-75

MONTHS RUNNABLE: All

RUNNABLE WATER LEVEL (cfs) Minimum 200
    Maximum Up to flood stage

MEAN WATER TEMPERATURE (°F)

Jan. 43	Feb. 42	Mar. 46	Apr. 54	May 68	Jun. 77
Jul. 79	Aug. 77	Sep. 69	Oct. 61	Nov. 45	Dec. 42

SOURCE OF ADDITIONAL INFORMATION ON WATER CONDITIONS
    Cynthiana Police Dept. (606) 234-4242

HAZARDS: Dams, deadfalls

RESCUE INDEX: C-D
    A Extremely remote; evacuation only with expert help—6 hours to secure assistance
    B Remote; 3-6 hours to secure assistance
    C Accessible but difficult; up to 3 hours to secure assistance—evacuation difficult
    D Accessible; up to 1 hour to secure assistance, evacuation not difficult

PORTAGES: Around dams at Berry and Falmouth

SCOUTING: As required to portage around dams

INTEREST HIGHLIGHTS: Scenery, history, local culture and industry

SCENERY: Pretty to pretty in spots

ACCESS POINT	ACCESS CODE	KEY
F	1 3 5 8	1 Paved Road
G	1 3 5 8	2 Unpaved Road
H	1 3 6 7	3 Short Carry
I	1 3 6 8	4 Long Carry
J*	1 3 6 8	5 Easy Grade
		6 Steep Grade
		7 Clear Trail
		8 Brush and Trees
		9 Private Property, Permission Needed
		10 Launching Fee Charged
		11 No Access—For Reference Only

*On the Middle Fork of the Licking River

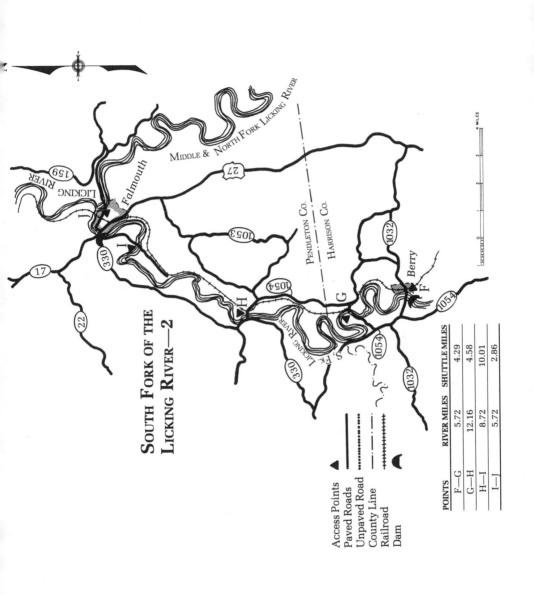

SOUTH FORK OF THE LICKING RIVER—2

Middle & North Fork Licking River

LICKING RIVER

Falmouth

Berry

Pendleton Co.
Harrison Co.

S. Fk. Licking River

Access Points
Paved Roads
Unpaved Road
County Line
Railroad
Dam

POINTS	RIVER MILES	SHUTTLE MILES
F–G	5.72	4.29
G–H	12.16	4.58
H–I	8.72	10.01
I–J	5.72	2.86

4 MILES

SECTION: Falmouth to Ohio River (Pendleton Co., Kenton Co., Campbell Co.)

USGS QUADS: Falmouth, Butler, DeMossville, Alexandria, Newport, Covington

LEVEL OF DIFFICULTY International Class I   Numerical Points 4

SUITABLE FOR: Cruising   **GRADIENT** (feet per mile): 1.25

APPROPRIATE FOR: Beginners, Intermediates, Advanced

VELOCITY (mph): 2.6-5.0   **AVERAGE WIDTH** (ft): 80-130

MONTHS RUNNABLE: All

RUNNABLE WATER LEVEL (cfs) Minimum   240
Maximum   Up to flood stage

MEAN WATER TEMPERATURE (°F)

| Jan. 42 | Feb. 42 | Mar. 45 | Apr. 53 | May 64 | Jun. 74 |
| Jul. 76 | Aug. 75 | Sep. 68 | Oct. 60 | Nov. 45 | Dec. 39 |

SOURCE OF ADDITIONAL INFORMATION ON WATER CONDITIONS
Corps of Engineers (606) 783-7001

HAZARDS: Powerboats

RESCUE INDEX: C-D
A Extremely remote; evacuation only with expert help—6 hours to secure assistance
B Remote; 3-6 hours to secure assistance
C Accessible but difficult; up to 3 hours to secure assistance—evacuation difficult
D Accessible; up to 1 hour to secure assistance, evacuation not difficult

PORTAGES: None required

SCOUTING: None required

INTEREST HIGHLIGHTS: Scenery, local culture and industry

SCENERY: Pleasant in spots to pretty in spots

ACCESS POINT	ACCESS CODE	KEY
A	1 3 6 8	1 Paved Road
B	1 3 6 8	2 Unpaved Road
C	1 3 6 8	3 Short Carry
D	2 3 5 8	4 Long Carry
		5 Easy Grade
		6 Steep Grade
		7 Clear Trail
		8 Brush and Trees
		9 Private Property, Permission Needed
		10 Launching Fee Charged
		11 No Access—For Reference Only

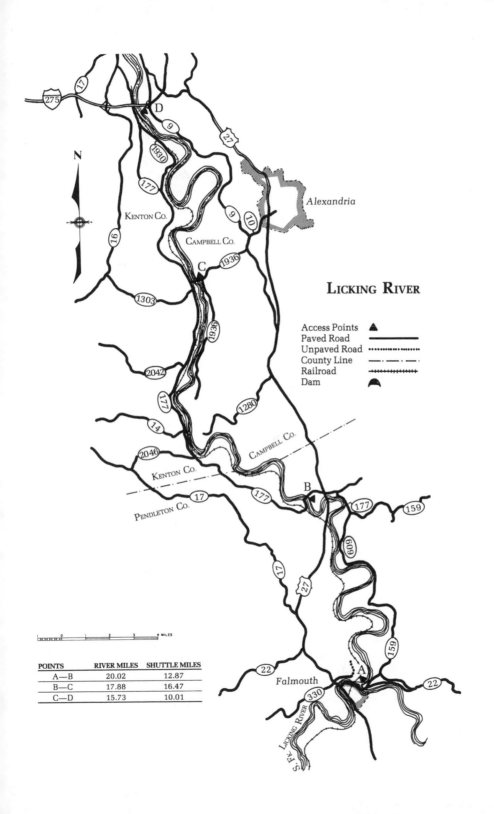

LICKING RIVER

Access Points ▲
Paved Road ———
Unpaved Road ••••••••••
County Line —·—·—
Railroad ++++++++
Dam ⌒

N

275 17

D
9
1930
177
16   KENTON CO.
9
10   Alexandria
CAMPBELL CO.
C   1936
1303
1936
2042
177
14
2046   CAMPBELL CO.
KENTON CO.
17   B
PENDLETON CO.   177   177   159
609
17
27
159
22   A   22
Falmouth
330
S. FK. LICKING RIVER

POINTS	RIVER MILES	SHUTTLE MILES
A—B	20.02	12.87
B—C	17.88	16.47
C—D	15.73	10.01

0   1   2   3   4 MILES

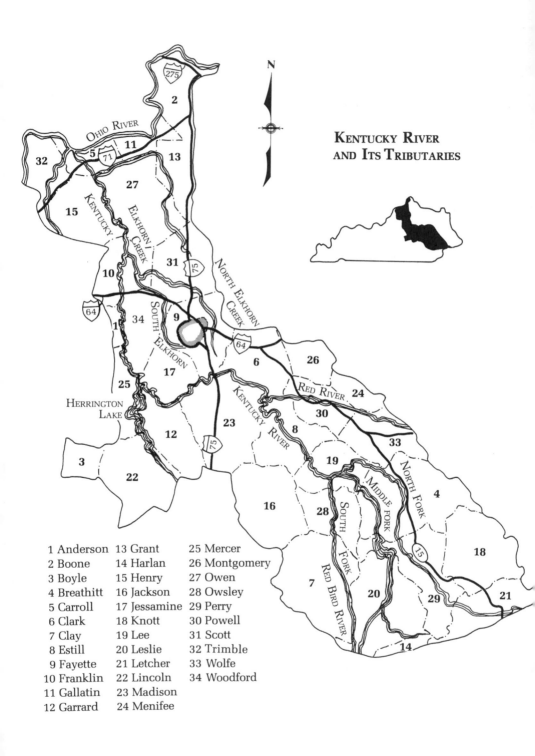

KENTUCKY RIVER AND ITS TRIBUTARIES

N

OHIO RIVER

KENTUCKY RIVER

ELKHORN CREEK

NORTH ELKHORN CREEK

SOUTH ELKHORN

HERRINGTON LAKE

RED RIVER

KENTUCKY RIVER

SOUTH FORK

MIDDLE FORK

NORTH FORK

RED BIRD RIVER

1 Anderson	13 Grant	25 Mercer
2 Boone	14 Harlan	26 Montgomery
3 Boyle	15 Henry	27 Owen
4 Breathitt	16 Jackson	28 Owsley
5 Carroll	17 Jessamine	29 Perry
6 Clark	18 Knott	30 Powell
7 Clay	19 Lee	31 Scott
8 Estill	20 Leslie	32 Trimble
9 Fayette	21 Letcher	33 Wolfe
10 Franklin	22 Lincoln	34 Woodford
11 Gallatin	23 Madison	
12 Garrard	24 Menifee	

3
THE KENTUCKY RIVER AND ITS TRIBUTARIES

NORTH FORK OF THE KENTUCKY RIVER

The North Fork of the Kentucky River originates in the mountains of southeastern Kentucky near Whitesburg and flows northwest draining the counties of Letcher, Perry, Breathitt, and Lee. The North Fork is runnable in its upper reaches (Roxana to Viper) during the winter and early spring only. Downstream, from Viper to Jackson, the river can be paddled from late October to mid-June. Below Jackson, the North Fork of the Kentucky is usually runnable all year.

In the upper sections, the river is 35 to 40 feet wide and flows over a mud and gravel bed through steep, wooded valleys and coal country. Although the terrain is rugged, man and his habitat are visible all along the upper North Fork. While detracting from the wilderness atmosphere, the small towns, frame houses, wooden footbridges, and porch-front rockers present an enduring and picturesque perspective of Eastern Kentucky mountain living. The river itself is winding and has steep banks that make access generally difficult, even at bridges. Trees overhang the stream in the extreme upper section (above Blackey) but give way to thick scrub vegetation further downstream. Paddling is interesting with numerous small shoals and rapids (Class I+). Deadfalls pose the only major peril to navigation.

As Line Fork enters the stream at the Perry–Letcher county line, water volume increases significantly, and the river widens to approximately 55 to 60 feet. As KY 15 intersects the river south of Hazard, the North Fork sinks into increasingly deep banks. Even with a highway on the west and a railroad on the east, access is difficult. Scenery, however, remains beautiful.

Downstream of Hazard, the water's quality diminishes due to mining discharge, and there is less vegetation along the banks.

Signs of human habitation are more frequent and far less pictu-resque than farther upstream. The river valley broadens here and farm fields become more common. Rapids and shoals disappear as the stream settles into mud banks. As the North Fork flows north through Jackson towards Beattyville, the surrounding hills (known locally as mountains) become smaller and the river wid-ens to an average of 80 feet and expands to 110 feet at its conflu-ence with the Middle Fork of the Kentucky. Though runnable all year, this section lacks the intimacy and beauty typical of the upper sections.

MIDDLE FORK OF THE KENTUCKY RIVER

The Middle Fork of the Kentucky River originates in the south-eastern Kentucky mountains of Leslie County and flows north through the tip of Perry County into Buckhorn Lake, and from there north through Breathitt County into Lee County where it joins the North Fork of the Kentucky near Beattyville.

The upper waters of the Middle Fork roll out of the hills in the western portion of Leslie County in the Daniel Boone National Forest. Although the upper reaches are crowded with small mountain communities, the river valley and surrounding hills are nevertheless extremely beautiful. The river flows over a rock and gravel bed with almost continuous Class-I+ and Class-II rapids and shoals. Runnable in late winter and early spring, the upper section is paralleled by KY 1780 from which the run can be scouted. Hazards, including deadfalls, low bridges, and two con-crete fords, are easily spotted. The river is small, averaging 25 to 35 feet in width. Banks are 6 to 10 feet in height and easily traversed; access is good. The river side of the banks is well vege-tated, but most trees are situated somewhat back on the floodplain away from the river providing the mixed blessing of being able to see both the human habitation and the truly spectacular surround-ing hills ("mountains") as you paddle along.

Near the intersection of KY 1780 and U.S. 421, the river collects several major tributaries and proceeds to follow U.S. 421 north towards Hyden. This section is also characterized by extremely mild whitewater (Class I+), but it is of a more intermittent nature. Access once again is good, and the scenery is much improved as the river moves away from the line of houses and barns that dot the headwaters. Runnable from late November to early June, this section passes through beautiful wilderness hill terrain before emer-ging in Hoskinston. Beyond Hoskinston and Stinnett the river again slips into the forest to rejoin civilization in Hyden. Occa-sional deadfalls and a five-foot dam as the river approaches the

86

Leslie County High School complex south of Hyden are the only dangers to navigation.

At Hyden, the river averages 50 feet in width and has descended into a luxurious green valley sprinkled with cabins on the hills overlooking the river. Its banks are mud and are extremely tall and steep. Above the steep banks a gorge rises with exposed rock visible. This can best be appreciated during the colder months when the foliage of trees along the banks does not obstruct the view. From Hyden to Buckhorn Lake the river smooths considerably and has only a few riffles and small waves. Access is good where it is available. This section is normally runnable from November to early June.

From the tailwaters of the Buckhorn Dam to the mouth of Turkey Creek in Breathitt County, the river widens somewhat but otherwise remains essentially the same. Habitation along the Middle Fork increases sharply along this section as the river departs the national forest. This section is runnable almost all year and access is good.

From the mouth of Turkey Creek (near Guerrant) to the Lee County line, the Middle Fork flows through hilly woods and farm country, but population is sparse and fewer dwellings are visible from the river. Between Turkey Creek and its confluence with the North Fork of the Kentucky, the Middle Fork swells to 110 to 130 feet in width. Like the North Fork, the Middle Fork in Lee County lacks the dramatic scenery and continually changing vistas of the upper sections.

RED BIRD RIVER

The Red Bird River is the main tributary of the South Fork of the Kentucky River. Running over a bed of rock, gravel, and mud, the Red Bird winds through the Daniel Boone National Forest draining the eastern half of Clay County. Runnable in late fall and spring, the river can best be described as a busy Class I with almost continuous riffles, small waves, and shoals. At higher water, several of the shoals and small rapids may be classified as borderline Class II. The Red Bird valley is one of the most beautiful in the Daniel Boone National Forest with steep hills looming above the river and lush vegetation everywhere. Some human habitation is in evidence along the Red Bird River, but it does not usually detract from the beauty of the stream. Banks are 5 to 8 feet high and of varying steepness. Access is good from the Red Bird Hospital to the KY 80 bridge, average width is 30 to 40 feet throughout, and concrete fords and deadfalls represent the only navigational hazards.

SOUTH FORK OF THE KENTUCKY RIVER

The South Fork of the Kentucky River originates at the confluence of the Red Bird River and Bullskin Creek (at Eriline) in Clay County and flows north over primarily mud banks through Owsley County to its confluence with the North and Middle Forks of the Kentucky River near Beattyville in Lee County.

From the mouth of the Red Bird River to Oneida, the South Fork averages 35 to 50 feet in width and is primarily Class I with some occasional small shoals. The surrounding scenery is very pleasant as the river meanders through a broad valley bordered with high, wooded hills. Access is fair, at best, in this section because of a scarcity of crossings and high, steep banks. Vegetation is thick and trees line the streamside. Navigational hazards consist mainly of deadfalls.

North of Oneida (which is further downstream), the banks remain very high and steep. Trees are less frequent at streamside and much of the surrounding floodplain has been terraced and farmed. The river is less scenic here than upstream but the general absence of trees along the immediate banks allows a good view of the bordering hillsides.

Approximately three miles north of Oneida, near Teges, the river turns sharply to the east away from KY 11 (which follows the stream downstream of Oneida) into a dense, secluded woodland. From here to the Clay–Owsley county line lies the most scenic and interesting paddling of the entire South Fork. Runnable from November to mid-June, this section is alive with small shoals and several borderline Class-II rapids. Sloping hillsides bring the forest right down to the river bank. Average width is 45 to 55 feet and access is good. Navigational dangers are limited to an occasional deadfall and a concrete ford.

As the South Fork flows through Owsley County leaving behind the national forest, it encounters broader valleys, scenic, pastoral farmland, and increased human habitation. Riffles and shoals are infrequent here and disappear altogether after the South Fork passes Booneville. Between Booneville and its confluence with the North and Middle Forks, the South Fork averages 70 to 90 feet in width and is runnable all year. Access is fair to good.

KENTUCKY RIVER BELOW THE FORKS

BEATTYVILLE TO VALLEY VIEW TO FRANKFORT. The Kentucky River from Beattyville to Frankfort would be a good canoeing stream were it not for the abundance of powerboats, both pleasure and commercial. The Kentucky River is scenic, running first through forested hills and well-kept farmland, later curving beneath 400-foot exposed rock palisades, and finally emerging into a broad, fertile plain bordered by tall, wooded ridges. Access is plentiful and usually good. Dangers to navigation include ten dams (exclusive of No. 4 below Frankfort), floating debris, and of course, the ever-present armada of powercraft. A Class-I river, the Kentucky is runnable all year. Its banks are mud and usually steep. Numerous trip possibilities exist along this 83-mile stretch. Points of interest include Fort Boonesborough State Park (with beach and campground) just below Lock No. 10, a 30-foot waterfall one-half mile up Boone Creek (entering the Kentucky River on the right just upstream of the I-75 bridge), numerous small tributary streams worthy of exploration between Lock 9 and Lock 8, historic Camp Nelson downstream of Lock 8, High Bridge and the mouth of the Dix River below Dix Dam (Herrington Lake) just upstream of Lock 7, and the City of Frankfort (the capital of Kentucky) above Lock 4. The most scenic run between Beattyville and Frankfort is between Lock 8 and Lock 7 where magnificient exposed rock palisades grace the river on both sides. This can be made into a canoe-camping run with an overnight stop at Camp Nelson.

Visitors are welcome at all of the locks, and the lock grounds are as well kept and pretty as any park and are eminently suitable for picnicking, putting-in, or taking-out. Two locks (10 and 8) have beaches adjoining them. You can usually leave shuttle vehicles parked at the locks while running the river, but be sure to check with the Lockmaster to find out what time the grounds are closed.

When approaching the locks from the river, all must obviously be portaged. This presents no problem except at Locks 9, 10, and 5 where no good landing areas exist. If you expect to portage Lock 9, 10, or 5, carry two 30-foot lengths of line to hoist your boat up the side of the lock (there will be a ladder for you). If you are in a large group or arrive at the lock at the same time as a powerboat, the Lockmaster will normally allow you to lock through. While not as fast as carrying around, locking through is fun and interesting, particularly if there are children in the group.

FRANKFORT TO THE OHIO RIVER. From Frankfort to the Ohio River, the Kentucky River continues through farm valleys bordered by steep ridges. The level of difficulty remains Class I throughout with portages being limited to four locks (including No. 4 at Frankfort). Access is generally good and dangers to navigation are the same as those listed for Frankfort to Beattyville.

RED RIVER

Originating in Wolfe County, the Red River (of Kentucky) flows northwest through Powell County and along the Estill–Clark county line before emptying into the Kentucky River south of Winchester. During the early seventies, national attention was focused on the river and on the beautiful Red River Gorge through which it flows, when Kentuckians and conservationists from throughout the country successfully fought the Corps of Engineers over the building of a dam. Hanging in the balance as the battle raged was the heart of the Red River and some of the most spectacular canoeing waters anywhere in the eastern United States.

For paddling purposes the Red River is popularly divided into three sections: the Upper, the Middle, and the Lower Red River.

UPPER RED RIVER. The Upper Red River is a Class-II to -III whitewater stream of unparalleled beauty winding among boulders and beneath cavernous overhangs. Only 20 feet wide at the put-in near the KY 746 bridge, the Upper Red remains intimate throughout with hardwoods shading the water and mountain laurel growing thick above the rock ledges. The first three miles are scenic Class-I water with a good current and a few small riffles and ledges. Below the mouth of Stillwater Creek the gradient increases with a technical, Class-II rapid.

From here downstream the Red winds below imposing bluffs assuming a pattern of alternating pools and small rapids (Class I+), with the only interruption coming in the form of a river-wide ledge ranging from 1½ to 2½ feet in height and often referred to as the "Falls." This ledge is sometimes difficult to get over at low to moderate water levels and is best run far left or far right. Continuing downstream, the river remains well behaved until it reaches the mouth of Peck Branch. For the next half mile the Upper Red twists through a series of three borderline Class-III rapids popularly known as the "Narrows of the Red." The first rapid is a long series of ledges with a healthy sampling of rocks to dodge, ending with a 2½-foot plunge into a beautiful pool. Enter at the top left-center, skirt the obstructing rocks as water level allows, and pull into the eddy behind the last midstream rock before the vertical drop. Run the vertical drop by hugging the large boulder on the far left. The second rapid, 30 yards downstream is known as "Dog Drowning Hole" and should probably be scouted (on the right). It consists of a turning chute accompanied by a great deal of water turbulence. At low water it is very technical and at higher water very squirrely with irregular waves and currents. The total drop along the length of this rapid is approximately five feet. At the third rapid of the "Narrows," the river appears to come to a dead end. The current is deflected along the upstream face of a large boulder to the left bank where it cuts right, down a fast sluice with an inclined three-foot drop, finally washing up on an undercut rock 30 feet downstream. Run the sluice right center and grab an eddy on the right before the undercut rock grabs you.

From here downstream to the take-out at the KY 715 bridge the run is an easy Class II with delightful scenery and lots of hikers and backpackers to wave at.

The Upper Red is runnable from late December to late May in years of average rainfall. Since there are no reliable regular sources of information on water level (sometimes the rangers from the Stanton Ranger Station can provide some information), the Upper Red is difficult to catch at an appropriate paddling level. At very low water the run can turn into a hike. At very high water the Red is extremely dangerous, practically running in the trees. Rapids on the Red are not especially difficult but on the other hand they allow little margin for error. Each year dozens of canoes are demolished on the Upper Red. Dangers other than those already described include frequent deadfalls, several undercut rocks, and the potential of the river to rise rapidly following a rain. The best time to run the Upper Red is in the morning because of the afternoon sun that shines directly into your eyes after about 2 P.M.

MIDDLE RED RIVER. The middle section of the Red River begins at KY 715 bridge and twists through the center of the Red River Gorge, past Sky Bridge Arch, Tower Rock, and Chimney Top Rock and works its way between boulders in the stream eventually ending in the shadow of Raven Rock at the KY 77 bridge. Its level of difficulty is Class I throughout, but numerous sharp turns, sandbars, riffles, and small ledges make the paddling interesting. The scenery is spectacular without exception, with enormous hardwoods shading the stream and wildflowers in abundance. The middle section of the Red is runnable from late fall to early summer most years. Access is excellent. Navigational hazards consist of deadfalls, occasional logjams, and periodic overcrowding. Canoe camping is allowed but the steep, uncompromising terrain militates against it.

LOWER RED RIVER. The Lower Red River, downstream of KY 77, remains very scenic for the first several miles, winding along below Courthouse Rock and finally running out of the Red River Gorge. From here downstream, the river is pleasant and meanders through hilly farm country and woodlands, but it does not compare to the upper and middle sections. Additionally, the lower section is almost always clogged with deadfalls that force portaging or swinging continually back and forth across the river to navigate around them. Flowing over a bed of gravel and mud between steep banks, the Lower Red is bordered by private property and is not suitable for camping. Aside from deadfalls and logjams mentioned above, there are no navigational hazards. The

Lower Red River averages 35 to 55 feet in width and is runnable from late fall to early summer.

BOONE CREEK

Boone Creek is a small, intense stream flowing over a rock bed along the eastern border of Fayette County. Runnable only ten or twelve days a year, it just may be the most singularly beautiful run in the entire state. The upper section (above the Iroquois Hunt Club) snakes over ledges between 20-foot high rock walls. Passing the hunt club, Boone Creek's gradient increases as it descends into a narrow, vertical-walled rock gorge that funnels the stream at furious speed toward its mouth at the Kentucky River. Frequently the constricting gorge walls recede permitting trees to grow along the water's edge. At higher water levels these trees create the only eddies on the run. At several points below the hunt club feeder streams join Boone Creek. Two of these enter the creek after dropping over large waterfalls that are easily visible from Boone Creek. During the spring, wildflowers, particularly bluebells, further enhance the beauty of the stream.

While Boone Creek is beautiful, it is also dangerous. At higher water it is a continuous Class-III run (which many have classified as Class IV because of the scarcity of eddies). Its gradient averages 31 feet per mile but ranges as high as 44 feet per mile in certain sections. Fortunately, however, the gradient is evenly distributed and no single drops exceeding three feet are encountered. Strainers in the form of deadfalls and logjams present the greatest danger. There are three fences—cattle gates on the upper section of the creek. These strainers are particularly dangerous in light of the scarcity of eddies and the fast, pushy current that allows the paddler very little time to react. Action is continuous and generally nontechnical, and consists primarily of standing waves, holes, and small drops. The main channel is easy to discern except at two points on the lower section where the stream splits around small islands. In both cases the right affords the better channel but unfortunately also seems to be the most likely to clog with strainers. Boone Creek at high water is recommended only for intermediate and advanced decked boaters with dependable rolls (rescue of swimming paddlers and their boats is extremely difficult). At moderate levels Boone Creek is a good Class-II to -III run for open boats. First timers (with decked or open boats) should make every effort to go down with someone who knows the run. Access is good at put-in and take-out points. Dangers other than those mentioned include several undercut ledges.

DIX RIVER

The Dix River originates in Rockcastle County and flows northwest through Lincoln County before being impounded to form Herrington Lake along the Garrard–Boyle county line. From the Dix River Dam, the river flows a short two miles before emptying into the Kentucky River. Flowing primarily through farmland and wooded hills, the Dix is a pleasant, intimate river shaded by hardwoods and occasionally graced with some small bluffs and exposed rock ledges. Running over a mud bottom in the upper stretches between often-steep mud banks, the stream bed changes to a rock bottom with boulders along the bank as the Dix approaches the mouth of the Hanging Fork. Its level of difficulty is Class I although several tight spots require good boat control. Riffles, small ledges, and shoals are not uncommon. Dangers to navigation consist mainly of deadfalls and occasional logjams. The Dix is runnable from late fall to late spring downstream of the U.S. 27 bridge at Logantown. Canoe camping is possible if adjoining sections of the river and lake are combined. Campgrounds are all privately owned and charge for camping space.

HANGING FORK OF THE DIX RIVER

The Hanging Fork, a tributary of the Dix River flowing northeast along the Boyle–Lincoln county line, is runnable from late fall to early May below the KY 590 bridge. An interesting little stream (15 to 30 feet wide), the Hanging Fork twists through a small, shady gorge interrupted occasionally as grassy grazing plains insinuate themselves between the steep ridges. The paddling is rated a busy Class I and borderline Class II with almost continuous small shoals and rapids. There are numerous deadfalls and immense logjams to avoid. There is also a small dam near the confluence with the Dix that may be portaged or (at favorable water levels) run on the left where the dam is partially collapsed. Emerging on the Dix River, the take-out is three-quarters of a mile downstream below the KY 52 bridge.

BENSON CREEK

Benson Creek, along with its south fork, flows northeast out of Anderson County, through Franklin County to the Kentucky River at Frankfort. Runnable above the confluence of the forks after heavy rains, and below the confluence from late fall through the spring, Benson Creek offers a variety of surprises. The north fork, below Sheeppen Road, meanders lazily along through fields and pastureland until suddenly it veers to the right and drops over a 13-foot vertical falls. The south fork, averaging only 20 feet in width downstream of the Pea Ridge Road put-in, drops swiftly over Class-I and -II ledges and through five barbed wire cattle fences. Neither fork is runnable. Fortunately, Benson Creek below the confluence of the forks (just downstream of the large falls) is somewhat more predictable. Flowing between tall, beautiful, wooded bluffs (many with exposed rock), Benson Creek becomes a scenic and delightful Class-II run. Rapids consist primarily of riverwide ledges ranging from one to three feet in height that can be run just about anywhere. Holes occurring below the drops are generally friendly at most water levels. Several rapids disappear around curves and should be scouted for possible obstructions (deadfalls). Hazards include deadfalls, logjams, and a five-foot dam at the distillery that must be portaged on the right. Access is good except at the end of the run. Probably the easiest take-out is to paddle a half mile upstream after reaching the Kentucky River to the Frankfort Boat Dock.

ELKHORN CREEK

Elkhorn Creek, with its North and South Forks, flows northwest draining portions of Jessamine, Fayette, Scott, Woodford, and Franklin counties before emptying into the Kentucky River north of Frankfort. Because of its mild whitewater, beautiful scenery, plentiful access, and proximity to four major urban areas, the Elkhorn is fast becoming Kentucky's most popular canoeing stream.

NORTH FORK OF ELKHORN CREEK. The North Fork of Elkhorn Creek flows through Scott County and is runnable from late fall to late spring from Georgetown downstream. Several dams in the Georgetown vicinity create pools that permit the paddling of certain two- to four-mile stretches year-round. These stretches have been used for several years as a training site for a group of USCA marathon canoe-racing contenders. The absence of current in the dam pool stretches makes round trips possible and thus eliminates the need for a shuttle. By and large, the North Fork winds through rolling farmland. Trees line the mud and rock banks that vary markedly in height and steepness. The most popular run on the North Fork begins at the covered bridge near Switzer and terminates at the confluence of the North and South Forks. In this stretch the stream grows progressively more rocky and many small ledges and rapids appear (all Class I). Access is good all along the North Fork. Dangers to navigation include dams (as mentioned) that must be portaged, and deadfalls. The level of difficulty is Class I throughout and the average width is 35 to 40 feet.

SOUTH FORK OF ELKHORN CREEK. Similar to the North Fork, the South Fork of Elkhorn Creek is also very seasonal, being runnable only during the winter and spring. Treelined and flowing through gently rolling terrain amidst fertile fields and picturesque Bluegrass horse farms, the South Fork can be paddled below (downstream of) Fishers Mill in Woodford County. An exceptionally winding stream with continually changing vistas, the South Fork of Elkhorn Creek sports a variety of small riffles and ledges to enliven the paddling. Access is good and the level of difficulty is Class I. Hazards to navigation include deadfalls, cattle gates, and a large dam near the confluence with the North Fork.

FORKS OF ELKHORN TO THE KENTUCKY RIVER. Northeast of Frankfort at Forks of Elkhorn, the two forks of the creek come together. Here begins the most popular and scenic of the Elkhorn's many offerings; six miles of lively Class-I and Class-II whitewater. Runnable from late fall to early summer, this six-mile stretch is a perfect training ground for the novice whitewater paddler. Running through a deep gorge with exposed rock walls sometimes reaching 200 feet in height, the rapids, riffles, and ledges are almost continuous. In all there are four legitimate Class-II rapids on this run with perhaps eight additional high Class I or borderline Class II's. Several islands punctuate the stream, all except the first of which (at the very beginning of the run) are normally run along the right side. At low water the run is technical and helpful in developing water reading skills. At high water (3 feet) large standing waves predominate. Access is good. Dangers to navigation include a dam (mandatory portage) adjacent to the Old Grand-Dad Distillery, low-hanging branches, spring logjams, and a huge, uprooted tree trunk in the middle of a rapid as one approaches the railroad bridge about a half mile below the dam.

Downstream of the whitewater section, the Elkhorn continues swift and beautiful, flowing over a rock bed as it moves towards its rendezvous with the Kentucky. This final section clears the rocky gorge and drops into an intimate valley. Ledges, riffles, and small rapids persist, as do some more, fairly large islands. The stream's width fluctuates widely in this section from a constricting 35 feet to a broad and shallow 90 feet. Access is good and deadfalls and logjams are the only navigational dangers. The level of difficulty is Class I.

EAGLE CREEK

Eagle Creek originates in Scott County and flows northwest over a mud and rock bottom through Owen, Grant, Carroll, and Gallatin counties before emptying into the Kentucky River near

Worthville. Runnable from November through May downstream of the KY 36 bridge in Grant County, Eagle Creek flows through the farmland and woods of the Northern Kentucky Knobs. Throughout the upper stretches of the stream (upstream of Sparta), the Eagle flows through a broad and frequently saturated floodplain. Banks are inclined gently in this section allowing seasonal rains to flatten all streamside vegetation. Brush islands formed on river curves following the recession of high water are common and provide navigational challenge to the paddler. Below (downstream of) Sparta, the 45-foot stream runs more deeply as steeper banks channel the flow, and some very small ledges and rapids are encountered. The banks are treelined all along the Eagle, but very thinly so. The level of difficulty is Class I throughout with deadfalls being the foremost danger to paddlers. Access is excellent between the KY 36 bridge and Worthville.

Kentucky River   Photograph courtesy of the Commonwealth of Kentucky, Department of Public Information

SECTION: Roxana to Viper (Letcher Co., Perry Co.)

USGS QUADS: Roxana, Blackey, Vicco, Hazard South

LEVEL OF DIFFICULTY International Class I (II) Numerical Points 6

SUITABLE FOR: Cruising   **GRADIENT** (feet per mile): 7.05

APPROPRIATE FOR: Advanced Beginners, Intermediates, Advanced

VELOCITY (mph): 2.6-5.0   **AVERAGE WIDTH** (ft): 25-45

MONTHS RUNNABLE: December to April

RUNNABLE WATER LEVEL (cfs) Minimum   150
    Maximum   Up to flood stage

MEAN WATER TEMPERATURE (°F)

Jan. 43	Feb. 44	Mar. 48	Apr. 49	May 58	Jun. 69
Jul. 75	Aug. 81	Sep. 72	Oct. 65	Nov. 49	Dec. 44

SOURCE OF ADDITIONAL INFORMATION ON WATER CONDITIONS
    Hazard Police Dept. (606) 436-2222

HAZARDS: Deadfalls, low bridges, low trees

RESCUE INDEX: B-D
    A Extremely remote; evacuation only with expert help—6 hours to secure assistance
    B Remote; 3-6 hours to secure assistance
    C Accessible but difficult; up to 3 hours to secure assistance—evacuation difficult
    D Accessible; up to 1 hour to secure assistance, evacuation not difficult

PORTAGES: None required

SCOUTING: None required

INTEREST HIGHLIGHTS: Scenery, local culture and industry

SCENERY: Pretty to pretty in spots

ACCESS POINT	ACCESS CODE	KEY
A	1 3 6 8	1 Paved Road
B	1 3 6 8	2 Unpaved Road
C	1 3 6 8	3 Short Carry
D	1 3 6 8	4 Long Carry
E	1 3 6 7	5 Easy Grade
F*	1 3 6 8	6 Steep Grade
		7 Clear Trail
		8 Brush and Trees
		9 Private Property, Permission Needed
		10 Launching Fee Charged
		11 No Access—For Reference Only

*KY 7 bridge at mouth of Maces Creek in Viper

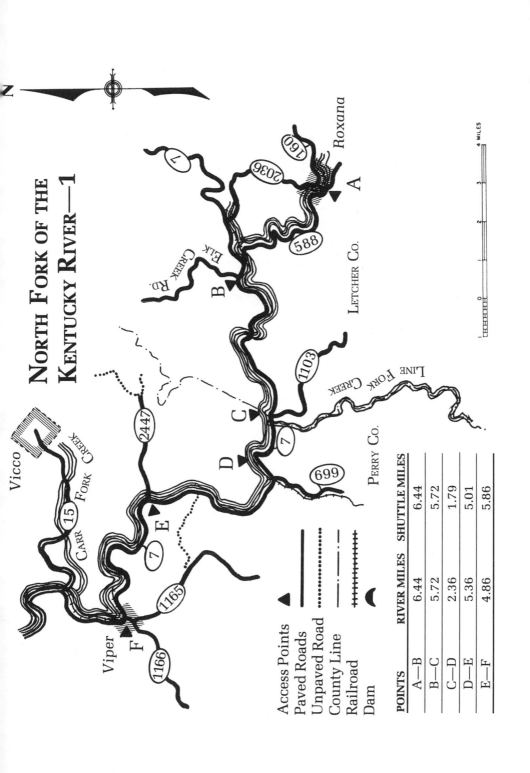

North Fork of the Kentucky River—1

N

Roxana

Vicco

Viper

LETCHER CO.

PERRY CO.

Line Fork Creek

Elk Creek Rd.

Carr Fork Creek

Access Points	▲
Paved Roads	▬▬▬
Unpaved Road	•••••••
County Line	—•—•—
Railroad	＋＋＋＋＋
Dam	◖

POINTS	RIVER MILES	SHUTTLE MILES
A–B	6.44	6.44
B–C	5.72	5.72
C–D	2.36	1.79
D–E	5.36	5.01
E–F	4.86	5.86

0   1   2   3   4 MILES

SECTION: Viper to Chavies (Perry Co.)

USGS QUADS: Hazard South, Hazard North, Krypton, Haddix

LEVEL OF DIFFICULTY International Class I   Numerical Points **4**

SUITABLE FOR: Cruising   **GRADIENT** (feet per mile): 2.81

APPROPRIATE FOR: Beginners, Intermediates, Advanced

VELOCITY (mph): 2.6-5.0   **AVERAGE WIDTH** (ft): 40-60

MONTHS RUNNABLE: Late October to mid-June

RUNNABLE WATER LEVEL (cfs) Minimum **175**
Maximum **Up to flood stage**

MEAN WATER TEMPERATURE ($^\circ$F)

Jan. 45	Feb. 45	Mar. 48	Apr. 56	May 67	Jun. 77
Jul. 81	Aug. 82	Sep. 74	Oct. 66	Nov. 49	Dec. 42

SOURCE OF ADDITIONAL INFORMATION ON WATER CONDITIONS
Jackson Police Dept. (606) 666-2424
Hazard Police Dept. (606) 436-2222

HAZARDS: Deadfalls

RESCUE INDEX: D
A   Extremely remote; evacuation only with expert help—6 hours to secure assistance
B   Remote; 3-6 hours to secure assistance
C   Accessible but difficult; up to 3 hours to secure assistance—evacuation difficult
D   Accessible; up to 1 hour to secure assistance, evacuation not difficult

PORTAGES: None required

SCOUTING: None required

INTEREST HIGHLIGHTS: Scenery, local culture and industry

SCENERY: Pretty to pretty in spots

ACCESS POINT	ACCESS CODE	KEY
F*	1 3 6 8	1 Paved Road
G	1 3 6 7	2 Unpaved Road
H	1 3 6 8	3 Short Carry
I	1 3 6 8	4 Long Carry
J	1 3 6 8 9	5 Easy Grade
K	1 3 6 7	6 Steep Grade
		7 Clear Trail
		8 Brush and Trees
		9 Private Property, Permission Needed
		10 Launching Fee Charged
		11 No Access—For Reference Only

*KY 7 bridge at the mouth of Maces Creek in Viper

NORTH FORK OF THE KENTUCKY RIVER—2

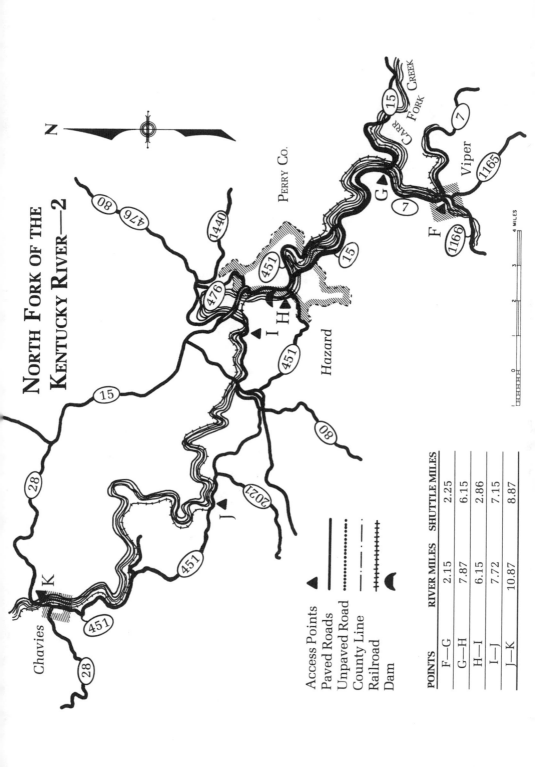

	Access Points
▲	
⋯⋯	Paved Roads
—·—·	Unpaved Road
┼┼┼┼	County Line
	Railroad
◖	Dam

POINTS	RIVER MILES	SHUTTLE MILES
F–G	2.15	2.25
G–H	7.87	6.15
H–I	6.15	2.86
I–J	7.72	7.15
J–K	10.87	8.87

SECTION: Chavies to Jackson (Perry Co., Breathitt Co.)

USGS QUADS: Haddix, Quicksand, Jackson

LEVEL OF DIFFICULTY International Class I   Numerical Points **4**

SUITABLE FOR: Cruising   **GRADIENT** (feet per mile): **2.65**

APPROPRIATE FOR: Beginners, Intermediates, Advanced

VELOCITY (mph): 2.6-5.0   **AVERAGE WIDTH** (ft): 40-60

MONTHS RUNNABLE: Late October to mid-June

RUNNABLE WATER LEVEL (cfs) Minimum **175**
    Maximum **Up to flood stage**

MEAN WATER TEMPERATURE (°F)

Jan. 45	Feb. 45	Mar. 48	Apr. 56	May 67	Jun. 77
Jul. 81	Aug. 82	Sep. 74	Oct. 66	Nov. 49	Dec. 42

SOURCE OF ADDITIONAL INFORMATION ON WATER CONDITIONS
    Jackson Police Dept. (606) 666-2424

HAZARDS: Deadfalls

RESCUE INDEX: D
  A Extremely remote; evacuation only with expert help—6 hours to secure assistance
  B Remote; 3-6 hours to secure assistance
  C Accessible but difficult; up to 3 hours to secure assistance—evacuation difficult
  D Accessible; up to 1 hour to secure assistance, evacuation not difficult

PORTAGES: None required

SCOUTING: None required

INTEREST HIGHLIGHTS: Scenery, local culture and industry

SCENERY: Pretty to pretty in spots

ACCESS POINT	ACCESS CODE	KEY
K	1 3 6 7	1 Paved Road
L	2 3 6 7	2 Unpaved Road
M	2 3 6 8	3 Short Carry
N*	1 3 6 8	4 Long Carry
O	1 3 6 8	5 Easy Grade
		6 Steep Grade
		7 Clear Trail
		8 Brush and Trees
		9 Private Property, Permission Needed
		10 Launching Fee Charged
		11 No Access—For Reference Only

*KY 1812 bridge at the mouth of Quicksand Creek

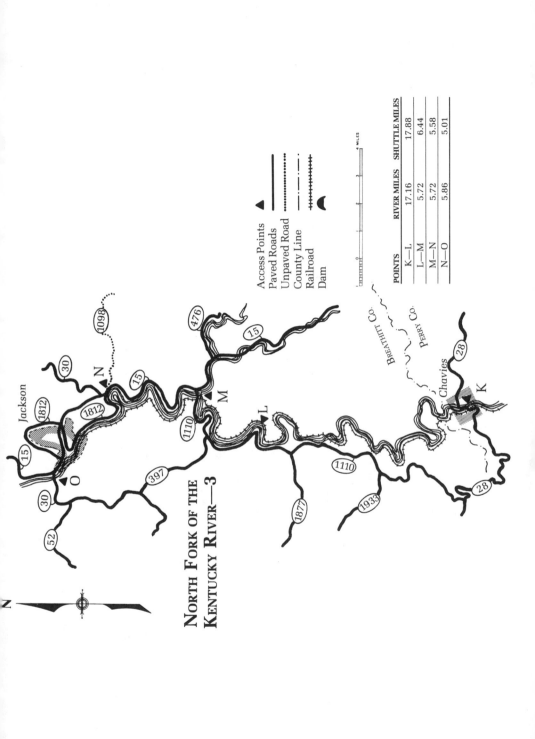

NORTH FORK OF THE
KENTUCKY RIVER—3

Jackson

Access Points
Paved Roads
Unpaved Road
County Line
Railroad
Dam

BREATHITT CO.
PERRY CO.
Chavies

POINTS	RIVER MILES	SHUTTLE MILES
K–L	17.16	17.88
L–M	5.72	6.44
M–N	5.72	5.58
N–O	5.86	5.01

MILES

SECTION: Jackson to Beattyville (Breathitt Co., Lee Co.)

USGS QUADS: Jackson, Tallega, Campton, Zachariah, Beattyville

LEVEL OF DIFFICULTY International Class I   Numerical Points 3

SUITABLE FOR: Cruising   **GRADIENT** (feet per mile): 1.33

APPROPRIATE FOR: Beginners, Intermediates, Advanced

VELOCITY (mph): 2.6-5.0   **AVERAGE WIDTH** (ft): 80-110

MONTHS RUNNABLE: All

RUNNABLE WATER LEVEL (cfs) Minimum 260
Maximum   Up to flood stage

MEAN WATER TEMPERATURE (°F)

Jan. 45	Feb. 45	Mar. 48	Apr. 56	May 68	Jun. 78
Jul. 81	Aug. 81	Sep. 75	Oct. 66	Nov. 48	Dec. 42

SOURCE OF ADDITIONAL INFORMATION ON WATER CONDITIONS
Jackson Police Dept. (606) 666-2424

HAZARDS: Deadfalls

RESCUE INDEX: C-D
 A Extremely remote; evacuation only with expert help—6 hours to secure assistance
 B Remote; 3-6 hours to secure assistance
 C Accessible but difficult; up to 3 hours to secure assistance—evacuation difficult
 D Accessible; up to 1 hour to secure assistance, evacuation not difficult

PORTAGES: None required

SCOUTING: None required

INTEREST HIGHLIGHTS: Scenery, local culture and industry

SCENERY: Uninspiring to pleasant in spots to pleasant

ACCESS POINT	ACCESS CODE	KEY
O	1 3 6 8	1 Paved Road
P	1 3 6 7	2 Unpaved Road
Q	1 3 6 8	3 Short Carry
R	1 3 6 7	4 Long Carry
		5 Easy Grade
		6 Steep Grade
		7 Clear Trail
		8 Brush and Trees
		9 Private Property, Permission Needed
		10 Launching Fee Charged
		11 No Access—For Reference Only

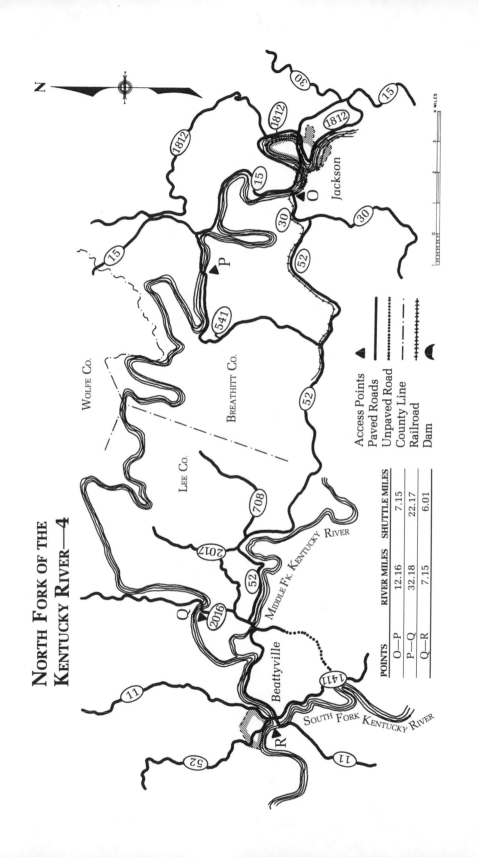

North Fork of the Kentucky River—4

POINTS	RIVER MILES	SHUTTLE MILES
O–P	12.16	7.15
P–Q	32.18	22.17
Q–R	7.15	6.01

Access Points
Paved Roads
Unpaved Road
County Line
Railroad
Dam

Wolfe Co.

Lee Co.

Breathitt Co.

Jackson

Beattyville

Middle Fk. Kentucky River

South Fork Kentucky River

N

4 MILES

SECTION: War Branch to Buckhorn Lake (Leslie Co.)

USGS QUADS: Hoskinston, Cutshin, Hyden East, Hyden West

LEVEL OF DIFFICULTY International Class I-II† I+‡   Numerical Points 8,4

SUITABLE FOR: Cruising, camping* **GRADIENT** (feet per mile): 13.66

APPROPRIATE FOR: Intermediate, Advanced†; Families, Beginners, Intermediates, Advanced‡
VELOCITY (mph): 2.6-5.0   **AVERAGE WIDTH** (ft): 25-45

MONTHS RUNNABLE: January to mid-April†; late November to early June‡

RUNNABLE WATER LEVEL (cfs) Minimum   175
Maximum   Up to flood stage

MEAN WATER TEMPERATURE (°F)

Jan. 42	Feb. 42	Mar. 43	Apr. 53	May 66	Jun. 75
Jul. 77	Aug. 76	Sep. 68	Oct. 62	Nov. 43	Dec. 39

SOURCE OF ADDITIONAL INFORMATION ON WATER CONDITIONS
City of Hyden (606) 672-2300

HAZARDS: Dams, deadfalls, low bridges

RESCUE INDEX: D
A   Extremely remote; evacuation only with expert help—6 hours to secure assistance
B   Remote; 3-6 hours to secure assistance
C   Accessible but difficult; up to 3 hours to secure assistance—evacuation difficult
D   Accessible; up to 1 hour to secure assistance, evacuation not difficult

PORTAGES: Around dam south of Hyden near county high school

SCOUTING: Upper section along KY 1780 (scout from road)

INTEREST HIGHLIGHTS: Scenery, local culture and history

SCENERY: Pretty to pretty in spots

ACCESS POINT	ACCESS CODE	KEY
A	1 3 5 7	1 Paved Road
B	1 3 5 7	2 Unpaved Road
C	1 3 5 7	3 Short Carry
D	1 3 5 7	4 Long Carry
E	1 3 5 7	5 Easy Grade
F	1 3 5 7	6 Steep Grade
G	1 3 6 8	7 Clear Trail
H	1 3 5 7	8 Brush and Trees
I	1 3 5 8	9 Private Property, Permission Needed
		10 Launching Fee Charged
		11 No Access—For Reference Only

*At Buckhorn Lake
†Along KY 1780
‡Below Asher

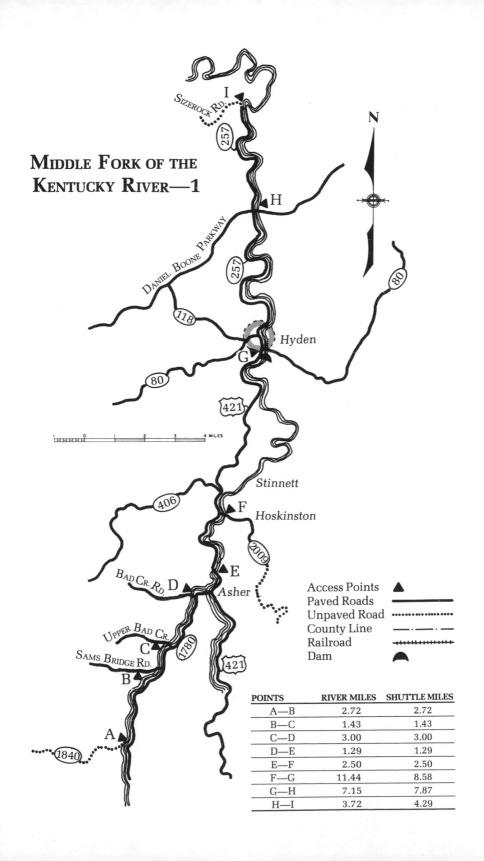

MIDDLE FORK OF THE
KENTUCKY RIVER—1

I

SIZEROCK RD.

257

H

N

DANIEL BOONE PARKWAY

257

118

80

Hyden

G

80

421

0   1   2   3   4 MILES

Stinnett

406

F

Hoskinston

2009

E

BAD CR. RD. D

Asher

UPPER BAD CR.

C

1780

SAMS BRIDGE RD.

B

421

Access Points ▲
Paved Roads ————
Unpaved Road ·············
County Line —·—·—·—
Railroad ++++++++++
Dam

A

1840

POINTS	RIVER MILES	SHUTTLE MILES
A—B	2.72	2.72
B—C	1.43	1.43
C—D	3.00	3.00
D—E	1.29	1.29
E—F	2.50	2.50
F—G	11.44	8.58
G—H	7.15	7.87
H—I	3.72	4.29

SECTION: Below Buckhorn Dam to Beattyville (Perry Co., Breathitt Co., Lee Co.)

USGS QUADS: Buckhorn Canoe, Cowcreek, Tallega, Beattyville

LEVEL OF DIFFICULTY International Class I   Numerical Points 4

SUITABLE FOR: Cruising   **GRADIENT** (feet per mile): 1.72

APPROPRIATE FOR: Families, Beginners, Intermediates, Advanced

VELOCITY (mph): 2.6-5.0   **AVERAGE WIDTH** (ft): 60-90

MONTHS RUNNABLE: All when dam is releasing

RUNNABLE WATER LEVEL (cfs) Minimum 210
Maximum Up to flood stage

MEAN WATER TEMPERATURE (°F)

Jan. 42	Feb. 43	Mar. 44	Apr. 53	May 67	Jun. 76
Jul. 79	Aug. 78	Sep. 68	Oct. 63	Nov. 43	Dec. 41

SOURCE OF ADDITIONAL INFORMATION ON WATER CONDITIONS
Corps of Engineers (606) 398-7157

HAZARDS: Deadfalls, low bridges

RESCUE INDEX: C-D
A Extremely remote; evacuation only with expert help—6 hours to secure assistance
B Remote; 3-6 hours to secure assistance
C Accessible but difficult; up to 3 hours to secure assistance—evacuation difficult
D Accessible; up to 1 hour to secure assistance, evacuation not difficult

PORTAGES: None required

SCOUTING: None required

INTEREST HIGHLIGHTS: Scenery, local culture and industry

SCENERY: Pretty to pretty in spots

ACCESS POINT	ACCESS CODE	KEY
J	1 3 5 7	1 Paved Road
K	2 3 5 7	2 Unpaved Road
L	1 3 6 8	3 Short Carry
M	1 3 6 7	4 Long Carry
N	2 3 5 7	5 Easy Grade
O	1 3 6 7	6 Steep Grade
P	1 3 6 7	7 Clear Trail
		8 Brush and Trees
		9 Private Property, Permission Needed
		10 Launching Fee Charged
		11 No Access—For Reference Only

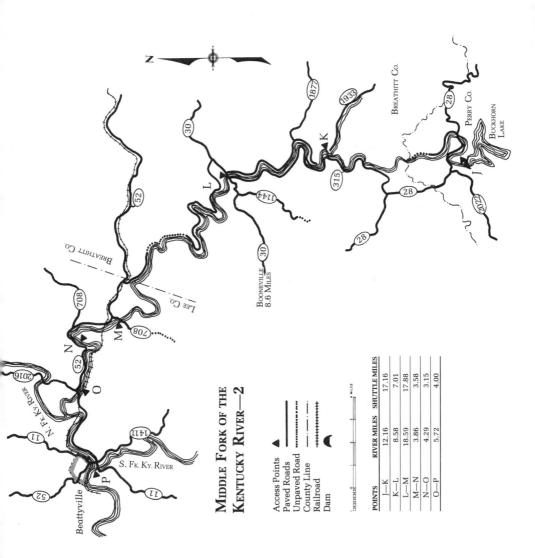

MIDDLE FORK OF THE
KENTUCKY RIVER—2

Access Points ◀
Paved Roads ▬▬▬
Unpaved Road ••••••••
County Line —··—··—
Railroad ✕✕✕✕✕✕✕
Dam ◖

POINTS	RIVER MILES	SHUTTLE MILES
J—K	12.16	17.16
K—L	8.58	7.01
L—M	18.59	17.88
M—N	3.86	3.58
N—O	4.29	3.15
O—P	5.72	4.00

SECTION: Queensdale to mouth (Clay Co.)

USGS QUADS: Creekville, Big Creek

LEVEL OF DIFFICULTY International Class I+   Numerical Points 5

SUITABLE FOR: Cruising   **GRADIENT** (feet per mile): 7.20

APPROPRIATE FOR: Beginners, Intermediates, Advanced

VELOCITY (mph): 2.6-5.0   **AVERAGE WIDTH** (ft): 25-40

MONTHS RUNNABLE: December to April

RUNNABLE WATER LEVEL (cfs) Minimum 180
   Maximum Up to flood stage

MEAN WATER TEMPERATURE (°F)

Jan. 41	Feb. 42	Mar. 43	Apr. 52	May 64	Jun. 74
Jul. 76	Aug. 76	Sep. 67	Oct. 63	Nov. 53	Dec. 39

SOURCE OF ADDITIONAL INFORMATION ON WATER CONDITIONS
   Redbird Ranger Headquarters (606) 598-2192

HAZARDS: Deadfalls, low bridges, low trees

RESCUE INDEX: D
   A Extremely remote; evacuation only with expert help—6 hours to secure assistance
   B Remote; 3-6 hours to secure assistance
   C Accessible but difficult; up to 3 hours to secure assistance—evacuation difficult
   D Accessible; up to 1 hour to secure assistance, evacuation not difficult

PORTAGES: Over concrete fords at low water

SCOUTING: None required

INTEREST HIGHLIGHTS: Scenery, wildlife, local culture and industry

SCENERY: Pretty to beautiful in spots

ACCESS POINT	**ACCESS CODE**	**KEY**
A	1 3 6 7	1 Paved Road
B	2 3 5 7	2 Unpaved Road
C	2 3 5 7	3 Short Carry
D	1 3 5 7	4 Long Carry
E	2 3 5 7	5 Easy Grade
F	1 3 6 8	6 Steep Grade
G*	2 3 6 8	7 Clear Trail
		8 Brush and Trees
		9 Private Property, Permission Needed
		10 Launching Fee Charged
		11 No Access—For Reference Only

*On South Fork of the Kentucky River near Eriline

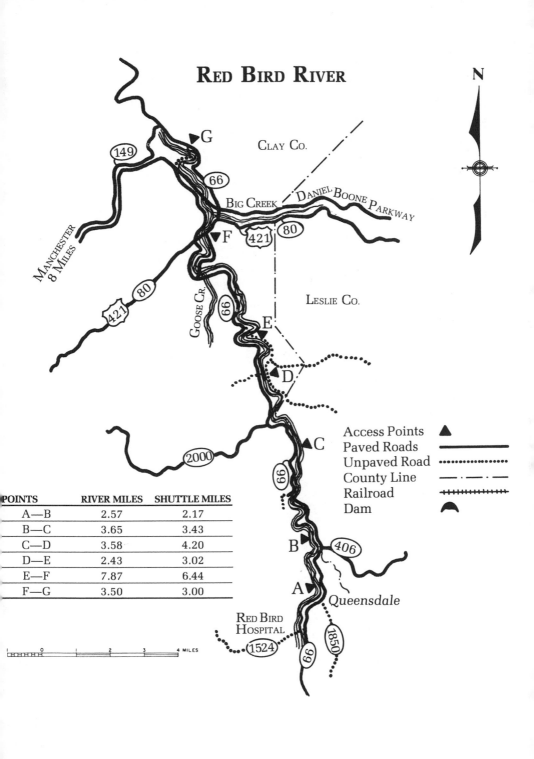

RED BIRD RIVER

N

CLAY CO.

149

G

66

BIG CREEK   DANIEL BOONE PARKWAY

421   80

F

MANCHESTER
8 MILES

80

LESLIE CO.

421

GOOSE CR.

66

E

D

2000

C

Access Points   ▲
Paved Roads   ————
Unpaved Road   ············
County Line   —·—·—
Railroad   +++++++++
Dam   ◠

POINTS	RIVER MILES	SHUTTLE MILES
A—B	2.57	2.17
B—C	3.65	3.43
C—D	3.58	4.20
D—E	2.43	3.02
E—F	7.87	6.44
F—G	3.50	3.00

66

B   406

A   Queensdale

RED BIRD
HOSPITAL   1524   1850

99

0   1   2   3   4 MILES

SECTION: Eriline to Beattyville (Clay Co., Owsley Co., Lee Co.)

USGS QUADS: Big Creek, Mistletoe, Oneida, Booneville, Beattyville

LEVEL OF DIFFICULTY International Class I,II† Numerical Points 6

SUITABLE FOR: Cruising   **GRADIENT** (feet per mile): 3.33

APPROPRIATE FOR: Beginners, Intermediates, Advanced

VELOCITY (mph): 2.6-5.0   **AVERAGE WIDTH** (ft): 35-60

MONTHS RUNNABLE: November to mid-June (Eriline to Booneville);
all (Booneville to Beattyville)

RUNNABLE WATER LEVEL (cfs) Minimum 225
Maximum Up to flood stage

MEAN WATER TEMPERATURE (°F)

Jan. 44	Feb. 43	Mar. 47	Apr. 55	May 68	Jun. 78
Jul. 78	Aug. 77	Sep. 70	Oct. 62	Nov. 46	Dec. 41

SOURCE OF ADDITIONAL INFORMATION ON WATER CONDITIONS
Redbird Ranger Headquarters (606) 598-2192

HAZARDS: Deadfalls, low bridges, low trees

RESCUE INDEX: C-D
A Extremely remote; evacuation only with expert help—6 hours to secure assistance
B Remote; 3-6 hours to secure assistance
C Accessible but difficult; up to 3 hours to secure assistance—evacuation difficult
D Accessible; up to 1 hour to secure assistance, evacuation not difficult

PORTAGES: None required

SCOUTING: None required

INTEREST HIGHLIGHTS: Scenery, local culture and history

SCENERY: Pretty in spots to beautiful in spots

ACCESS POINT	ACCESS CODE	KEY
A	2 3 6 8	1 Paved Road
B	2 3 5 7	2 Unpaved Road
C*	1 3 5 8	3 Short Carry
D	2 3 5 8	4 Long Carry
E	2 3 5 7	5 Easy Grade
F	2 3 5 7	6 Steep Grade
G	2 3 5 8	7 Clear Trail
H	2 3 5 7	8 Brush and Trees
I	1 3 6 7	9 Private Property, Permission Needed
J	1 3 6 7	10 Launching Fee Charged
K	1 3 6 7	11 No Access—For Reference Only

*Bridge over Goose Creek, south of Oneida
†At points C and F

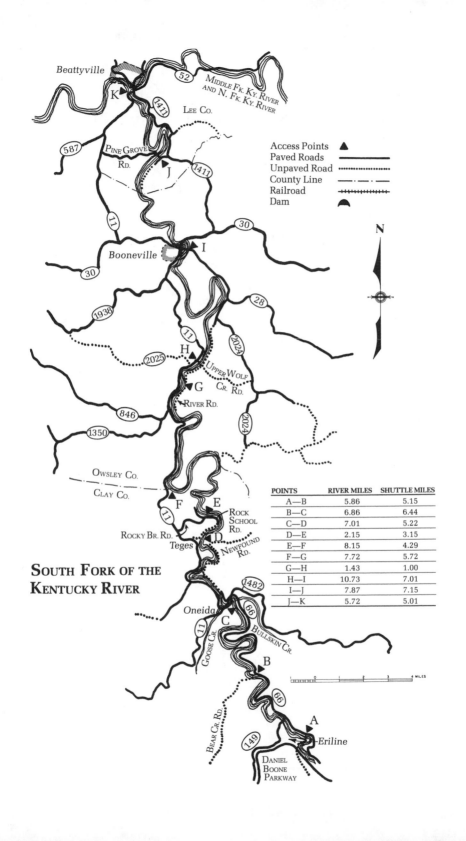

Beattyville

52

MIDDLE FK. KY. RIVER
AND N. FK. KY. RIVER

K

1411

LEE CO.

587

PINE GROVE
RD.

J

1411

11

30

30

Booneville

I

1938

28

11

2024A

H

2025

UPPER WOLF
CR. RD.

G

RIVER RD.

846

2024

1350

OWSLEY CO.

CLAY CO.

F   E

ROCK
SCHOOL
RD.

11

ROCKY BR. RD.

D

NEWFOUND
RD.

Teges

SOUTH FORK OF THE
KENTUCKY RIVER

1482

Oneida

66

11

C

GOOSE CR.

BULLSKIN CR.

B

66

BEAR CR. RD.

A

Eriline

1149

DANIEL
BOONE
PARKWAY

Access Points   ▲
Paved Roads
Unpaved Road   ·············
County Line   ─·─·─·─
Railroad   ┼┼┼┼┼┼┼
Dam

N

POINTS	RIVER MILES	SHUTTLE MILES
A—B	5.86	5.15
B—C	6.86	6.44
C—D	7.01	5.22
D—E	2.15	3.15
E—F	8.15	4.29
F—G	7.72	5.72
G—H	1.43	1.00
H—I	10.73	7.01
I—J	7.87	7.15
J—K	5.72	5.01

0   1   2   3   4 MILES

SECTION: Beattyville to Lock No. 11 (Lee Co., Estill Co., Madison Co.)

USGS QUADS: Beattyville, Heidleberg, Cobhill, Irvine, Panola

LEVEL OF DIFFICULTY International Class I   Numerical Points 4

SUITABLE FOR: Cruising   **GRADIENT** (feet per mile): 0.72

APPROPRIATE FOR: Families, Beginners, Intermediates, Advanced

VELOCITY (mph): 2.6-5.0   **AVERAGE WIDTH** (ft): 80-105

MONTHS RUNNABLE: All

RUNNABLE WATER LEVEL (cfs) Minimum **600**
  Maximum Up to flood stage

MEAN WATER TEMPERATURE (°F)

Jan. 46	Feb. 45	Mar. 49	Apr. 50	May 64	Jun. 75
Jul. 80	Aug. 82	Sep. 74	Oct. 65	Nov. 54	Dec. 45

SOURCE OF ADDITIONAL INFORMATION ON WATER CONDITIONS
  Corps of Engineers (502) 582-5647

HAZARDS: Dams, powerboats

RESCUE INDEX: C-D
  A Extremely remote; evacuation only with expert help—6 hours to secure assistance
  B Remote; 3-6 hours to secure assistance
  C Accessible but difficult; up to 3 hours to secure assistance—evacuation difficult
  D Accessible; up to 1 hour to secure assistance, evacuation not difficult

PORTAGES: Lock Nos. 14 (Beattyville), 13 (Evelyn), 12 (Ravenna), 11 (near mouth of Flint Creek)
SCOUTING: None required

INTEREST HIGHLIGHTS: Scenery, local culture and industry

SCENERY: Pleasant to pretty in spots

ACCESS POINT	ACCESS CODE	KEY
A	1 3 5 7	1 Paved Road
B	1 3 6 7	2 Unpaved Road
C	2 3 6 7	3 Short Carry
D	1 3 5 7	4 Long Carry
E	2 3 5 7	5 Easy Grade
F	2 3 6 7	6 Steep Grade
G	2 3 6 7	7 Clear Trail
		8 Brush and Trees
		9 Private Property, Permission Needed
		10 Launching Fee Charged
		11 No Access—For Reference Only

KENTUCKY RIVER—1

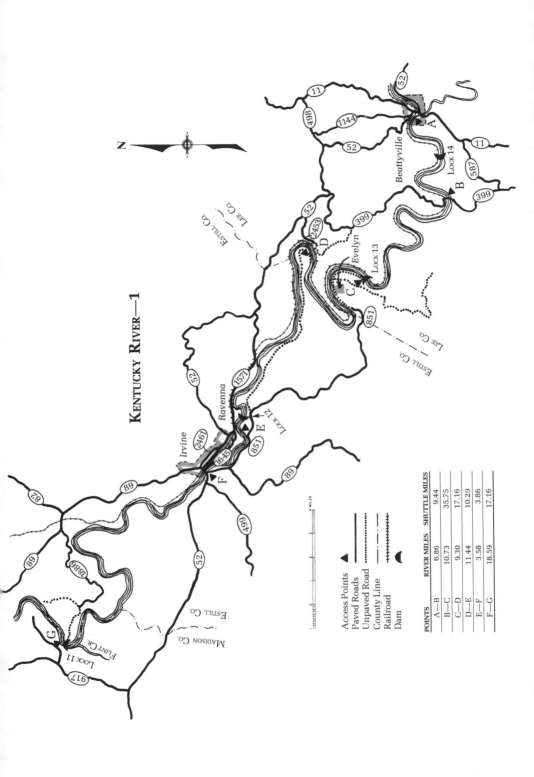

POINTS	RIVER MILES	SHUTTLE MILES
A–B	6.86	9.44
B–C	10.73	35.75
C–D	9.30	17.16
D–E	11.44	10.29
E–F	3.58	3.86
F–G	18.59	17.16

Access Points

Paved Roads

Unpaved Road

County Line

Railroad

Dam

SECTION: Lock No. 11 to Lock No. 9 near Valley View (Estill Co., Clark Co., Madison Co., Fayette Co.)

USGS QUADS: Panola, Palmer, Union City, Winchester, Ford, Richmond North, Valley View

LEVEL OF DIFFICULTY International Class I   Numerical Points   4

SUITABLE FOR: Cruising   **GRADIENT** (feet per mile): 0.72

APPROPRIATE FOR: Families, Beginners, Intermediates, Advanced

VELOCITY (mph): 2.6-5.0   **AVERAGE WIDTH** (ft): 95-125

MONTHS RUNNABLE: All

RUNNABLE WATER LEVEL (cfs) Minimum 600
   Maximum Up to flood stage

MEAN WATER TEMPERATURE (°F)

Jan. 46	Feb. 45	Mar. 49	Apr. 50	May 64	Jun. 75
Jul. 80	Aug. 82	Sep. 74	Oct. 65	Nov. 54	Dec. 45

SOURCE OF ADDITIONAL INFORMATION ON WATER CONDITIONS
   Corps of Engineers (502) 582-5647

HAZARDS: Dams, powerboats

RESCUE INDEX: C-D
   A Extremely remote; evacuation only with expert help—6 hours to secure assistance
   B Remote; 3-6 hours to secure assistance
   C Accessible but difficult; up to 3 hours to secure assistance—evacuation difficult
   D Accessible; up to 1 hour to secure assistance, evacuation not difficult

PORTAGES: Lock Nos. 11 (near mouth of Flint Creek), 10 (Ft. Boonesborough), 9 (near Valley View)

SCOUTING: None required

INTEREST HIGHLIGHTS: Scenery, local culture and industry

SCENERY: Pleasant to pretty in spots

ACCESS POINT	ACCESS CODE	KEY
G	2 3 6 7	1 Paved Road
H	1 3 5 7 (10)	2 Unpaved Road
I	1 3 5 7	3 Short Carry
J	1 3 5 7	4 Long Carry
K	1 3 5 7	5 Easy Grade
L	1 3 5 7 (10)	6 Steep Grade
M	1 3 5 7	7 Clear Trail
		8 Brush and Trees
		9 Private Property, Permission Needed
		10 Launching Fee Charged
		11 No Access—For Reference Only

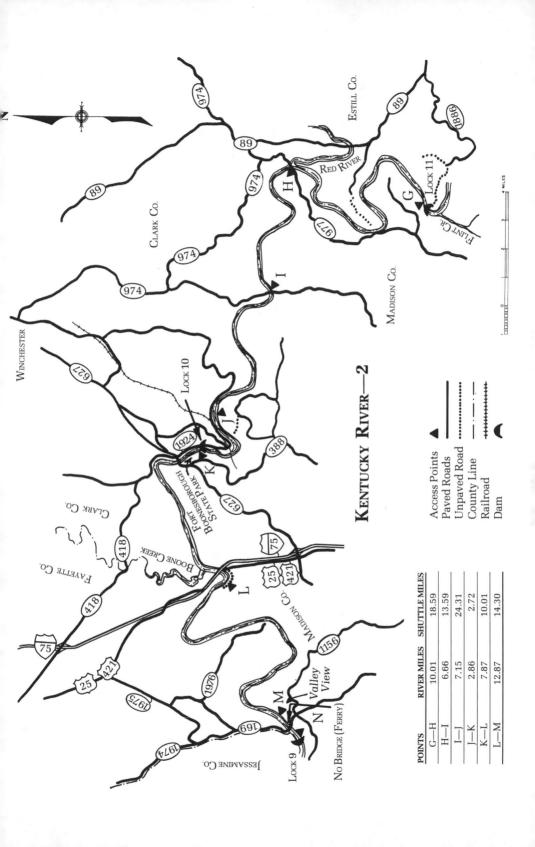

KENTUCKY RIVER—2

Access Points ▲
Paved Roads ━━━━
Unpaved Road ∙∙∙∙∙∙∙∙
County Line ─∙─∙─∙─
Railroad ┼┼┼┼┼┼┼
Dam ◖

POINTS	RIVER MILES	SHUTTLE MILES
G–H	10.01	18.59
H–I	6.66	13.59
I–J	7.15	24.31
J–K	2.86	2.72
K–L	7.87	10.01
L–M	12.87	14.30

SECTION: Lock No. 9 near Valley View to Lock No. 6 near Salvisa (Fayette Co., Madison Co., Garrard Co., Jessamine Co., Woodford Co., Mercer Co.)

USGS QUADS: Valley View, Little Hickman, Buckeye, Wilmore, Harrodsburg, Salvisa

LEVEL OF DIFFICULTY International Class I   Numerical Points   4

SUITABLE FOR: Cruising (Camping) **GRADIENT** (feet per mile): 0.99

APPROPRIATE FOR: Families, Beginners, Intermediates, Advanced

VELOCITY (mph): 2.6-5.0   **AVERAGE WIDTH** (ft): 110-130

MONTHS RUNNABLE: All

RUNNABLE WATER LEVEL (cfs) Minimum 800
  Maximum Up to flood stage

MEAN WATER TEMPERATURE (°F)

Jan. 44	Feb. 44	Mar. 47	Apr. 53	May 66	Jun. 76
Jul. 80	Aug. 79	Sep. 75	Oct. 65	Nov. 53	Dec. 44

SOURCE OF ADDITIONAL INFORMATION ON WATER CONDITIONS
  Corps of Engineers (502) 582-5647

HAZARDS: Dams, powerboats

RESCUE INDEX: C-D
  A Extremely remote; evacuation only with expert help—6 hours to secure assistance
  B Remote; 3-6 hours to secure assistance
  C Accessible but difficult; up to 3 hours to secure assistance—evacuation difficult
  D Accessible; up to 1 hour to secure assistance, evacuation not difficult

PORTAGES: Lock Nos. 9 (near Valley View), 8, 7 (near High Bridge), 6 (near Salvisa)

SCOUTING: None required

INTEREST HIGHLIGHTS: Scenery, history, local culture and industry

SCENERY: Pretty to beautiful in spots

ACCESS POINT	ACCESS CODE	KEY
M	1 3 5 7	1 Paved Road
N	1 3 6 7	2 Unpaved Road
O	1 3 5 7	3 Short Carry
P	1 3 5 7	4 Long Carry
Q	1 4 5 7	5 Easy Grade
R	1 3 5 7 (10)	6 Steep Grade
S	1 3 6 7	7 Clear Trail
T	1 3 6 7	8 Brush and Trees
U	1 3 5 7	9 Private Property, Permission Needed
V	2 3 6 8	10 Launching Fee Charged
		11 No Access—For Reference Only

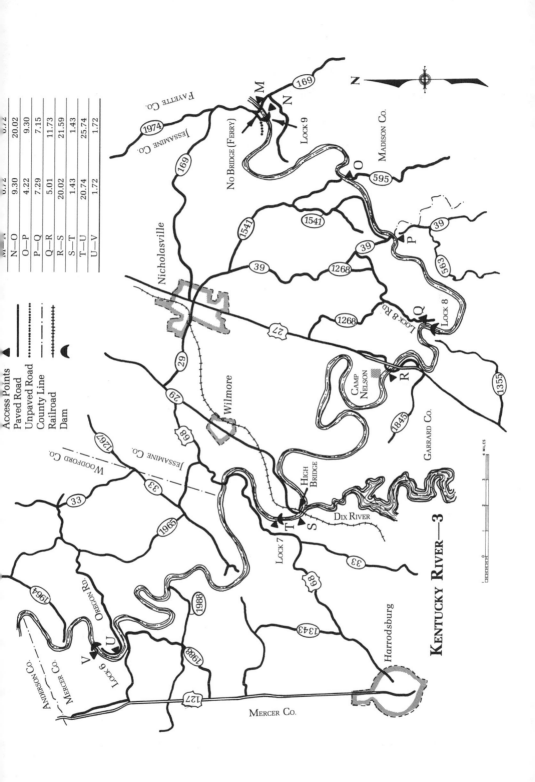

M–N	6.72	6.72
N–O	9.30	20.02
O–P	4.22	9.30
P–Q	7.29	7.15
Q–R	5.01	11.73
R–S	20.02	21.59
S–T	1.43	1.43
T–U	20.74	25.74
U–V	1.72	1.72

Access Points

Paved Road

Unpaved Road

County Line

Railroad

Dam

KENTUCKY RIVER—3

SECTION: Lock No. 6 near Salvisa to Frankfort Boat Dock (Woodford Co., Mercer Co., Anderson Co., Franklin Co.)

USGS QUADS: Salvisa, Tyrone, Frankfort East, Frankfort West

LEVEL OF DIFFICULTY International Class I   Numerical Points 4

SUITABLE FOR: Cruising (Camping) **GRADIENT** (feet per mile): 0.99

APPROPRIATE FOR: Families, Beginners, Intermediates, Advanced

VELOCITY (mph): 2.6-5.0   **AVERAGE WIDTH** (ft): 110-135

MONTHS RUNNABLE: All

RUNNABLE WATER LEVEL (cfs) Minimum **800**
Maximum Up to flood stage

MEAN WATER TEMPERATURE (°F)

Jan.	44	Feb.	44	Mar.	47	Apr.	53	May	66	Jun.	76
Jul.	80	Aug.	79	Sep.	75	Oct.	65	Nov.	53	Dec.	44

SOURCE OF ADDITIONAL INFORMATION ON WATER CONDITIONS
Corps of Engineers (502) 582-5647

HAZARDS: Dams, powerboats

RESCUE INDEX: C-D
- A Extremely remote; evacuation only with expert help—6 hours to secure assistance
- B Remote; 3-6 hours to secure assistance
- C Accessible but difficult; up to 3 hours to secure assistance—evacuation difficult
- D Accessible; up to 1 hour to secure assistance, evacuation not difficult

PORTAGES: Lock Nos. 6 (near Salvisa), 5 (near Lawrenceburg)

SCOUTING: None required

INTEREST HIGHLIGHTS: Scenery, history, local culture and industry

SCENERY: Pretty to beautiful in spots

ACCESS POINT	ACCESS CODE	KEY
V	2 3 6 8	1 Paved Road
W	1 3 5 7	2 Unpaved Road
X	1 3 6 7 (10)	3 Short Carry
Y	2 3 6 8	4 Long Carry
Z	1 3 5 7 (10)	5 Easy Grade
A A	1 3 5 7 9	6 Steep Grade
B B	1 3 5 7	7 Clear Trail
		8 Brush and Trees
		9 Private Property, Permission Needed
		10 Launching Fee Charged
		11 No Access—For Reference Only

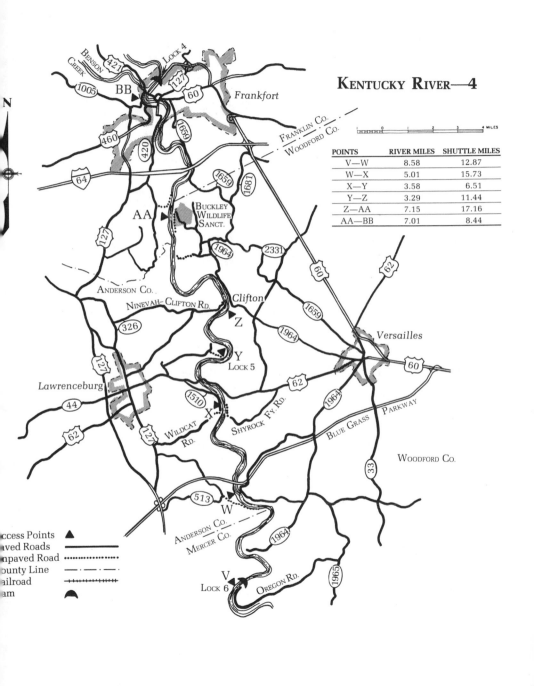

KENTUCKY RIVER—4

POINTS	RIVER MILES	SHUTTLE MILES
V—W	8.58	12.87
W—X	5.01	15.73
X—Y	3.58	6.51
Y—Z	3.29	11.44
Z—AA	7.15	17.16
AA—BB	7.01	8.44

Access Points ▲
Paved Roads ────
Unpaved Road ••••••••••
County Line ─·─·─
Railroad ┼┼┼┼┼┼
Dam ◣

SECTION: Frankfort Boat Dock to Springport Ferry Rd. (Franklin Co., Henry Co., Owen Co.)

USGS QUADS: Frankfort East, Frankfort West, Polsgrove, Switzer, Gratz, New Liberty

LEVEL OF DIFFICULTY International Class   I   Numerical Points   **4**

SUITABLE FOR: Cruising   **GRADIENT** (feet per mile): 0.53

APPROPRIATE FOR: Families, Beginners, Intermediates, Advanced

VELOCITY (mph): 2.6-5.0   **AVERAGE WIDTH** (ft): 120-190

MONTHS RUNNABLE: All

RUNNABLE WATER LEVEL (cfs) Minimum   N/A
   Maximum   Up to flood stage

MEAN WATER TEMPERATURE (°F)

| Jan. | 44 | Feb. | 45 | Mar. | 47 | Apr. | 53 | May | 66 | Jun. | 75 |
| Jul. | 80 | Aug. | 79 | Sep. | 75 | Oct. | 65 | Nov. | 54 | Dec. | 58 |

SOURCE OF ADDITIONAL INFORMATION ON WATER CONDITIONS

Corps of Engineers, Lock 4 (502) 223-8338

HAZARDS: Dams, powerboats

RESCUE INDEX: C-D
   A   Extremely remote; evacuation only with expert help—6 hours to secure assistance
   B   Remote; 3-6 hours to secure assistance
   C   Accessible but difficult; up to 3 hours to secure assistance—evacuation difficult
   D   Accessible; up to 1 hour to secure assistance, evacuation not difficult

PORTAGES: Lock Nos. 4 (Frankfort), 3 (Monterey), 2 (Lockport)

SCOUTING: None required

INTEREST HIGHLIGHTS: Scenery, history, local culture and industry

SCENERY: Pretty to pretty in spots

ACCESS POINT	ACCESS CODE	KEY
BB	1 3 5 7	1 Paved Road
CC	1 3 6 7	2 Unpaved Road
DD	1 3 5 7	3 Short Carry
EE	1 3 5 7 9	4 Long Carry
FF	2 3 6 7	5 Easy Grade
GG	1 3 5 7	6 Steep Grade
HH	1 3 5 7 9	7 Clear Trail
		8 Brush and Trees
		9 Private Property, Permission Needed
		10 Launching Fee Charged
		11 No Access—For Reference Only

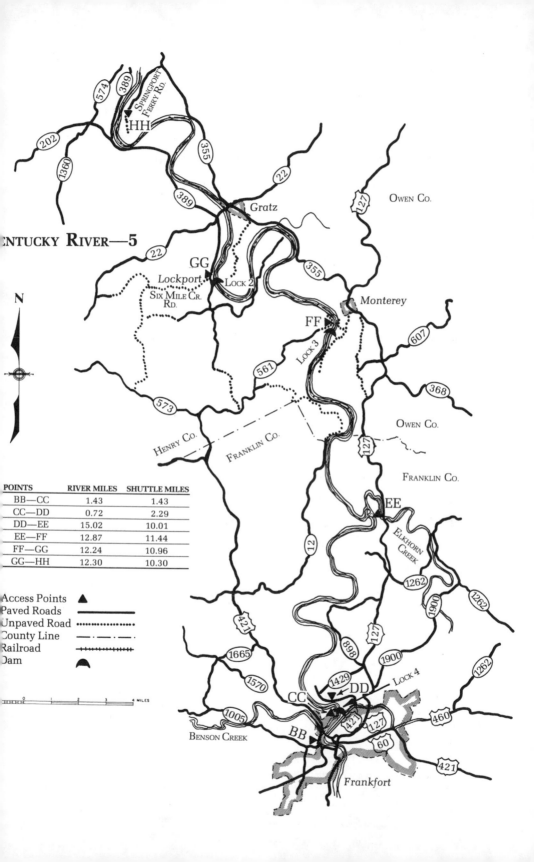

POINTS	RIVER MILES	SHUTTLE MILES
BB—CC	1.43	1.43
CC—DD	0.72	2.29
DD—EE	15.02	10.01
EE—FF	12.87	11.44
FF—GG	12.24	10.96
GG—HH	12.30	10.30

Access Points ▲
Paved Roads ——
Unpaved Road ••••••••••
County Line —•—•—•—
Railroad +++++++++
Dam

0   1   2   3   4 MILES

SECTION: Springport Ferry Rd. to Carrollton Boat Dock (Henry Co., Owen Co., Carroll Co.)

USGS QUADS: New Liberty, Worthville, Vevay South, Carrollton

LEVEL OF DIFFICULTY International Class I   **Numerical Points** 4

SUITABLE FOR: Cruising   **GRADIENT** (feet per mile): 0.53

APPROPRIATE FOR: Families, Beginners, Intermediates, Advanced

VELOCITY (mph): 2.6-5.0   **AVERAGE WIDTH** (ft): 140-205

MONTHS RUNNABLE: All

RUNNABLE WATER LEVEL (cfs) Minimum N/A
Maximum Up to flood stage

MEAN WATER TEMPERATURE (°F)

Jan. 44	Feb. 45	Mar. 47	Apr. 53	May 66	Jun. 75
Jul. 80	Aug. 79	Sep. 75	Oct. 65	Nov. 54	Dec. 58

SOURCE OF ADDITIONAL INFORMATION ON WATER CONDITIONS

Corps of Engineers, Lock 4 (502) 223-8338

HAZARDS: Dams, powerboats

RESCUE INDEX: C-D
  A Extremely remote; evacuation only with expert help—6 hours to secure assistance
  B Remote; 3-6 hours to secure assistance
  C Accessible but difficult; up to 3 hours to secure assistance—evacuation difficult
  D Accessible; up to 1 hour to secure assistance, evacuation not difficult

PORTAGES: Lock No. 1 (near Butler State Park)

SCOUTING: None required

INTEREST HIGHLIGHTS: Scenery, history, local culture and industry

SCENERY: Pretty to pretty in spots

ACCESS POINT	ACCESS CODE	KEY
HH	1 3 5 7 9	1 Paved Road
II	1 3 6 7 9	2 Unpaved Road
JJ	1 3 5 7	3 Short Carry
KK*	1 3 5 7	4 Long Carry
		5 Easy Grade
		6 Steep Grade
		7 Clear Trail
		8 Brush and Trees
		9 Private Property, Permission Needed
		10 Launching Fee Charged
		11 No Access—For Reference Only

*One-half mile upstream on the Ohio River

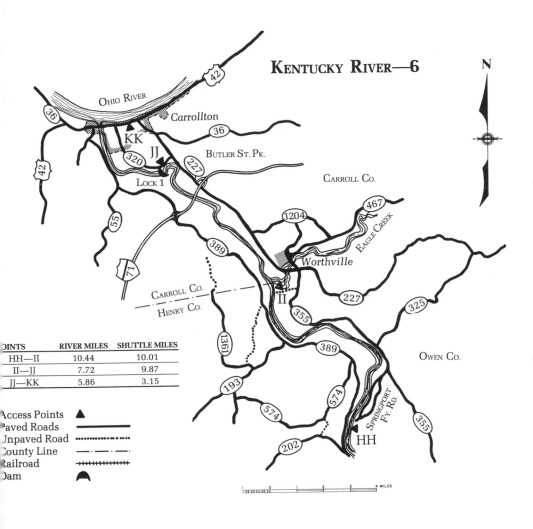

KENTUCKY RIVER—6

N

OHIO RIVER

42

36

Carrollton

36

KK

320 JJ

BUTLER ST. PK.

227

CARROLL CO.

42

LOCK 1

467

55

1204

EAGLE CREEK

71

389

Worthville

CARROLL CO.

HENRY CO.

227

325

II

355

OWEN CO.

1361

389

OINTS	RIVER MILES	SHUTTLE MILES
HH—II	10.44	10.01
II—JJ	7.72	9.87
JJ—KK	5.86	3.15

193

574

355

574

SPRINGPORT FY. RD.

Access Points

Paved Roads

Unpaved Road

County Line

Railroad

Dam

202

HH

0   1   2   3   4 MILES

SECTION: KY 746 to KY 715 (Wolfe Co.)

USGS QUADS: Lee City, Cannel City, Hazel Green, Pomeroyton

LEVEL OF DIFFICULTY International Class II (III) Numerical Points 16

SUITABLE FOR: Cruising   **GRADIENT** (feet per mile): 13.19

APPROPRIATE FOR: Intermediates, Advanced

VELOCITY (mph): 2.6-5.0+   **AVERAGE WIDTH** (ft): 25-45

MONTHS RUNNABLE: December to early May (with luck)

RUNNABLE WATER LEVEL (cfs) Minimum 175
   Maximum   Open: 350   Decked: 500

MEAN WATER TEMPERATURE (°F)

Jan. 41	Feb. 41	Mar. 46	Apr. 54	May 66	Jun. 73
Jul. 74	Aug. 73	Sep. 67	Oct. 61	Nov. 44	Dec. 40

SOURCE OF ADDITIONAL INFORMATION ON WATER CONDITIONS

Stanton Ranger Headquarters (606) 663-2852

HAZARDS: Deadfalls, undercut rocks, low trees, flash floods, difficult rapids

RESCUE INDEX: B
   A Extremely remote; evacuation only with expert help—6 hours to secure assistance
   B Remote; 3-6 hours to secure assistance
   C Accessible but difficult; up to 3 hours to secure assistance—evacuation difficult
   D Accessible; up to 1 hour to secure assistance, evacuation not difficult

PORTAGES: At deadfalls across stream

SCOUTING: At major rapids (5) and at blind curves for strainers

INTEREST HIGHLIGHTS: Scenery, wildlife, geology

SCENERY: Exceptionally beautiful to spectacular

ACCESS POINT	ACCESS CODE	KEY
A	2 3 5 7	1 Paved Road
B	1 3 6 7	2 Unpaved Road
		3 Short Carry
		4 Long Carry
		5 Easy Grade
		6 Steep Grade
		7 Clear Trail
		8 Brush and Trees
		9 Private Property, Permission Needed
		10 Launching Fee Charged
		11 No Access—For Reference Only

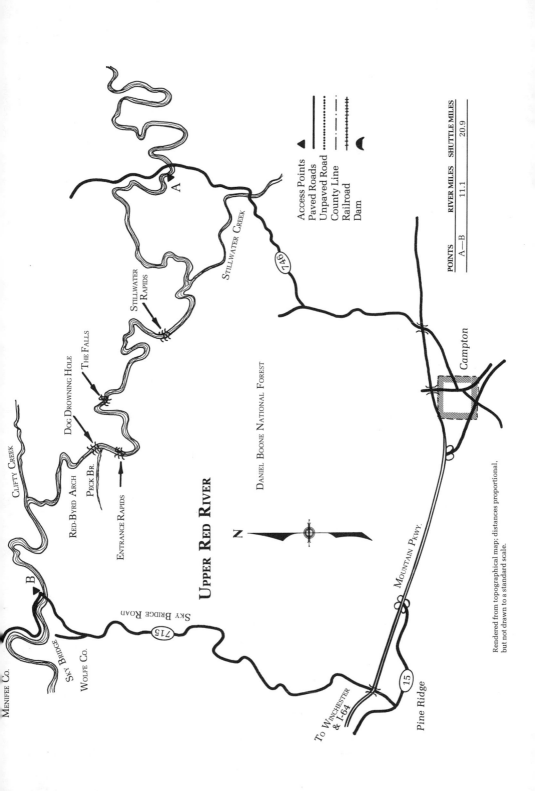

UPPER RED RIVER

Menifee Co.

Clifty Creek

Sky Bridge
Wolfe Co.

Red-Byrd Arch

Dog Drowning Hole

The Falls

Peck Br.

Entrance Rapids

Stillwater Rapids

Stillwater Creek

Sky Bridge Road

715

746

DANIEL BOONE NATIONAL FOREST

N

Mountain Pkwy.

To Winchester & I-64

Pine Ridge

15

Campton

POINTS	RIVER MILES	SHUTTLE MILES
A—B	11.1	20.9

Access Points ◀

Paved Roads ▬▬▬▬

Unpaved Road ·······

County Line —·—·—·—

Railroad ─┼─┼─┼─

Dam ◗

Rendered from topographical map; distances proportional, but not drawn to a standard scale.

SECTION: KY 715 to KY 77 (Wolfe Co., Powell Co.)

USGS QUADS: Pomeroyton, Slade

LEVEL OF DIFFICULTY International Class I+   Numerical Points   **4**

SUITABLE FOR: Cruising   **GRADIENT** (feet per mile): 2.53

APPROPRIATE FOR: Beginners, Intermediates, Advanced

VELOCITY (mph): 2.6-5.0   **AVERAGE WIDTH** (ft): 30-50

MONTHS RUNNABLE: November to mid-June

RUNNABLE WATER LEVEL (cfs) Minimum   180
  Maximum   Up to flood stage

MEAN WATER TEMPERATURE (°F)

Jan.	41	Feb.	41	Mar.	46	Apr.	54	May	66	Jun.	73
Jul.	74	Aug.	73	Sep.	67	Oct.	61	Nov.	44	Dec.	40

SOURCE OF ADDITIONAL INFORMATION ON WATER CONDITIONS
  Stanton Ranger Headquarters (606) 663-2852

HAZARDS: Deadfalls

RESCUE INDEX: D
  A Extremely remote; evacuation only with expert help—6 hours to secure assistance
  B Remote; 3-6 hours to secure assistance
  C Accessible but difficult; up to 3 hours to secure assistance—evacuation difficult
  D Accessible; up to 1 hour to secure assistance, evacuation not difficult

PORTAGES: None required

SCOUTING: None required

INTEREST HIGHLIGHTS: Scenery, history, wildlife, geology

SCENERY: Beautiful to exceptionally beautiful

ACCESS POINT	ACCESS CODE	KEY
B	1 3 6 7	1 Paved Road
C	1 4 6 7	2 Unpaved Road
		3 Short Carry
		4 Long Carry
		5 Easy Grade
		6 Steep Grade
		7 Clear Trail
		8 Brush and Trees
		9 Private Property, Permission Needed
		10 Launching Fee Charged
		11 No Access—For Reference Only

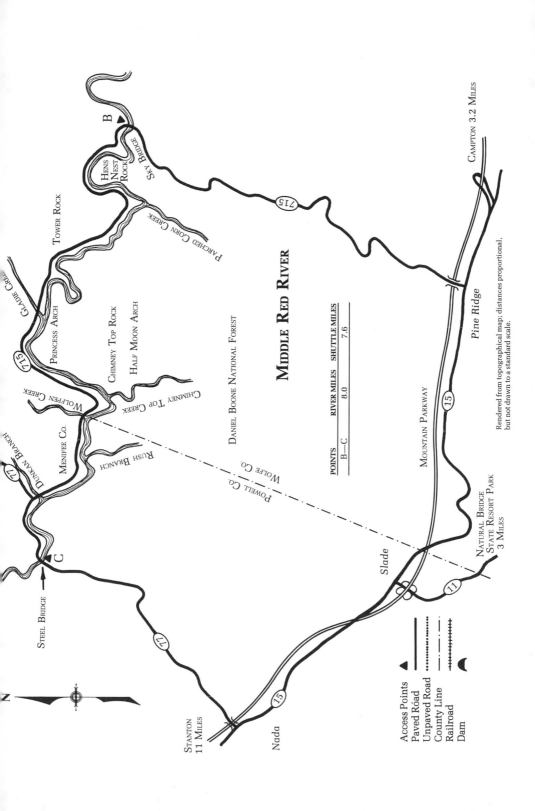

MIDDLE RED RIVER

POINTS	RIVER MILES	SHUTTLE MILES
B—C	8.0	7.6

Rendered from topographical map; distances proportional,
but not drawn to a standard scale.

DANIEL BOONE NATIONAL FOREST

POWELL CO.
WOLFE CO.

MENIFEE CO.

Access Points
Paved Road
Unpaved Road
County Line
Railroad
Dam

N

B

HENS NEST ROCK
SKY BRIDGE
TOWER ROCK
PARCHED CORN CREEK
715
CAMPTON 3.2 MILES
PINE RIDGE
15
MOUNTAIN PARKWAY
NATURAL BRIDGE STATE RESORT PARK 3 MILES
11
SLADE
NADA
15
STANTON 11 MILES
77
STEEL BRIDGE
C
DUNCAN BRANCH
77
RUSH BRANCH
WOLPPEN CREEK
PRINCESS ARCH
CHIMNEY TOP ROCK
HALF MOON ARCH
CHIMNEY TOP CREEK
GLADIE CREEK
715

SECTION: KY 77 to Kentucky River (Powell Co., Estill Co., Clark Co.)

USGS QUADS: Stanton, Clay City, Palmer

LEVEL OF DIFFICULTY International Class I   Numerical Points **4**

SUITABLE FOR: Cruising   **GRADIENT** (feet per mile): **2.46**

APPROPRIATE FOR: Beginners, Intermediates, Advanced

VELOCITY (mph): 2.6-5.0   **AVERAGE WIDTH** (ft): 30-55

MONTHS RUNNABLE: November to mid-June

RUNNABLE WATER LEVEL (cfs) Minimum **180**
   Maximum   Up to flood stage

MEAN WATER TEMPERATURE (°F)

Jan. 41	Feb. 41	Mar. 47	Apr. 56	May 67	Jun. 74
Jul. 76	Aug. 75	Sep. 68	Oct. 62	Nov. 44	Dec. 42

SOURCE OF ADDITIONAL INFORMATION ON WATER CONDITIONS
   Stanton Ranger Headquarters (606) 663-2852

HAZARDS: Deadfalls, low trees

RESCUE INDEX: C-D
   A Extremely remote; evacuation only with expert help—6 hours to secure assistance
   B Remote; 3-6 hours to secure assistance
   C Accessible but difficult; up to 3 hours to secure assistance—evacuation difficult
   D Accessible; up to 1 hour to secure assistance, evacuation not difficult

PORTAGES: Around numerous deadfalls

SCOUTING: None required

INTEREST HIGHLIGHTS: Scenery, local culture and industry

SCENERY: Pretty

ACCESS POINT	ACCESS CODE	KEY
C	1 4 6 7	1 Paved Road
D	1 3 6 8	2 Unpaved Road
E	1 3 6 8	3 Short Carry
F	1 3 6 8	4 Long Carry
G	1 3 5 8	5 Easy Grade
H	1 3 6 7	6 Steep Grade
I	1 3 5 8	7 Clear Trail
J	1 3 5 7 (10)	8 Brush and Trees
		9 Private Property, Permission Needed
		10 Launching Fee Charged
		11 No Access—For Reference Only

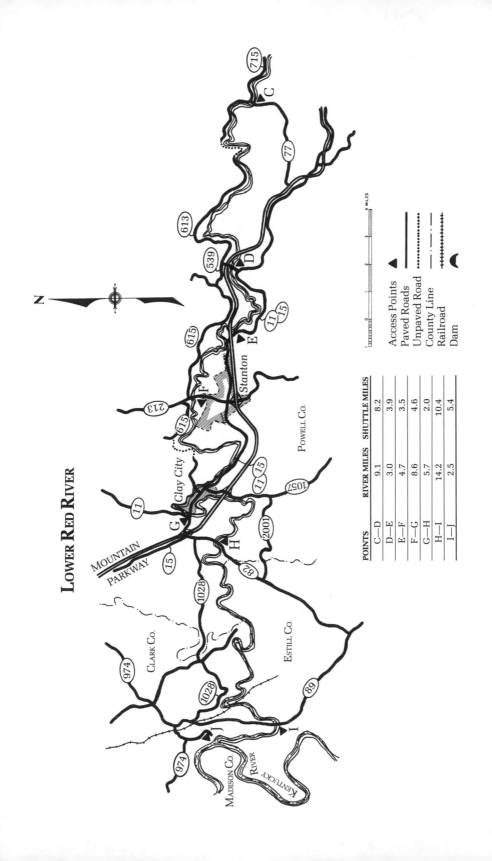

LOWER RED RIVER

N

POINTS	RIVER MILES	SHUTTLE MILES
C–D	9.1	8.2
D–E	3.0	3.9
E–F	4.7	3.5
F–G	8.6	4.6
G–H	5.7	2.0
H–I	14.2	10.4
I–J	2.5	5.4

Access Points
Paved Roads
Unpaved Road
County Line
Railroad
Dam

MILES

CLARK CO.
MADISON CO.
ESTILL CO.
POWELL CO.

KENTUCKY RIVER

MOUNTAIN PARKWAY

Clay City
Stanton

SECTION: KY 418 to Kentucky River (Fayette Co., Clark Co.)

USGS QUADS: Clintonville, Ford

LEVEL OF DIFFICULTY International Class III-IV‡ Numerical Points 23

SUITABLE FOR: Cruising   **GRADIENT** (feet per mile): 31.31

APPROPRIATE FOR: Intermediates, Advanced

VELOCITY (mph): 2.6-5.0+   **AVERAGE WIDTH** (ft): 20-40

MONTHS RUNNABLE: Following heavy rains

RUNNABLE WATER LEVEL (cfs) Minimum 170
Maximum   Open: 400   Decked: 900

MEAN WATER TEMPERATURE (°F) (Data not available)

| Jan. | Feb. | Mar. | Apr. | May | Jun. |
| Jul. | Aug. | Sep. | Oct. | Nov. | Dec. |

SOURCE OF ADDITIONAL INFORMATION ON WATER CONDITIONS
None available

HAZARDS: Deadfalls, undercut rocks, low bridges, low trees, fences, difficult rapids*, powerboats

RESCUE INDEX: C
A Extremely remote; evacuation only with expert help—6 hours to secure assistance
B Remote; 3-6 hours to secure assistance
C Accessible but difficult; up to 3 hours to secure assistance—evacuation difficult
D Accessible; up to 1 hour to secure assistance, evacuation not difficult

PORTAGES: Around deadfalls

SCOUTING: Must be done from eddy to eddy as creek runs through a gorge

INTEREST HIGHLIGHTS: Scenery, whitewater

SCENERY: Exceptionally beautiful to spectacular

ACCESS POINT	ACCESS CODE	KEY
A	1 3 5 7	1 Paved Road
B	1 3 5 7 9	2 Unpaved Road
C†	1 3 5 7	3 Short Carry
		4 Long Carry
		5 Easy Grade
		6 Steep Grade
		7 Clear Trail
		8 Brush and Trees
		9 Private Property, Permission Needed
		10 Launching Fee Charged
		11 No Access—For Reference Only

‡For decked boats at higher water levels; Class II-III for open boats at lower water levels
*Individual **rapids** not difficult, but whitewater continuous
†Take out under the bridge, not at the nearby boat ramps where a fee is charged.

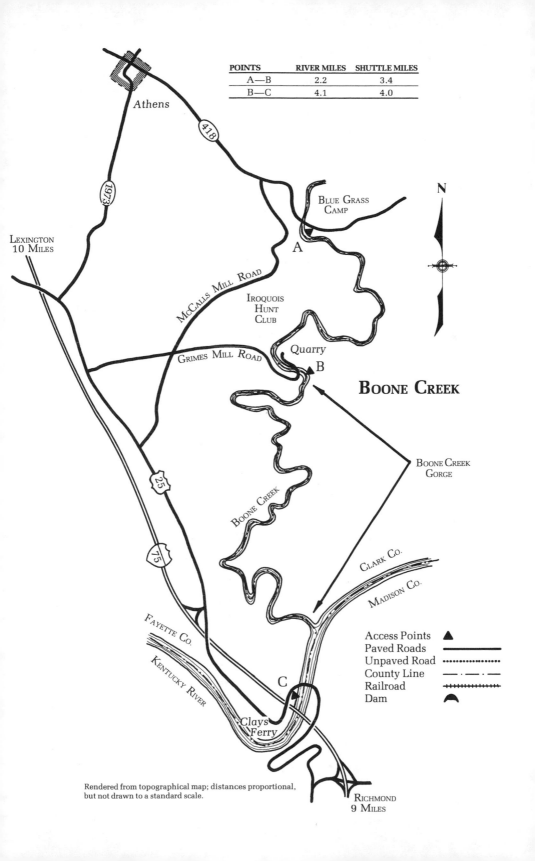

POINTS	RIVER MILES	SHUTTLE MILES
A—B	2.2	3.4
B—C	4.1	4.0

Athens

418

1973

Blue Grass Camp

A

N

Lexington
10 Miles

McCalls Mill Road

Iroquois
Hunt
Club

Grimes Mill Road

Quarry

B

BOONE CREEK

Boone Creek Gorge

25

Boone Creek

75

Clark Co.

Madison Co.

Access Points ▲
Paved Roads ——
Unpaved Road ••••••••
County Line —·—·—·
Railroad +++++++
Dam ⌒

Fayette Co.

Kentucky River

C

Clays
Ferry

Rendered from topographical map; distances proportional,
but not drawn to a standard scale.

Richmond
9 Miles

SECTION: Logantown to Herrington Lake (Lincoln Co., Boyle Co.)

USGS QUADS: Lancaster, Stanford, Bryantsville, Wilmore

LEVEL OF DIFFICULTY International Class I++ Numerical Points 6

SUITABLE FOR: Cruising, camping* **GRADIENT** (feet per mile): 2.37

APPROPRIATE FOR: Advanced Beginners, Intermediates, Advanced

VELOCITY (mph): 2.6-5.0 **AVERAGE WIDTH** (ft): 30-50

MONTHS RUNNABLE: Mid-November to mid-May

RUNNABLE WATER LEVEL (cfs) Minimum 200
Maximum Up to flood stage

MEAN WATER TEMPERATURE (°F)

Jan. 42	Feb. 40	Mar. 46	Apr. 54	May 66	Jun. 74
Jul. 74	Aug. 73	Sep. 67	Oct. 61	Nov. 43	Dec. 39

SOURCE OF ADDITIONAL INFORMATION ON WATER CONDITIONS
Lancaster Police Dept. (606) 792-3032

HAZARDS: Deadfalls, low trees

RESCUE INDEX: C
A Extremely remote; evacuation only with expert help—6 hours to secure assistance
B Remote; 3-6 hours to secure assistance
C Accessible but difficult; up to 3 hours to secure assistance—evacuation difficult
D Accessible; up to 1 hour to secure assistance, evacuation not difficult

PORTAGES: None required

SCOUTING: Several blind curves between the mouth of the Hanging Fork and KY 52 should be scouted for strainers

INTEREST HIGHLIGHTS: Scenery

SCENERY: Pretty to pretty in spots

ACCESS POINT	ACCESS CODE	KEY
A	1 3 5 8	1 Paved Road
B	2 3 6 7	2 Unpaved Road
C	1 3 5 7	3 Short Carry
D	2 3 5 7	4 Long Carry
E	1 4 5 7 9	5 Easy Grade
F	1 3 5 7 9	6 Steep Grade
		7 Clear Trail
		8 Brush and Trees
		9 Private Property, Permission Needed
		10 Launching Fee Charged
		11 No Access—For Reference Only

*Very nice fee campground below KY 52 bridge

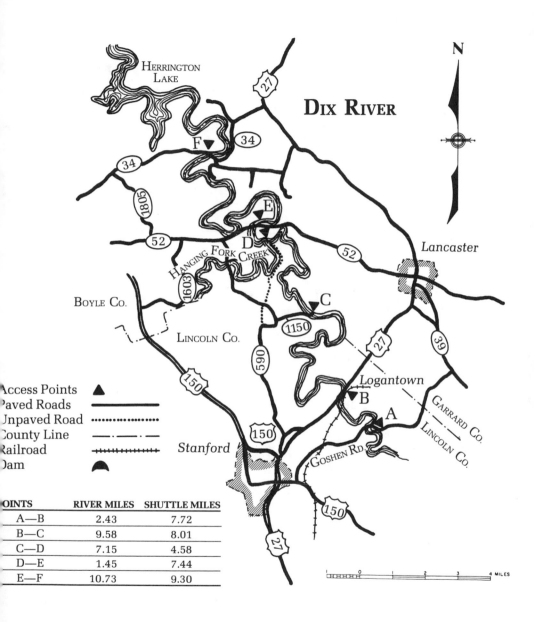

HERRINGTON LAKE

27

34

DIX RIVER

N

34

1805

52

E

D

HANGING FORK CREEK

1603

Lancaster

52

BOYLE CO.

C

LINCOLN CO.

1150

590

39

27

Logantown

B

GARRARD CO.

LINCOLN CO.

A

150

Access Points ▲
Paved Roads ━━━━
Unpaved Road ••••••••
County Line ━·━·━·
Railroad ┿┿┿┿┿┿
Dam ⌒

150

Stanford

GOSHEN RD.

150

27

4 MILES

POINTS	RIVER MILES	SHUTTLE MILES
A—B	2.43	7.72
B—C	9.58	8.01
C—D	7.15	4.58
D—E	1.45	7.44
E—F	10.73	9.30

SECTION: KY 590 to Dix River (Boyle Co.)

USGS QUADS: Stanford

LEVEL OF DIFFICULTY International Class I (II) Numerical Points 6

SUITABLE FOR: Cruising　　　**GRADIENT** (feet per mile): 13.94

APPROPRIATE FOR: Very advanced Beginners, Intermediates, Advanced

VELOCITY (mph): 2.6-5.0　　　**AVERAGE WIDTH** (ft): 20-35

MONTHS RUNNABLE: December to early May

RUNNABLE WATER LEVEL (cfs) Minimum 120
　Maximum　　Open: 400　Decked: 400

MEAN WATER TEMPERATURE (°F)
Jan. 41	Feb. 40	Mar. 46	Apr. 53	May 67	Jun. 75
Jul. 77	Aug. 75	Sep. 67	Oct. 61	Nov. 44	Dec. 41

SOURCE OF ADDITIONAL INFORMATION ON WATER CONDITIONS
　None available

HAZARDS: Dams, deadfalls, low trees

RESCUE INDEX: C
　A　Extremely remote; evacuation only with expert help—6 hours to secure assistance
　B　Remote; 3-6 hours to secure assistance
　C　Accessible but difficult; up to 3 hours to secure assistance—evacuation difficult
　D　Accessible; up to 1 hour to secure assistance, evacuation not difficult

PORTAGES: Around dam near mouth at Dix River*

SCOUTING: Blind curves

INTEREST HIGHLIGHTS: Scenery, local culture and industry

SCENERY: Pretty

ACCESS POINT	ACCESS CODE	KEY
AA	1 3 6 8	1 Paved Road
E†	1 4 5 7 9	2 Unpaved Road
		3 Short Carry
		4 Long Carry
		5 Easy Grade
		6 Steep Grade
		7 Clear Trail
		8 Brush and Trees
		9 Private Property, Permission Needed
		10 Launching Fee Charged
		11 No Access—For Reference Only

*Sometimes can be run on the left where it has caved in—scout first!
†On the Dix River

Hanging Fork of the Dix River

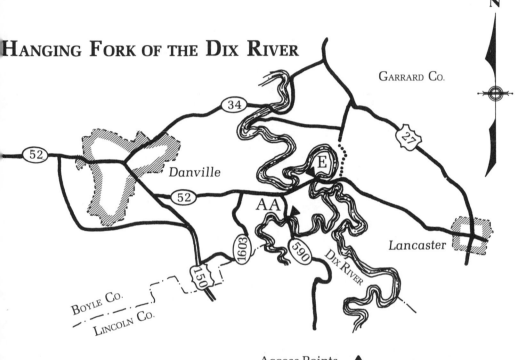

POINTS	RIVER MILES	SHUTTLE MILES
AA—E	5.72	1.72

Access Points ▲
Paved Roads ───
Unpaved Road ••••••••••
County Line ─ · ─ · ─
Railroad ┼┼┼┼┼┼┼┼┼
Dam ◗

SECTION: KY 1005 to Kentucky River (Franklin Co.)

USGS QUADS: Frankfort West

LEVEL OF DIFFICULTY International Class II   Numerical Points 8

SUITABLE FOR: Cruising   **GRADIENT** (feet per mile): 15.78

APPROPRIATE FOR: Intermediates, Advanced

VELOCITY (mph): 2.6-5.0   **AVERAGE WIDTH** (ft): 30-65

MONTHS RUNNABLE: November to mid-May

RUNNABLE WATER LEVEL (cfs) Minimum   200
   Maximum   Up to flood stage

MEAN WATER TEMPERATURE (°F)

Jan. 42	Feb. 42	Mar. 47	Apr. 55	May 66	Jun. 77
Jul. 78	Aug. 77	Sep. 69	Oct. 61	Nov. 45	Dec. 42

SOURCE OF ADDITIONAL INFORMATION ON WATER CONDITIONS
   None available

HAZARDS: Dams, deadfalls

RESCUE INDEX: D
   A Extremely remote; evacuation only with expert help—6 hours to secure assistance
   B Remote; 3-6 hours to secure assistance
   C Accessible but difficult; up to 3 hours to secure assistance—evacuation difficult
   D Accessible; up to 1 hour to secure assistance, evacuation not difficult

PORTAGES: Around dam at distillery

SCOUTING: At blind curves for strainers

INTEREST HIGHLIGHTS: Scenery, wildlife, geology, local culture and industry

SCENERY: Pretty to beautiful in spots

ACCESS POINT	ACCESS CODE	KEY
A	1 3 5 7	1 Paved Road
B*	1 3 5 7	2 Unpaved Road
		3 Short Carry
		4 Long Carry
		5 Easy Grade
		6 Steep Grade
		7 Clear Trail
		8 Brush and Trees
		9 Private Property, Permission Needed
		10 Launching Fee Charged
		11 No Access—For Reference Only

*On Kentucky River upstream of mouth of Benson Creek at Frankfort boat dock

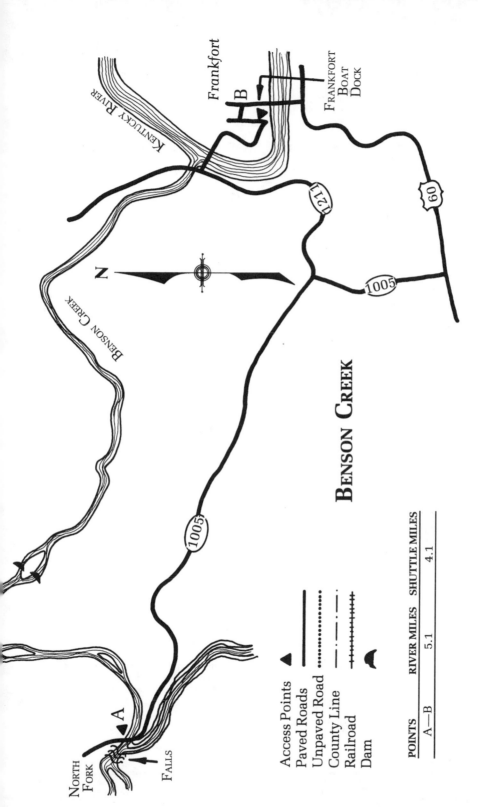

NORTH FORK

FALLS

A

BENSON CREEK

1005

KENTUCKY RIVER

Frankfort

B

FRANKFORT BOAT DOCK

121

60

1005

N

BENSON CREEK

Access Points ▲
Paved Roads ▬▬▬
Unpaved Road ••••••••
County Line —•—•—
Railroad ┼┼┼┼┼┼
Dam ◗

POINTS	RIVER MILES	SHUTTLE MILES
A—B	5.1	4.1

Rendered from topographical map; distances proportional, but not drawn to a standard scale.

SECTION: Georgetown to Forks of Elkhorn (Scott Co., Franklin Co.)

USGS QUADS: Georgetown, Midway, Stamping Ground, Switzer

LEVEL OF DIFFICULTY International Class I+ Numerical Points 5

SUITABLE FOR: Cruising, camping*GRADIENT (feet per mile): 4.07

APPROPRIATE FOR: Beginners, Intermediates, Advanced

VELOCITY (mph): 2.6-5.0   **AVERAGE WIDTH** (ft): 35-40

MONTHS RUNNABLE: December to early May

RUNNABLE WATER LEVEL (cfs) Minimum 180
Maximum   Up to flood stage

MEAN WATER TEMPERATURE (°F)

Jan. 43	Feb. 43	Mar. 47	Apr. 55	May 66	Jun. 77
Jul. 78	Aug. 77	Sep. 69	Oct. 61	Nov. 45	Dec. 41

SOURCE OF ADDITIONAL INFORMATION ON WATER CONDITIONS
City of Georgetown (502) 863-7850

HAZARDS: Dams, deadfalls

RESCUE INDEX: D
A Extremely remote; evacuation only with expert help—6 hours to secure assistance
B Remote; 3-6 hours to secure assistance
C Accessible but difficult; up to 3 hours to secure assistance—evacuation difficult
D Accessible; up to 1 hour to secure assistance, evacuation not difficult

PORTAGES: Around dams approaching U.S. 25 in Georgetown, Great Crossing, and around 2 dams between Great Crossing and Switzer
SCOUTING: None required

INTEREST HIGHLIGHTS: Scenery, local culture and industry

SCENERY: Pretty to pretty in spots

ACCESS POINT	ACCESS CODE	KEY
A	1 3 6 8	1 Paved Road
B	1 3 5 7	2 Unpaved Road
C	1 3 5 7	3 Short Carry
D	1 3 5 7	4 Long Carry
E	1 3 5 7	5 Easy Grade
F	1 3 6 7 9	6 Steep Grade
G	1 3 5 7 9	7 Clear Trail
		8 Brush and Trees
		9 Private Property, Permission Needed
		10 Launching Fee Charged
		11 No Access—For Reference Only

*Public fee campground only

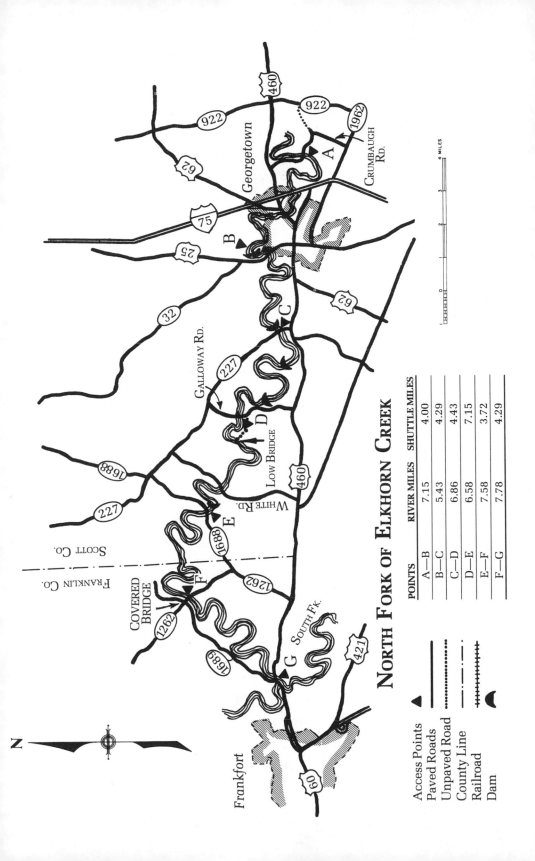

NORTH FORK OF ELKHORN CREEK

POINTS	RIVER MILES	SHUTTLE MILES
A–B	7.15	4.00
B–C	5.43	4.29
C–D	6.86	4.43
D–E	6.58	7.15
E–F	7.58	3.72
F–G	7.78	4.29

Access Points	◀	
Paved Roads	▬▬▬▬	
Unpaved Road	••••••••	
County Line	—•—•—	
Railroad	┼┼┼┼┼	
Dam	◖	

SECTION: Fishers Mill to Forks of Elkhorn (Woodford Co., Franklin Co.)

USGS QUADS: Versailles, Midway, Frankfort East, Switzer

LEVEL OF DIFFICULTY International Class I+ Numerical Points 4

SUITABLE FOR: Cruising   **GRADIENT** (feet per mile): 1.38

APPROPRIATE FOR: Beginners, Intermediates, Advanced

VELOCITY (mph): 2.6-5.0   **AVERAGE WIDTH** (ft): 25-40

MONTHS RUNNABLE: December to April

RUNNABLE WATER LEVEL (cfs) Minimum 125
    Maximum Up to flood stage

MEAN WATER TEMPERATURE (°F)

Jan. 43	Feb. 43	Mar. 47	Apr. 55	May 66	Jun. 77
Jul. 78	Aug. 77	Sep. 69	Oct. 61	Nov. 45	Dec. 41

SOURCE OF ADDITIONAL INFORMATION ON WATER CONDITIONS
    None available

HAZARDS: Dams, deadfalls, low bridges, low trees, fences

RESCUE INDEX: D
    A Extremely remote; evacuation only with expert help—6 hours to secure assistance
    B Remote; 3-6 hours to secure assistance
    C Accessible but difficult; up to 3 hours to secure assistance—evacuation difficult
    D Accessible; up to 1 hour to secure assistance, evacuation not difficult

PORTAGES: Around cattle gates, low bridges, and dam at Forks of Elkhorn

SCOUTING: As required to portage

INTEREST HIGHLIGHTS: Scenery, history, wildlife, local culture and industry

SCENERY: Pretty to pretty in spots

ACCESS POINT	ACCESS CODE	KEY
A	1 3 5 7	1 Paved Road
B	1 3 5 8	2 Unpaved Road
C	1 3 5 7 9	3 Short Carry
		4 Long Carry
		5 Easy Grade
		6 Steep Grade
		7 Clear Trail
		8 Brush and Trees
		9 Private Property, Permission Needed
		10 Launching Fee Charged
		11 No Access—For Reference Only

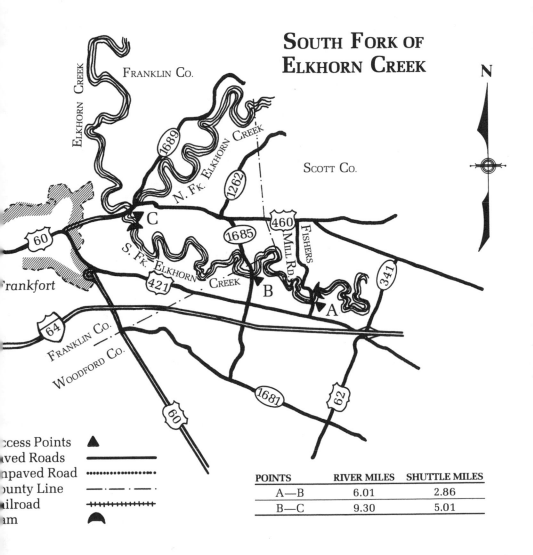

SOUTH FORK OF ELKHORN CREEK

ELKHORN CREEK

FRANKLIN CO.

SCOTT CO.

N. FK. ELKHORN CREEK

1689

1262

460

C

FISHERS

1685

MILL RD.

S. FK. ELKHORN CREEK

421

B

341

A

Frankfort

60

64

FRANKLIN CO.

WOODFORD CO.

60

1681

62

N

Access Points   ▲
Paved Roads
Unpaved Road
County Line
Railroad
Dam

POINTS	RIVER MILES	SHUTTLE MILES
A—B	6.01	2.86
B—C	9.30	5.01

4 MILES

0   2   3

SECTION: Forks of Elkhorn to Kentucky River (Franklin Co.)

USGS QUADS: Switzer, Polsgrove

LEVEL OF DIFFICULTY International Class II (G-H) Numerical Points 9, 4 (re-
I+ (H-L)   spectively)
SUITABLE FOR: Cruising   **GRADIENT** (feet per mile): 9.55

APPROPRIATE FOR: Very advanced Beginners, Intermediates, Advanced (G-H);
Beginners, Intermediates, Advanced (H-L)
VELOCITY (mph): 2.6-5.0   **AVERAGE WIDTH** (ft): 30-55

MONTHS RUNNABLE: November to mid-June

RUNNABLE WATER LEVEL (cfs) Minimum 200 (0 ft.)
Maximum Open: 850   Decked: Up to flood stage

MEAN WATER TEMPERATURE ($^\circ$F)

Jan. 43	Feb. 43	Mar. 47	Apr. 55	May 66	Jun. 77
Jul. 78	Aug. 77	Sep. 69	Oct. 61	Nov. 45	Dec. 41

SOURCE OF ADDITIONAL INFORMATION ON WATER CONDITIONS
City of Georgetown (502) 863-7850

HAZARDS: Dams, deadfalls, low trees

RESCUE INDEX: D
A Extremely remote; evacuation only with expert help—6 hours to secure assistance
B Remote; 3-6 hours to secure assistance
C Accessible but difficult; up to 3 hours to secure assistance—evacuation difficult
D Accessible; up to 1 hour to secure assistance, evacuation not difficult

PORTAGES: Around dam at distillery below Forks of Elkhorn

SCOUTING: For deadfalls on any blind rapid

INTEREST HIGHLIGHTS: Scenery, wildlife, mild whitewater

SCENERY: Pretty to beautiful in spots

ACCESS POINT	ACCESS CODE	KEY
G	1 3 5 7 9	1 Paved Road
H	1 3 5 7	2 Unpaved Road
I	1 3 6 7	3 Short Carry
J	1 3 5 8	4 Long Carry
K	2 3 5 8	5 Easy Grade
L	2 3 6 8	6 Steep Grade
		7 Clear Trail
		8 Brush and Trees
		9 Private Property, Permission Needed
		10 Launching Fee Charged
		11 No Access—For Reference Only

ELKHORN CREEK

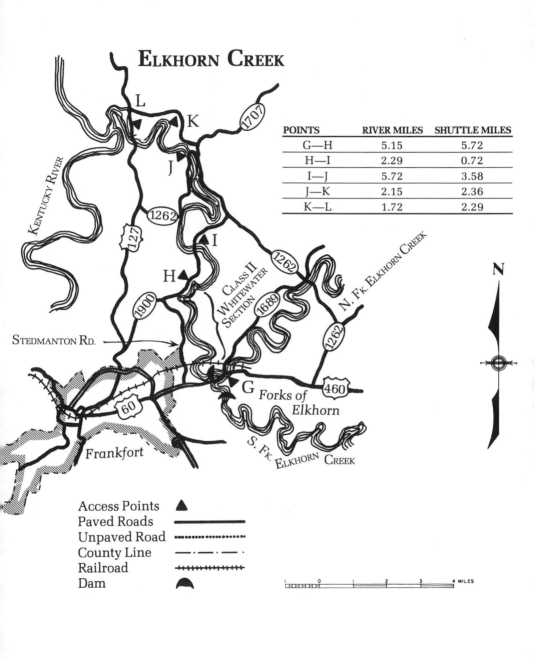

POINTS	RIVER MILES	SHUTTLE MILES
G—H	5.15	5.72
H—I	2.29	0.72
I—J	5.72	3.58
J—K	2.15	2.36
K—L	1.72	2.29

Access Points
Paved Roads
Unpaved Road
County Line
Railroad
Dam

4 MILES

SECTION: KY 36 bridge to Kentucky River (Grant Co., Gallatin Co., Carroll Co.)

USGS QUADS: Lawrenceville, Elliston, Glencoe, Sanders, Vevay South, Worthville

LEVEL OF DIFFICULTY International Class I+   Numerical Points 5

SUITABLE FOR: Cruising   **GRADIENT** (feet per mile): 4.72

APPROPRIATE FOR: Beginners, Intermediates, Advanced

VELOCITY (mph): 2.6-5.0   **AVERAGE WIDTH** (ft): 35-55

MONTHS RUNNABLE: November to early June

RUNNABLE WATER LEVEL (cfs) Minimum   190
Maximum   Up to flood stage

MEAN WATER TEMPERATURE (°F)

Jan. 40	Feb. 41	Mar. 46	Apr. 54	May 68	Jun. 76
Jul. 81	Aug. 79	Sep. 69	Oct. 61	Nov. 47	Dec. 40

SOURCE OF ADDITIONAL INFORMATION ON WATER CONDITIONS
Worthville Police Dept. (502) 732-6621

HAZARDS: Deadfalls, low trees

RESCUE INDEX: D
A Extremely remote; evacuation only with expert help—6 hours to secure assistance
B Remote; 3-6 hours to secure assistance
C Accessible but difficult; up to 3 hours to secure assistance—evacuation difficult
D Accessible; up to 1 hour to secure assistance, evacuation not difficult

PORTAGES: None required

SCOUTING: None required

INTEREST HIGHLIGHTS: Scenery, local culture and industry

SCENERY: Pleasant to pretty in spots

ACCESS POINT	ACCESS CODE	KEY
A	1 3 6 8	1 Paved Road
B	1 3 5 7	2 Unpaved Road
C	1 3 5 8	3 Short Carry
D	2 3 5 7	4 Long Carry
E	1 3 6 7	5 Easy Grade
F	1 3 6 7	6 Steep Grade
G	1 3 6 7	7 Clear Trail
H	1 4 6 8	8 Brush and Trees
II	1 3 5 7 9	9 Private Property, Permission Needed
		10 Launching Fee Charged
		11 No Access—For Reference Only

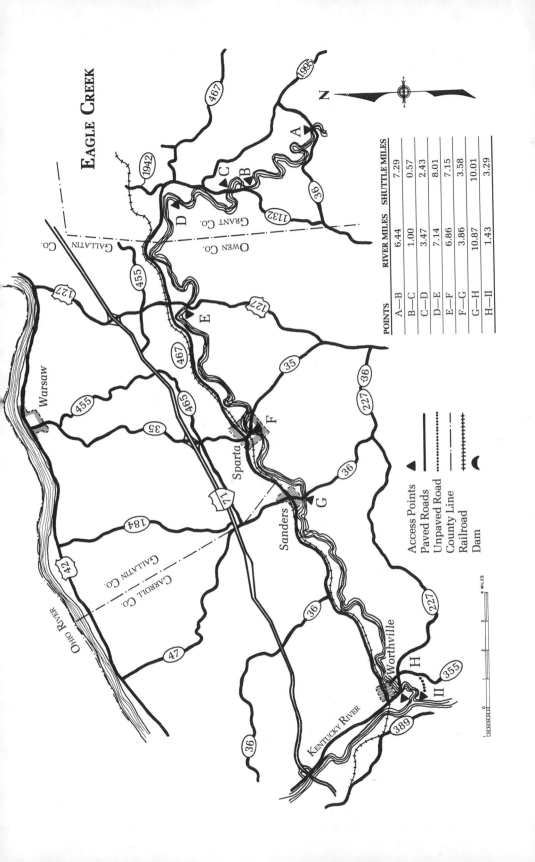

EAGLE CREEK

POINTS	RIVER MILES	SHUTTLE MILES
A–B	6.44	7.29
B–C	1.00	0.57
C–D	3.47	2.43
D–E	7.14	8.01
E–F	6.86	7.15
F–G	3.86	3.58
G–H	10.87	10.01
H–II	1.43	3.29

Access Points
Paved Roads
Unpaved Road
County Line
Railroad
Dam

4 MILES

N

OHIO RIVER
Warsaw
KENTUCKY RIVER
Worthville
Sanders
Sparta
CARROLL CO.
GALLATIN CO.
GALLATIN CO.
OWEN CO.
GRANT CO.

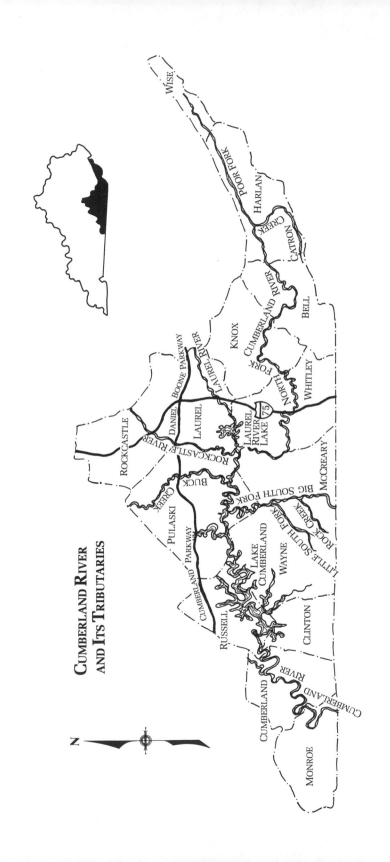

CUMBERLAND RIVER AND ITS TRIBUTARIES

N

WISE

POOR FORK

HARLAN

CREEK

CATRON

BELL

CUMBERLAND RIVER

KNOX

NORTH FORK

WHITLEY

DANIEL BOONE PARKWAY

LAUREL RIVER

LAUREL

75

LAUREL RIVER LAKE

ROCKCASTLE

ROCKCASTLE RIVER

BUCK CREEK

BIG SOUTH FORK

McCREARY

PULASKI

LITTLE SOUTH FORK

ROCK CREEK

CUMBERLAND PARKWAY

LAKE CUMBERLAND

WAYNE

RUSSELL

CLINTON

CUMBERLAND RIVER

MONROE

4

THE CUMBERLAND RIVER AND ITS TRIBUTARIES

POOR FORK OF THE CUMBERLAND RIVER

The Poor Fork of the Cumberland River drains Harlan and Letcher counties in southeastern Kentucky and is the largest of the headwater streams of the North Fork of the Cumberland River. Flowing swiftly over a bed of rock and gravel, the Poor Fork winds through one of the most deep and intimate mountain valleys in Eastern Kentucky. Human habitation is frequently in evidence along the Poor Fork but does surprisingly little to spoil the incredible beauty of this mountain stream. Trees envelop the stream only intermittently allowing the paddler frequent pano- ramic views of the surrounding mountains with their luxurious foliage and exposed rock bluffs. The banks are normally four to eight feet high and gently banked. The river varies in width from 25 to 40 feet and curves leisurely through the valley. Paddling is interesting with continually changing vistas and delightful Class-I and -II small shoals and rapids. The Poor Fork is runnable from January through mid-April, and occasionally following heavy rains. Access was less than desirable at the time of this writing but will be excellent on the completion of the new U.S. 119 through the valley. Lateral erosion is minimal on the Poor Fork so deadfalls are unusual. The only navigational hazards usually en- countered are man-made concrete fords that cross the stream from time to time.

NORTH FORK OF THE CUMBERLAND RIVER

The North Fork of the Cumberland River (locally referred to as simply the Cumberland) originates near Harlan at the confluence of the Poor Fork and Catron Creek, and flows west draining the East Kentucky counties of Knox, Bell, Harlan, Whitley, McCreary, and Pulaski.

HARLAN TO WILLIAMSBURG. Between Harlan and Pineville the North Fork flows over a mud and gravel bed with infrequent small shoals and rapids (Class I+) and occasional large rocks in evidence in the stream and along the banks. From a width of approximately 50 feet at its origin, the Cumberland broadens quickly to 85 to 105 feet. Running west through the steep, rugged hills of the Cumberland Plateau, the river winds through forest and coal country, under hanging wooden footbridges, and past the cabins of miners and the ever-present coal tipples along the railroad tracks. As the Cumberland passes Pineville, it settles down into a mud bottom with steep banks, broadens a bit, and flows smoothly as it progresses through the deep valleys past Barbourville towards Williamsburg. To canoe the Cumberland from Harlan to Williamsburg is to become intimately acquainted with the land and the people of Eastern Kentucky, their life-style and institutions visible and alive all along the river. Although only steep, wooded hillsides meet your searching eyes, you are never out of earshot of the rumbling coal trucks or the raspy barking of a dog defending an unseen cabin in some lonely hollow.

The Cumberland from Harlan to Pineville is frequently runnable from November through mid-May or whenever the Williamsburg gauge reads in excess of 1300 cfs. Access is reasonably good providing you are accustomed to steep banks. From Pineville to Williamsburg the river is usually runnable when the Williamsburg gauge reads in excess of 700 cfs. The section from Harlan to Williamsburg is best suited to one-day runs (pick your own) rather than canoe camping.

WILLIAMSBURG TO CUMBERLAND FALLS. From Williamsburg to Cumberland Falls, the river flows through the Daniel Boone National Forest. In this section the river continues to widen until in some places it is almost 200 feet across. The gradient increases here also and some mild whitewater (Class II) is encountered, with boulders in the stream and some shoals spanning the entire width of the river. This section (beyond the mouth of Jellico Creek) is extremely remote and makes a good canoe-camping run at moderate water levels (500 to 1100 cfs) and a fair whitewater run at higher levels (1100 to 1900 cfs). Rock replaces the mud bottom of the upper sections, and the current runs swift and continuously, with very few pools. Boulders line the banks in increasing numbers and some flat, accessible terraces have been carved along the streamside. In the last three miles before reaching the KY 90 bridge, exposed rock palisades become visible on the right as the Cumberland begins to enter the deep gorge that will carry it over the falls and beyond to Lake Cumberland. About one mile upstream of the falls the river curves sharply to the left and the KY 90 bridge becomes visible downstream. Move to the right of the river for the take-out on the upstream side of the bridge (at the picnic ground and parking lot). Failure to move promptly to the right can have tragic consequences for the un-lucky or inexperienced. One of the larger shoals (Class II) of this section is situated across the entire river just upstream of the take-out. If you run it on the left and fill up or capsize, you will find yourself in the main current heading for the entrance rapids to Cumberland Falls several hundred yards downstream. If you run the shoals on the right and take water or turn over, you will be in much slower current and (except at excessive levels, i.e., 1900+) will be washed into the bank as the river narrows near the bridge, or alternately swept downstream past the bridge into a huge eddy that forms along the bank near the visitors' parking lot.

Access for this section is not plentiful but is good where it exists. The Cumberland from Williamsburg to Cumberland Falls is normally runnable from November to early June or whenever the Williamsburg gauge reads 400 cfs or more.

CUMBERLAND RIVER BELOW THE FALLS. This section of the North Fork of Cumberland is a Kentucky-protected Wild River and is one of the most popular whitewater runs in the state. Re-ferred to as "The Cumberland Below the Falls" by local paddlers, the river here runs through a mammoth rock gorge with boulders lining the river marking the age-old headward erosion of the falls. The run should be attempted only by experienced boaters and extra flotation is recommended for open boats.

The run begins with a long carry from the visitors' parking lot at Cumberland Falls to a beach a quarter of a mile away at the bottom of the falls. Scenery is spectacular right from the put-in, and most paddlers take the opportunity to paddle back upstream for a truly awe-inspiring view of the falls (80 yards from the falls is as close as you can safely paddle without fighting a fantasti-cally strong reversal current seeking to pull you into the falls).

Moving downstream, several easy Class-II rapids that require no scouting are encountered before arriving at the Class-III "Center Rock Rapid." This rapid can be identified by the large boulders on each side that constrict the river to a channel of approximately 20 feet, and by the degree of drop that substantially exceeds that encountered previously. The rapid consists of a 25-foot-long, stairstep chute followed 50 feet later by a three-foot vertical drop directly in front of a huge boulder that splits the current. This is "Center Rock." The first drop is usually run straight down the center while the strategy for the second is to angle the bow to the right and drop straight into the eddy on the right at the bottom of the drop. An alternate strategy for the second drop is to ride the pillow off the right side of Center Rock. It is recommended that this rapid be scouted.

Continuing downstream, the river lapses into a series of pools followed by rock gardens (at low to moderate water) and Class-II rapids. The drops are small, but several of the rapids are quite technical. One of these, at about mile 4, has an undercut boulder situated in mid-channel splitting the flow. This should be run along the far right bank. Moving on, there are more long pools and small rapids. At mile 5 there is a slanting 2½-foot drop with a playful hole at the bottom that spans the entire river. This is known as "Surfing Rapid" and is a delightful place to stop for lunch.

Beyond "Surfing Rapid" the run becomes more intense. One-half mile downstream of "Surfing Rapid," the river disappears to the right around a house-sized rock and immediately cuts left again crashing into a boulder on the right and down a 30-foot-long chute. This fast and furious borderline Class-III run serves up an exciting ride. Run right center and play the pillow off the boulder.

The next rapid, a quarter mile distant, is a turning four-foot drop known as "Screaming Right-Hand Rapid." At low to moderate water levels the main flow drops over a 1½-foot ledge and splashes almost immediately on a rock that diverts the current sharply to the right over a three-foot slanted drop. The most popular strategy here is to cut right after the first ledge using the pillow to turn the boat. At higher water levels the river overflows the obstructing rock and a four-foot vertical drop and a mean hydraulic is created completely across the river. Scouting is definitely required in this situation.

The next large rapid, known as "Stair Steps," is a long, delightful, borderline Class-III stretch that looks much worse than it is. It is easily recognized by the large hole at the top with a shark-fin-shaped rock just below it. Decked boaters may want to punch the hole. For open boaters the best route is to run right of the hole and then hug the right bank all the way to the bottom. Scout on the right.

The last major rapid is appropriately named "Last Drop." In this Class-III area, the current winds to the right along the upstream side of a large boulder and then suddenly cuts left dropping vertically three feet. Next the current is split by a building-sized boulder in the middle of the river. Run to the right at the top, staying to the inside of the turn and away from the upstream face of the boulder. Cut hard left, taking the vertical drop as close to the boulder as possible. Go around the building-sized boulder that splits the current on the far right. At high water this rapid (like several others) changes drastically forming a super mean hole at the top. Scout (or portage) to the right.

"Last Drop" marks the end of the whitewater section of the Cumberland (although several small shoals are encountered farther downstream due to the low level of the lake pool). From here it is a scenic 3½-mile paddle through the lake to the take-out at the mouth of the Laurel River. Access is excellent at the take-out.

Dangers other than those already described include logs that occasionally become trapped in the more narrow chutes, and strong headwinds while paddling off the lake. Off the river dangers include the possible vandalizing of vehicles (especially vans) left at the take-out end of the shuttle.

The Cumberland River below the falls is the only whitewater river in Kentucky that is normally runnable all year.

ROCKCASTLE RIVER

The Rockcastle River originates in Laurel County and drains portions of Jackson, Rockcastle, Laurel, and Pulaski counties. One of Kentucky's most popular rivers, the Rockcastle offers something for every type of canoeist.

The upper sections from KY 490 to KY 80 flow over a sand and rock bed through hilly woods and farmland in the heart of the Daniel Boone National Forest. Runnable from late fall to midsummer, this section is scenic and has banks of varying steepness and some very mild (Class I+) whitewater. A favorite run for canoe campers, current is good and dangers to navigation are limited to deadfalls. Access on the upper sections is good (except for steep, mud banks at the KY 80 bridge) and canoe rental and shuttle service is available from nearby professional outfitters (see Appendix).

The lower Rockcastle, from KY 80 to KY 192 is a protected Wild River and is one of Kentucky's most popular whitewater runs. Scenery is splendid with tall, forested hills along the first miles of the run giving way to high, rock bluffs further downstream, with boxcar-sized boulders situated in the river and along the banks. Paddling the lower Rockcastle is both interesting and challenging. To begin with, the run is an exhausting 17 miles long. The first six miles are essentially Class I with a fair current and numerous riffles and small ledges. Throughout the next six miles the river picks up a little gradient and several honest Class-II rapids are encountered. While these rapids are not difficult, two or three do disappear around boulders or curves. If you are not intimately familiar with the river (this or any other), you should take the time to scout these. Guidebook or no, it is not healthy to get into the habit of running rapids you cannot see the end of. At about mile 12 the river curves hard right and then hard left tumbling down a Class-II (-III?) series of ledges and standing waves known as the "Stair Steps." Beyond this rapid, the Rockcastle reverts to long pools punctuated by short Class-II drops at the ends. At about mile 15 the river appears to come to a dead end in a large boulder garden, but closer inspection reveals that whole stream is grunting laboriously between two huge rocks and falling about four feet. This is Beech (Creek) Narrows. Above the drop an ill-placed boulder makes it difficult to set up. Below the drop is a very bad, highly aerated keeper hydraulic. Beyond the hydraulic the current washes directly into a large boulder. While this Class-IV rapid has been run both decked and open, I consider attempting to run it highly dangerous, with success more a function of luck (specifically, catching the rotation of the violent hydraulic on the "up cycle" where it helps to kick you free) than skill. A portage trail circles the boulders on the right. My advice: carry around. If you choose to run, set up a rescue person where you are certain you can reach a person trapped in the keeper on the first throw. Below Beech Narrows the Rockcastle assumes its normal pool and drop for another three-quarters of a mile before entering a second apparent cul-de-sac. Here the river forms a large tranquil pool before cutting hard right, churning down a fast chute, and smacking into a rock. This rapid marks the entrance to the Lower Narrows, a three-quarter mile stretch of intense and almost continuous, highly technical Class-III and -IV water. After the first rapid of the Lower Narrows (which is followed by a 200-yard pool), the remaining four rapids are lined up literally one behind the other in an amazing stretch of tumbling, turbulent whitewater that lambastes the paddler with every challenge in the book. There is a possibility that this section of rapids will be covered after May of 1978 as the pool level of Lake Cumberland is raised. In this section of the narrows there are no pools. There are, thankfully however, some large eddies that let an embattled paddler stop after each rapid to bail, collect wits, and scramble up the banks to scout whatever lurks ahead. The rapids of the Lower Narrows are all runnable, but they demand considerable expertise in water reading and whitewater tactics. They also demand considerable time. The whole narrows is a series of twisting, turning blind drops so that it is impossible to see what lies beyond the next ledge. Thus, each rapid must be scouted individually. This entails a seemingly endless routine of jumping in and out of boats and scrambling up immense boulders to sneak a look at the next rapid.

The scouting and the boulder hopping are necessary, of course, but also time-consuming. A good running time for the Lower

Narrows by an experienced group of four open-canoe tandem teams would be about two hours. The alternative to running the narrows is carrying via a nice trail on the east bank that is reached by climbing the bank at the end of the pool marking the entrance to the first rapid. In running the lower Rockcastle, time is always a prime consideration. The average paddler already has 15 miles (much of it flatwater), a lunch break, and a portage of Beech Narrows behind when the Lower Narrows are reached. Assuming dark to be around 7:30 P.M. in the spring, a paddler needs to reach the Lower Narrows by 3:00 or 3:30 P.M. to be assured of having enough time to get off the river by dark (allowing a little time for unforeseen circumstances). Needless to say, the larger the group the longer it will take to get through the narrows (although for safety's sake three boats in a group is considered a minimum). The portage is long (¾ mile) but is much faster than running a group through the narrows. A frequent mistake observed on the Rockcastle is committed by the experienced paddler who decides to save time by running through the boats of less-experienced companions. While this provides some additional enjoyment for the experienced paddler and is both safe and easy for those inexperienced companions, the amount of time it consumes is unbelievable. It is much quicker to let the inexperienced paddlers portage on the trail.

Beyond the lower narrows there are a Class-II and a borderline Class-III stretch that are blind turns and should be scouted. The first rapid (the Class II) particularly has a tendency to trap floating logs in the spring. Downstream from the Class III it is approximately one mile to the take-out at Bee Rock Boat Ramp.

As one might gather, the Rockcastle River is beautiful, challenging, and exhausting. The paddler has more than put in a full day before even reaching the most demanding part of the run. An early put-in (10:00 A.M. at the absolute latest) is a necessity. Only paddlers with a lot of experience on technical rivers should attempt the Lower Narrows. Extra flotation is a must for open canoes. Dangers other than those already mentioned include deadfalls on several turns along the first 12 miles. Access is good at both put-in and take-out. Average stream width is 40 to 60 feet.

BUCK CREEK

Buck Creek is a small, scenic, Class-II, whitewater stream that drains the eastern half of Pulaski County. Runnable from KY 461 to Lake Cumberland following periods of heavy rain, the stream winds through forested hillsides with some exposed rock visible, especially in the lower sections below KY 80. Several small caves along the run provide the opportunity for interesting side trips. The level of difficulty is easy Class II with most rapids consisting of very small ledges or small standing waves. Route selection is obvious and no scouting is required. Deadfalls constitute the primary hazard to navigation. The average stream width is 35 to 45 feet. Access is good. Water levels on Buck Creek are usually optimal when surrounding larger streams (the Rockcastle River and the North Fork of the Cumberland River) are high or marginally flooded.

BIG SOUTH FORK OF THE CUMBERLAND RIVER (LEATHERWOOD FORD TO LAKE CUMBERLAND)

Flowing out of Scott County (Tennessee), the Big South Fork of the Cumberland River flows north through McCreary County (Kentucky) before emptying into Lake Cumberland. One of the most popular canoe-camping runs in the southeastern United States, the Big South Fork winds through the wooded bluffs and ridges of the southern portion of the Daniel Boone National Forest. An exceptionally beautiful river flowing swiftly below stately exposed rock pinnacles, the Big South Fork is dotted with huge boulders midstream and along the banks, and padded along either side by steep hillsides of hardwoods and evergreens. Wild flowers brighten the vista in the spring and wildlife is plentiful.

Paddling is interesting with as many as five legitimate (and six borderline) Class-II rapids (some of them quite long) consisting primarily of nontechnical small ledges and standing waves. The main channel is easily discerned in these rapids and scouting is normally not required. At moderate to low water all the Class II's can be run with a loaded boat. At higher water, loaded, open boats can avail themselves of sneak routes to avoid swamping.

Two Class-III to -IV rapids are encountered on this section of the Big South Fork. Both are technical, complex, high-velocity chutes that are dangerous at certain water levels. The first is Angel Falls, 1½ miles into the run, where the river takes an eight-foot drop in closely spaced one- and two-foot increments with the main flow being forced between two large rocks toward the right of the river. After the first two ledges (normally run from the left), converging smaller chutes of water join the main flow from the right further aerating the water and causing the current to impact a large boulder to the left. A smaller boulder at the bottom of the rapid, in conjunction with the converging currents from the right, causes the current to turn left at the end of the rapid before pooling out. This rapid must be scouted and different strategies are appropriate at different water levels (though as a point of departure Angel Falls is usually run far left to left center to right center). Regardless of water level, boats should be emptied of all gear before attempting the run. Portage is possible via a trail on the right 50 yards upstream of the rapid and is recommended at all water levels except for competent, experienced boaters.

"Devil's Jump," a difficult Class-IV section, is closer to the end of the run upstream of the Blue Heron Mine. Here current flows into a house-sized boulder from whence it is diverted at an angle through a high-velocity chute. The trick is to align your boat for the chute by riding the pillow off the left of the house-sized boulder. This is done at low to moderate water levels by practically setting your bow on a collision course for the giant boulder and then allowing the pillow to divert your bow into the top of the chute. The route to the right of the giant boulder is usually avoided because of a mean hydraulic at the bottom. Once again, all boats should be run without gear and after careful scouting (if you do not understand the dynamics of converging currents, leave this rapid alone). Portage is possible and is recommended at all water levels except for competent, experienced boaters.

The Big South Fork is runnable from late fall through early June in this section. Due to the lack of immediate access, the shortest possible run beginning at Leatherwood Ford is approximately 20 miles. Because of the scouting required, etc., it is not recommended that the Big South Fork from Leatherwood Ford downstream be attempted in one day. Several nice camping locations are available along the run (which can be lengthened to three or more days by continuing on down into Lake Cumberland). Between Leatherwood and "Devil's Jump," the river averages 80 to 110 feet but sometimes broadens to as much as 150 feet. Below "Devil's Jump," the Big South Fork widens to an average of 115 to 150 feet and settles down conspicuously with fewer rapids in evidence. Downstream from Yamacraw the current comes to a halt as it reaches the lake pool. Dangers to navigation are as described above plus a damaged concrete ford between Blue Heron and Yamacraw that must be portaged on the right, and the potential of the river to rise at an alarming rate after heavy rains (remember this when you set up camp). Because of the remoteness of the Big South Fork, access points are few and far between with connecting roads often unpaved and rugged (but generally passable in a passenger car).

LITTLE SOUTH FORK
OF THE CUMBERLAND RIVER

The Little South Fork of the Cumberland River is a Kentucky Wild River. Little used by paddlers due to its seasonal nature and its remoteness, it is nevertheless one of the most beautiful and pristine of Kentucky's rivers. Draining the eastern portion of Wayne County and the western portion of McCreary County before emptying into the Big South Fork of the Cumberland River, the Little South Fork runs cool and clear over a rock and mud bottom through steep, wooded hills. Runnable from November through mid-May downstream from Parmleysville, the stream is primarily Class I with some small shoals and rapids that approach Class II. The river is 30 feet wide in the upstream sections and does not broaden beyond 60 feet as it flows toward its mouth. Access is difficult from all but one or two bridges, and shuttles are long, particularly for sections south of KY 92. Exposed rock and a variety of hardwoods grace the usually steep riverbank along with the common proliferation of willow upstream of KY 92. Downstream of KY 92, near Freedom Chapel, the stream enters a massive and beautiful vertical rock-wall gorge. Above all, the Little South Fork is amazingly pristine and rugged. Dangers to navigation include deadfalls and flash flood potential.

ROCK CREEK

Rock Creek is a small, beautiful, and threatened creek that drains the southwestern corner of McCreary County near the Tennessee border. The upper section of the creek, above White Oak Junction, is protected as a Kentucky Wild River. Unfortunately for paddlers, however, the only canoeable section is from below White Oak Junction where coal mining discharge pollutes the water. Runnable in the spring and following heavy rain, Rock Creek is a Class-II, whitewater run with numerous small ledges and a variety of boulders and rocks. Access is easy with White Oak Road running along the stream. The logical put-in would be at the bridge at Devil's Creek Road with take-out on the Big South Fork of the Cumberland near Yamacraw. Above Devil's Creek Road, Rock Creek is runnable in spots but would require excessive flow for an unobstructed run. At one spot a half mile upstream of Devil's Creek, the entire stream pools and drops over a ledge to the left under an undercut rock that makes portaging necessary at any water level. For the most part the stream is boulder strewn and approximately 25 to 40 feet in width. Rock Creek runs through the steep, wooded hillsides of the Daniel Boone National Forest. Banks on the road side of the stream vary in steepness while the far bank often approaches being vertical. The streamside is dense with scrub vegetation and some trees, with deadfalls not being unusual in the upper sections.

CUMBERLAND RIVER FROM WOLF CREEK
TO THE TENNESSEE BORDER

After passing through the ailing Wolf Creek Dam in Russell County, the Cumberland River turns south through Cumberland and Monroe counties before crossing once more into Tennessee. Averaging 200 to 400 feet in width, the Cumberland is runnable here all year. Access is easy and there are few dangers. While this section of the Cumberland lacks the wilderness quality of the Big South Fork, it does nevertheless flow through beautiful, steep woodland and farm country, and compared with other Kentucky rivers of similar size, it is generally remarkably free of powerboat traffic. Mud banks rise on the average 6 to 12 feet to a floodplain that varies in width and is lined with tall grass and willows.

(The Big South Fork Gorge of the Cumberland River, a popular canoeing run located in nearby Tennessee, is described with the streams in the "Special Mention" section of this guidebook.)

SECTION: Cumberland (Chad) to Harlan (Harlan Co.)

USGS QUADS: Louellen, Nolansburg, Evarts, Harlan

LEVEL OF DIFFICULTY International Class I-II   Numerical Points 7

SUITABLE FOR: Cruising   **GRADIENT** (feet per mile): 10.05

APPROPRIATE FOR: Advanced Beginners, Intermediates, Advanced

VELOCITY (mph): 2.6-5.0+   **AVERAGE WIDTH** (ft): 25-40

MONTHS RUNNABLE: January to mid-April and after heavy rains

RUNNABLE WATER LEVEL (cfs) Minimum 180
    Maximum Up to flood stage

MEAN WATER TEMPERATURE (°F)

Jan. 42	Feb. 42	Mar. 47	Apr. 52	May 66	Jun. 78
Jul. 80	Aug. 76	Sep. 69	Oct. 60	Nov. 44	Dec. 39

SOURCE OF ADDITIONAL INFORMATION ON WATER CONDITIONS
    USGS (606) 549-2406

HAZARDS: Deadfalls, low bridges

RESCUE INDEX: D
   A Extremely remote; evacuation only with expert help—6 hours to secure assistance
   B Remote; 3-6 hours to secure assistance
   C Accessible but difficult; up to 3 hours to secure assistance—evacuation difficult
   D Accessible; up to 1 hour to secure assistance, evacuation not difficult

PORTAGES: At collapsed concrete ford near Nolansburg

SCOUTING: None required

INTEREST HIGHLIGHTS: Scenery, local culture and industry

SCENERY: Pretty in spots to beautiful

ACCESS POINT	ACCESS CODE	KEY
A	1 3 5 7	1 Paved Road
B	1 3 6 7	2 Unpaved Road
All points ⎫		3 Short Carry
on new ⎬	1 3 5 7	4 Long Carry
U.S. 119 ⎭		5 Easy Grade
		6 Steep Grade
		7 Clear Trail
		8 Brush and Trees
		9 Private Property, Permission Needed
		10 Launching Fee Charged
		11 No Access—For Reference Only

160

Poor Fork of the
Cumberland River

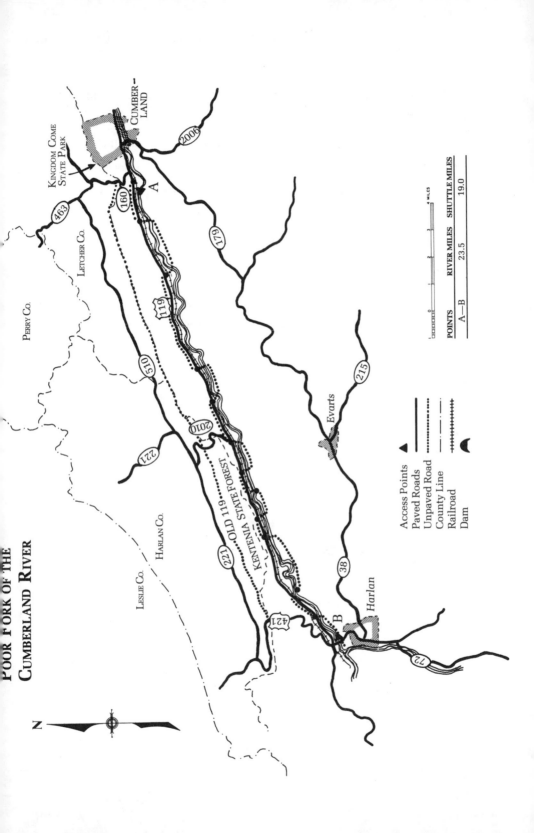

N

Kingdom Come State Park

Cumberland

Letcher Co.

Perry Co.

Harlan Co.

Leslie Co.

Evarts

Harlan

Old 119

Kentenia State Forest

463
160
2006
179
119
510
221
2010
215
221
38
72
421

Access Points
Paved Roads
Unpaved Road
County Line
Railroad
Dam

POINTS	RIVER MILES	SHUTTLE MILES
A—B	23.5	19.0

4 MILES

SECTION: Harlan to west of Pineville (Harlan Co., Bell Co., Knox Co., Whitley Co.)

USGS QUADS: Harlan, Wallins Creek, Balkan, Varilla, Middlesboro North, Pineville, Artemus, Barbourville, Rockholds, Saxton, Williamsburg

LEVEL OF DIFFICULTY International Class I+   Numerical Points   **5**

SUITABLE FOR: Cruising   **GRADIENT** (feet per mile): **2.54**

APPROPRIATE FOR: Families, Beginners, Intermediates, Advanced

VELOCITY (mph): 2.6-5.0   **AVERAGE WIDTH** (ft): 50-100

MONTHS RUNNABLE: November to mid-May

RUNNABLE WATER LEVEL (cfs) Minimum **300***
Maximum   Up to flood stage

MEAN WATER TEMPERATURE ($^\circ$F)

Jan. 42	Feb. 42	Mar. 47	Apr. 53	May 66	Jun. 79
Jul. 80	Aug. 78	Sep. 68	Oct. 60	Nov. 45	Dec. 40

SOURCE OF ADDITIONAL INFORMATION ON WATER CONDITIONS
USGS (606) 549-2406

HAZARDS: Deadfalls

RESCUE INDEX: C-D
A   Extremely remote; evacuation only with expert help—6 hours to secure assistance
B   Remote; 3-6 hours to secure assistance
C   Accessible but difficult; up to 3 hours to secure assistance—evacuation difficult
D   Accessible; up to 1 hour to secure assistance, evacuation not difficult

PORTAGES: None required

SCOUTING: None required

INTEREST HIGHLIGHTS: Scenery, local culture and industry

SCENERY: Pleasant to pretty in spots

ACCESS POINT	ACCESS CODE	KEY
A	1 3 6 7	1 Paved Road
B	1 4 6 8	2 Unpaved Road
C	1 3 6 8	3 Short Carry
D	1 3 6 8	4 Long Carry
		5 Easy Grade
		6 Steep Grade
		7 Clear Trail
		8 Brush and Trees
		9 Private Property, Permission Needed
		10 Launching Fee Charged
		11 No Access—For Reference Only

*This is approximately equal to a 1300 cfs reading (±100 cfs) on the Williamsburg gauge.

NORTH FORK OF THE CUMBERLAND RIVER—1

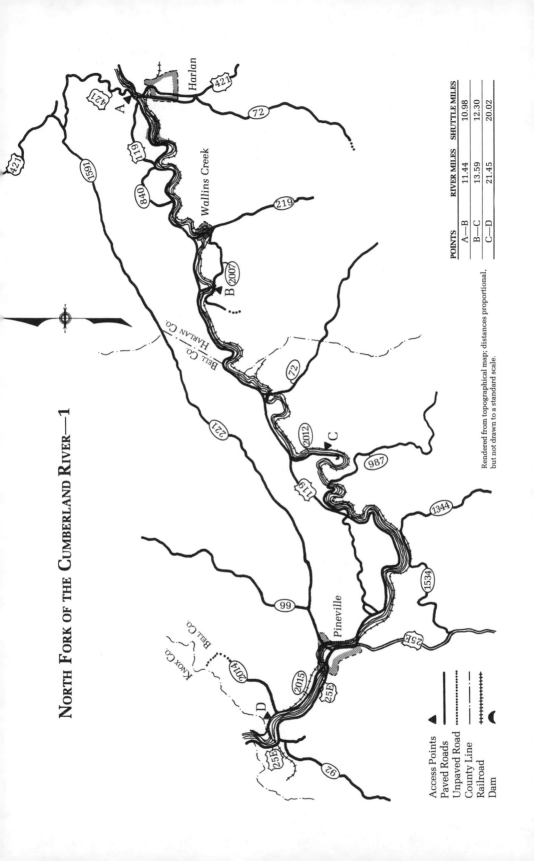

POINTS	RIVER MILES	SHUTTLE MILES
A—B	11.44	10.98
B—C	13.59	12.30
C—D	21.45	20.02

Rendered from topographical map; distances proportional, but not drawn to a standard scale.

Access Points

Paved Roads

Unpaved Road

County Line

Railroad

Dam

SECTION: West of Pineville to Williamsburg (Harlan Co., Bell Co., Knox Co., Whitley Co.)

USGS QUADS: Harlan, Wallins Creek, Balkan, Varilla, Middlesboro North, Pineville, Artemus, Barbourville, Rockholds, Saxton, Williamsburg

LEVEL OF DIFFICULTY International Class I+   Numerical Points 5

SUITABLE FOR: Cruising   **GRADIENT** (feet per mile):   2.54

APPROPRIATE FOR: Families, Beginners, Intermediates, Advanced

VELOCITY (mph): 2.6-5.0   **AVERAGE WIDTH** (ft): 50-100

MONTHS RUNNABLE: November to mid-May

RUNNABLE WATER LEVEL (cfs) Minimum 300*
Maximum Up to flood stage

MEAN WATER TEMPERATURE (°F)

Jan. 42	Feb. 42	Mar. 47	Apr. 53	May 66	Jun. 79
Jul. 80	Aug. 78	Sep. 68	Oct. 60	Nov. 45	Dec. 40

SOURCE OF ADDITIONAL INFORMATION ON WATER CONDITIONS
USGS (606) 549-2406

HAZARDS: Deadfalls, dams

RESCUE INDEX: C-D
  A Extremely remote; evacuation only with expert help—6 hours to secure assistance
  B Remote; 3-6 hours to secure assistance
  C Accessible but difficult; up to 3 hours to secure assistance—evacuation difficult
  D Accessible; up to 1 hour to secure assistance, evacuation not difficult

PORTAGES: Dam at power plant 9 miles below Pineville

SCOUTING: None required

INTEREST HIGHLIGHTS: Scenery, local culture and industry

SCENERY: Pleasant to pretty in spots

ACCESS POINT	ACCESS CODE	KEY
D	1 3 6 8	1 Paved Road
E	1 3 6 8	2 Unpaved Road
F	1 3 6 8	3 Short Carry
G	1 3 6 8	4 Long Carry
H	1 3 6 8	5 Easy Grade
I	1 3 5 7	6 Steep Grade
		7 Clear Trail
		8 Brush and Trees
		9 Private Property, Permission Needed
		10 Launching Fee Charged
		11 No Access—For Reference Only

*This is approximately equal to a 1300 cfs reading (± 100 cfs) on the Williamsburg gauge.

North Fork of the Cumberland River—2

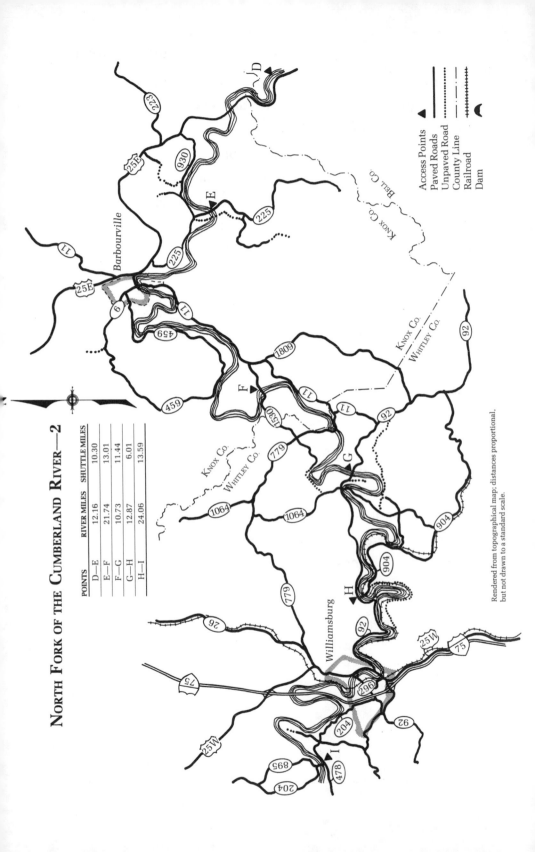

POINTS	RIVER MILES	SHUTTLE MILES
D–E	12.16	10.30
E–F	21.74	13.01
F–G	10.73	11.44
G–H	12.87	6.01
H–I	24.06	13.59

Access Points
Paved Roads
Unpaved Road
County Line
Railroad
Dam

Rendered from topographical map; distances proportional, but not drawn to a standard scale.

SECTION: Williamsburg to Cumberland Falls (Whitley Co., McCreary Co.)

USGS QUADS: Williamsburg, Wofford, Cumberland Falls

LEVEL OF DIFFICULTY International Class II   Numerical Points 8

SUITABLE FOR: Cruising, camping **GRADIENT** (feet per mile): 2.61

APPROPRIATE FOR: Advanced Beginners, Intermediates, Advanced

VELOCITY (mph): 2.6-5.0   **AVERAGE WIDTH** (ft): 70-105

MONTHS RUNNABLE: November to early June

RUNNABLE WATER LEVEL (cfs) Minimum   **500***
Maximum   Open: 2,000   Decked: Up to flood stage

MEAN WATER TEMPERATURE (°F)

Jan. 45	Feb. 45	Mar. 49	Apr. 58	May 68	Jun. 77
Jul. 80	Aug. 80	Sep. 73	Oct. 64	Nov. 47	Dec. 43

SOURCE OF ADDITIONAL INFORMATION ON WATER CONDITIONS
USGS (606) 549-2406

HAZARDS: Falls at end of run

RESCUE INDEX: A-B
A Extremely remote; evacuation only with expert help—6 hours to secure assistance
B Remote; 3-6 hours to secure assistance
C Accessible but difficult; up to 3 hours to secure assistance—evacuation difficult
D Accessible; up to 1 hour to secure assistance, evacuation not difficult

PORTAGES: None required, but you must take out before the falls

SCOUTING: None required

INTEREST HIGHLIGHTS: Scenery, wildlife

SCENERY: Pretty to beautiful in spots

ACCESS POINT	ACCESS CODE	KEY
I	1 3 5 7	1 Paved Road
J	1 3 5 7	2 Unpaved Road
		3 Short Carry
		4 Long Carry
		5 Easy Grade
		6 Steep Grade
		7 Clear Trail
		8 Brush and Trees
		9 Private Property, Permission Needed
		10 Launching Fee Charged
		11 No Access—For Reference Only

*This is approximately equal to a 1300 cfs reading (± 100 cfs) on the Williamsburg gauge.

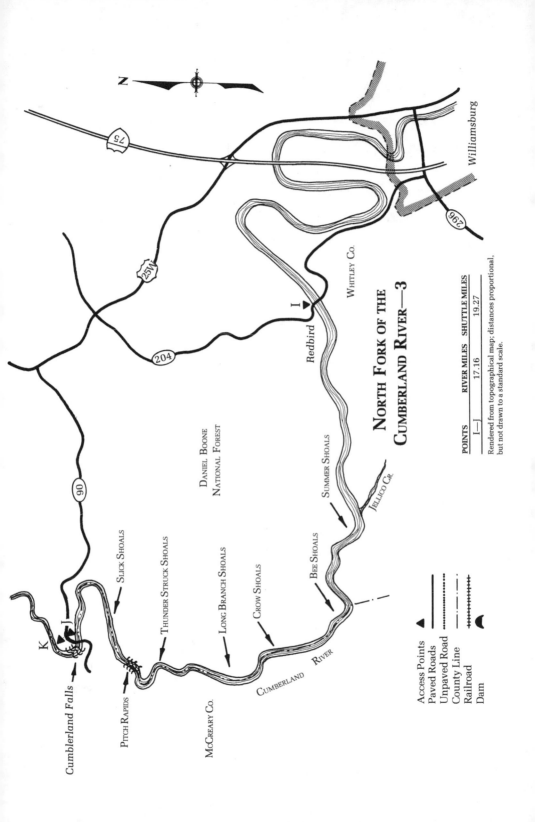

NORTH FORK OF THE CUMBERLAND RIVER—3

POINTS	RIVER MILES	SHUTTLE MILES
I–J	17.16	19.27

Rendered from topographical map; distances proportional, but not drawn to a standard scale.

Williamsburg

Whitley Co.

Redbird

Daniel Boone National Forest

Summer Shoals

Jellico Cr.

Bee Shoals

Crow Shoals

Long Branch Shoals

Thunder Struck Shoals

Slick Shoals

Cumberland Falls

Pitch Rapids

McCreary Co.

Cumberland River

Access Points
Paved Roads
Unpaved Road
County Line
Railroad
Dam

N

SECTION: Cumberland Falls to the mouth of the Laurel River (Lake Cumberland) (Whitley Co., McCreary Co.)

USGS QUADS: Cumberland Falls, Sawyer

LEVEL OF DIFFICULTY International Class III   Numerical Points 18

SUITABLE FOR: Cruising   **GRADIENT** (feet per mile): 11.75

APPROPRIATE FOR: Intermediates, Advanced

VELOCITY (mph): 2.6-5.0+   **AVERAGE WIDTH** (ft): 40-80

MONTHS RUNNABLE: All

RUNNABLE WATER LEVEL (cfs) Minimum   **300***
   Maximum   Open: 1,100   Decked: Up to flood·stage

MEAN WATER TEMPERATURE (°F)

Jan. 44	Feb. 44	Mar. 48	Apr. 54	May 68	Jun. 78
Jul. 81	Aug. 80	Sep. 75	Oct. 64	Nov. 47	Dec. 43

SOURCE OF ADDITIONAL INFORMATION ON WATER CONDITIONS
   USGS (606) 549-2406

HAZARDS: Undercut rocks, keeper hydraulics at certain water levels, difficult rapids

RESCUE INDEX: A-B

   A Extremely remote; evacuation only with expert help—6 hours to secure assistance
   B Remote; 3-6 hours to secure assistance
   C Accessible but difficult; up to 3 hours to secure assistance—evacuation difficult
   D Accessible; up to 1 hour to secure assistance, evacuation not difficult

PORTAGES: None required, but you should consider carrying at major rapids

SCOUTING: At major or "blind" rapids

INTEREST HIGHLIGHTS: Scenery, wildlife, geology

SCENERY: Beautiful to exceptionally beautiful

ACCESS POINT	ACCESS CODE	KEY
K	1 4 6 7	1 Paved Road
L	1 3 6 7	2 Unpaved Road
		3 Short Carry
		4 Long Carry
		5 Easy Grade
		6 Steep Grade
		7 Clear Trail
		8 Brush and Trees
		9 Private Property, Permission Needed
		10 Launching Fee Charged
		11 No Access—For Reference Only

*This is approximately equal to a 1300 cfs reading (± 100 cfs) on the Williamsburg gauge.

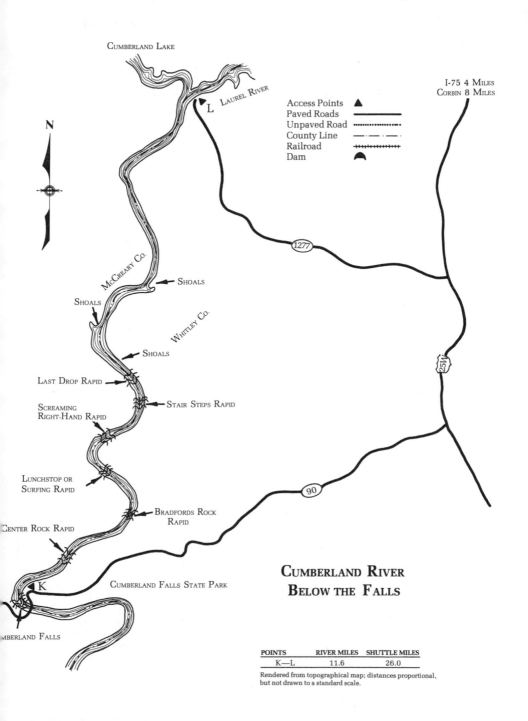

CUMBERLAND LAKE

L LAUREL RIVER

I-75 4 MILES
CORBIN 8 MILES

Access Points ▲
Paved Roads
Unpaved Road
County Line
Railroad
Dam

N

1277

MCCREARY CO.

SHOALS

SHOALS

WHITLEY CO.

SHOALS

LAST DROP RAPID

STAIR STEPS RAPID

SCREAMING
RIGHT-HAND RAPID

LUNCHSTOP OR
SURFING RAPID

BRADFORDS ROCK
RAPID

CENTER ROCK RAPID

25W

90

K

CUMBERLAND FALLS STATE PARK

CUMBERLAND FALLS

**CUMBERLAND RIVER
BELOW THE FALLS**

POINTS	RIVER MILES	SHUTTLE MILES
K—L	11.6	26.0

Rendered from topographical map; distances proportional,
but not drawn to a standard scale.

SECTION: KY 490 to KY 80 (Rockcastle Co., Laurel Co., Pulaski Co.)

USGS QUADS: Livingston, Bernstadt, Billows

LEVEL OF DIFFICULTY International Class I+ Numerical Points 5

SUITABLE FOR: Cruising, camping **GRADIENT** (feet per mile): 2.41

APPROPRIATE FOR: Families, Beginners, Intermediates, Advanced

VELOCITY (mph): 2.6-5.0 **AVERAGE WIDTH** (ft): 30-50

MONTHS RUNNABLE: November to late June

RUNNABLE WATER LEVEL (cfs) Minimum **220**
Maximum Up to flood stage

MEAN WATER TEMPERATURE ($^\circ$F)

Jan. 43	Feb. 43	Mar. 47	Apr. 54	May 64	Jun. 74
Jul. 77	Aug. 77	Sep. 71	Oct. 61	Nov. 46	Dec. 42

SOURCE OF ADDITIONAL INFORMATION ON WATER CONDITIONS

Rockcastle Adventures (606) 864-9407
USGS (606) 549-2406

HAZARDS: Deadfalls

RESCUE INDEX: C
A Extremely remote; evacuation only with expert help—6 hours to secure assistance
B Remote; 3-6 hours to secure assistance
C Accessible but difficult; up to 3 hours to secure assistance—evacuation difficult
D Accessible; up to 1 hour to secure assistance, evacuation not difficult

PORTAGES: None required

SCOUTING: None required

INTEREST HIGHLIGHTS: Scenery, wildlife

SCENERY: Pretty

ACCESS POINT	ACCESS CODE	KEY
A	1 3 6 8 9	1 Paved Road
B*	2 3 5 7	2 Unpaved Road
C	1 3 6 8	3 Short Carry
		4 Long Carry
		5 Easy Grade
		6 Steep Grade
		7 Clear Trail
		8 Brush and Trees
		9 Private Property, Permission Needed
		10 Launching Fee Charged
		11 No Access—For Reference Only

*Under I-75, reached via U.S. 25 and KY 1329

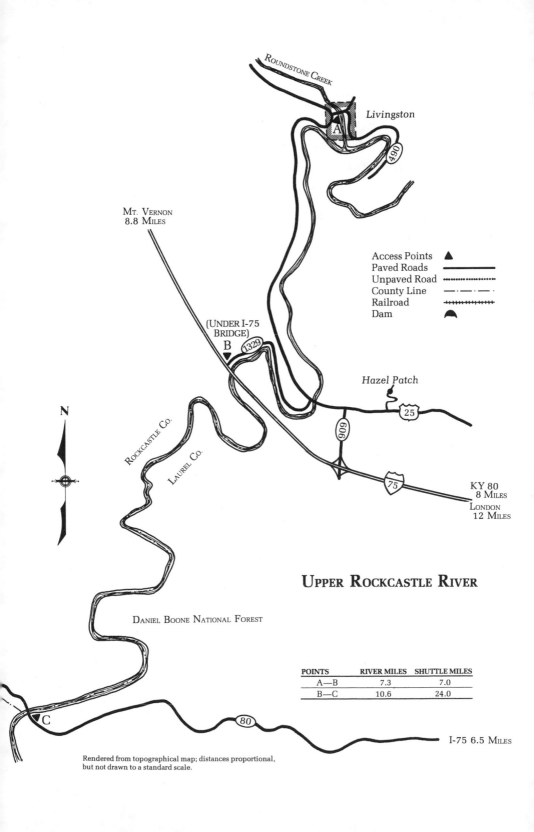

ROUNDSTONE CREEK

Livingston

A

490

MT. VERNON
8.8 MILES

Access Points ▲
Paved Roads ——————
Unpaved Road ••••••••••••••
County Line —·—·—·—·
Railroad ++++++++++++++
Dam

(UNDER I-75
BRIDGE)
B ▼ —1329

Hazel Patch

25

909

75

KY 80
8 MILES
LONDON
12 MILES

N

ROCKCASTLE CO.

LAUREL CO.

UPPER ROCKCASTLE RIVER

DANIEL BOONE NATIONAL FOREST

POINTS	RIVER MILES	SHUTTLE MILES
A—B	7.3	7.0
B—C	10.6	24.0

80

I-75 6.5 MILES

▼ C

Rendered from topographical map; distances proportional,
but not drawn to a standard scale.

SECTION: KY 80 to Cumberland River Lake (Laurel Co., Pulaski Co.)

USGS QUADS: Bernstadt, Billows, Ano, Sawyer

LEVEL OF DIFFICULTY International Class II   Numerical Points **5, 13**
(III-IV)   (21)*

SUITABLE FOR: Cruising, camping **GRADIENT** (feet per mile): 5.80

APPROPRIATE FOR: Very advanced Beginners, Intermediates, Advanced

VELOCITY (mph): 2.6-5.0+   **AVERAGE WIDTH** (ft): 30-60

MONTHS RUNNABLE: November to mid-June

RUNNABLE WATER LEVEL (cfs) Minimum **220**
Maximum   Open: **550**   Decked: Up to flood stage

MEAN WATER TEMPERATURE (°F)

Jan. 43	Feb. 43	Mar. 47	Apr. 54	May 64	Jun. 74
Jul. 77	Aug. 77	Sep. 71	Oct. 61	Nov. 46	Dec. 42

SOURCE OF ADDITIONAL INFORMATION ON WATER CONDITIONS

Rockcastle Adventures (606) 864-9407
USGS (606) 549-2406

HAZARDS: †Deadfalls, undercut rocks, keeper hydraulics, difficult rapids

RESCUE INDEX: A-B
A Extremely remote; evacuation only with expert help—6 hours to secure assistance
B Remote; 3-6 hours to secure assistance
C Accessible but difficult; up to 3 hours to secure assistance—evacuation difficult
D Accessible; up to 1 hour to secure assistance, evacuation not difficult

PORTAGES: Beech Narrows; Lower Narrows (optional)

SCOUTING: See "Portages"

INTEREST HIGHLIGHTS: Scenery, wildlife, geology

SCENERY: Beautiful to exceptionally beautiful

ACCESS POINT	ACCESS CODE	KEY
C	1 3 6 8	1 Paved Road
D	1 3 5 7	2 Unpaved Road
E	1 3 5 7	3 Short Carry
		4 Long Carry
		5 Easy Grade
		6 Steep Grade
		7 Clear Trail
		8 Brush and Trees
		9 Private Property, Permission Needed
		10 Launching Fee Charged
		11 No Access—For Reference Only

*5 points from Bee Rock Boat Ramp to Lake Cumberland; 13 points excluding "Narrows"; 21 points when running "Narrows."
†No hazards from Bee Rock Boat Ramp to Lake

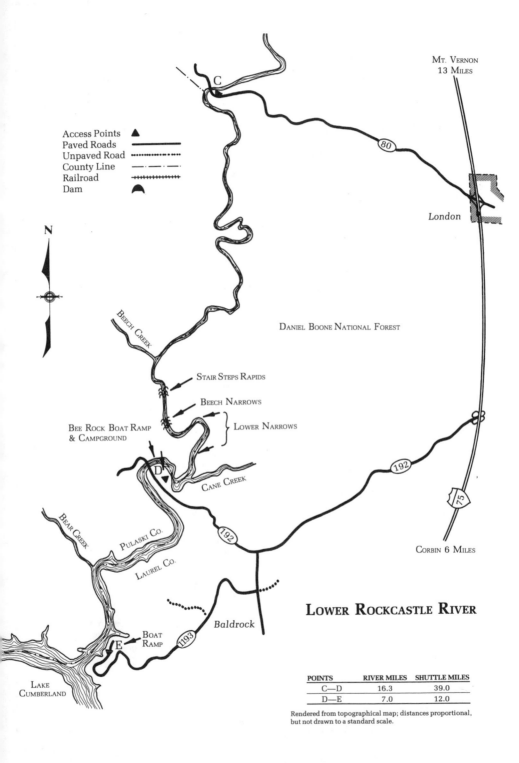

Access Points ▲
Paved Roads ————
Unpaved Road ••••••••••••
County Line —•—•—•—•—
Railroad ++++++++++++
Dam ◠

N

MT. VERNON
13 MILES

80

London

DANIEL BOONE NATIONAL FOREST

BEECH CREEK

STAIR STEPS RAPIDS

BEECH NARROWS

BEE ROCK BOAT RAMP
& CAMPGROUND

LOWER NARROWS

C

D

CANE CREEK

192

192

75

CORBIN 6 MILES

BEAR CREEK

PULASKI CO.

LAUREL CO.

Baldrock

1193

BOAT
RAMP

E

LAKE
CUMBERLAND

LOWER ROCKCASTLE RIVER

POINTS	RIVER MILES	SHUTTLE MILES
C—D	16.3	39.0
D—E	7.0	12.0

Rendered from topographical map; distances proportional,
but not drawn to a standard scale.

SECTION: KY 461 to Cumberland River (Pulaski Co.)

USGS QUADS: Shopville, Dykes

LEVEL OF DIFFICULTY International Class I (II) Numerical Points 8

SUITABLE FOR: Cruising   **GRADIENT** (feet per mile): 3.55

APPROPRIATE FOR: Advanced Beginners, Intermediates, Advanced

VELOCITY (mph): 2.6-5.0 (+)   **AVERAGE WIDTH** (ft): 30-50

MONTHS RUNNABLE: January to March and after heavy rains

RUNNABLE WATER LEVEL (cfs) Minimum 200*
Maximum   Up to flood stage

MEAN WATER TEMPERATURE (°F)

Jan. 42	Feb. 43	Mar. 46	Apr. 54	May 64	Jun. 75
Jul. 78	Aug. 77	Sep. 72	Oct. 61	Nov. 46	Dec. 43

SOURCE OF ADDITIONAL INFORMATION ON WATER CONDITIONS
None available

HAZARDS: Deadfalls

RESCUE INDEX: C
A Extremely remote; evacuation only with expert help—6 hours to secure assistance
B Remote; 3-6 hours to secure assistance
C Accessible but difficult; up to 3 hours to secure assistance—evacuation difficult
D Accessible; up to 1 hour to secure assistance, evacuation not difficult

PORTAGES: None required

SCOUTING: None required

INTEREST HIGHLIGHTS: Scenery, wildlife, geology

SCENERY: Pretty to beautiful in spots

ACCESS POINT	ACCESS CODE	KEY
A	1 3 5 7	1 Paved Road
B	1 3 6 8	2 Unpaved Road
C†	1 3 6 7	3 Short Carry
D	2 4 5 7	4 Long Carry
E	1 4 6 8	5 Easy Grade
F	1 3 5 7	6 Steep Grade
		7 Clear Trail
		8 Brush and Trees
		9 Private Property, Permission Needed
		10 Launching Fee Charged
		11 No Access—For Reference Only

*When billows gauge of Rockcastle River is 600+ cfs
†This access will change with the completion of the new highway.

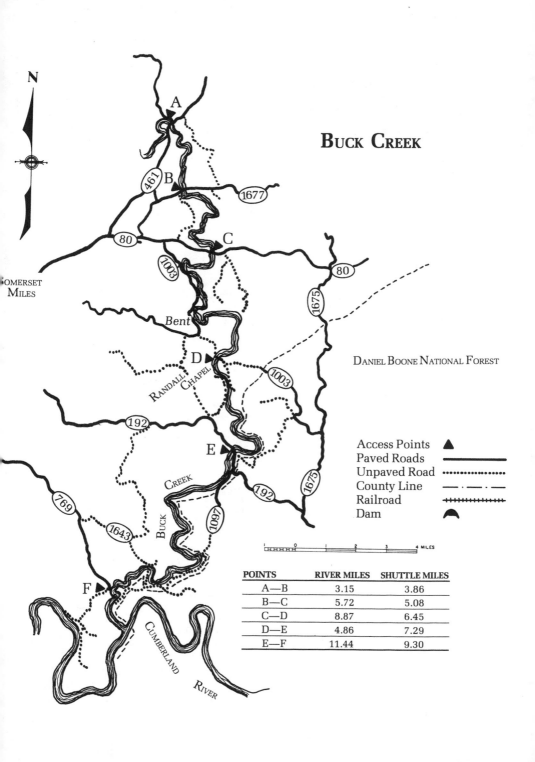

N

A

BUCK CREEK

461 B

1677

80

1003

SOMERSET
MILES

1675

80

Bent

DANIEL BOONE NATIONAL FOREST

D

RANDALL CHAPEL

1003

192

E

Access Points ▲
Paved Roads ━━━
Unpaved Road ⋯⋯⋯
County Line ─·─·─
Railroad ┼┼┼┼┼
Dam ⌒

769

CREEK

1097

1675

192

1643

BUCK

| 1 | 0 | | | 2 | 3 | 4 MILES |

POINTS	RIVER MILES	SHUTTLE MILES
A—B	3.15	3.86
B—C	5.72	5.08
C—D	8.87	6.45
D—E	4.86	7.29
E—F	11.44	9.30

F

CUMBERLAND

RIVER

SECTION: Leatherwood Ford (TN) to Lake Cumberland (Scott Co., TN, McCreary Co.)

USGS QUADS: Oneida South, Oneida North, Barthell, Nevelsville, Burnside

LEVEL OF DIFFICULTY International Class II (III-IV) Numerical Points 11* 7†

SUITABLE FOR: Camping   **GRADIENT** (feet per mile): 6.82

APPROPRIATE FOR: Advanced Beginners, Intermediates, Advanced

VELOCITY (mph): 2.6-5.0 (5.0+)   **AVERAGE WIDTH** (ft): 55-80 to Yamacraw, 100-150 below Yamacraw

MONTHS RUNNABLE: November to mid-June

RUNNABLE WATER LEVEL (cfs) Minimum 350
Maximum   Open: 1300   Decked: Up to flood stage

MEAN WATER TEMPERATURE (°F)

Jan. 45	Feb. 45	Mar. 49	Apr. 55	May 67	Jun. 79
Jul. 80	Aug. 80	Sep. 74	Oct. 64	Nov. 48	Dec. 42

SOURCE OF ADDITIONAL INFORMATION ON WATER CONDITIONS

USGS (606) 549-2406
Big South Fork National Park (615) 879-3625

HAZARDS: Undercut rocks, keeper hydraulics, flash floods, difficult rapids

RESCUE INDEX: A
A Extremely remote; evacuation only with expert help—6 hours to secure assistance
B Remote; 3-6 hours to secure assistance
C Accessible but difficult; up to 3 hours to secure assistance—evacuation difficult
D Accessible; up to 1 hour to secure assistance, evacuation not difficult

PORTAGES: Angel Falls and Devils Jump except for advanced paddlers

SCOUTING: Angel Falls, Devils Jump

INTEREST HIGHLIGHTS: Scenery, wildlife, whitewater

SCENERY: Beautiful to exceptionally beautiful

ACCESS POINT	ACCESS CODE	KEY
A	2 3 5 7	1 Paved Road
B	2 4 6 7	2 Unpaved Road
C	2 4 6 7	3 Short Carry
D	1 3 5 7	4 Long Carry
		5 Easy Grade
		6 Steep Grade
		7 Clear Trail
		8 Brush and Trees
		9 Private Property, Permission Needed
		10 Launching Fee Charged
		11 No Access—For Reference Only

*Leatherwood to Yamacraw, assumes a portage at Devils Jump and Angel Falls
†Yamacraw to Lake

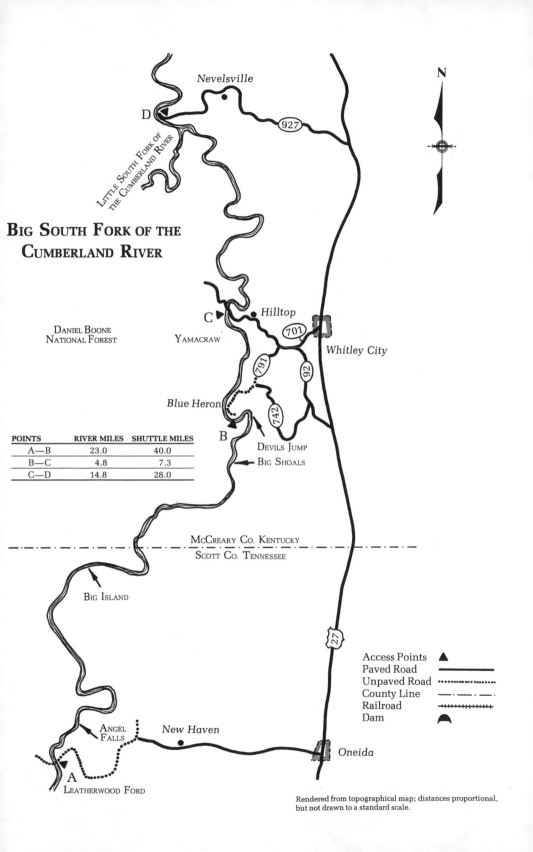

N

BIG SOUTH FORK OF THE
CUMBERLAND RIVER

Nevelsville

D

LITTLE SOUTH FORK OF
THE CUMBERLAND RIVER

927

DANIEL BOONE
NATIONAL FOREST

C Hilltop

YAMACRAW

701

Whitley City

791

92

Blue Heron

742

B

POINTS	RIVER MILES	SHUTTLE MILES
A—B	23.0	40.0
B—C	4.8	7.3
C—D	14.8	28.0

DEVILS JUMP

BIG SHOALS

McCREARY CO. KENTUCKY
SCOTT CO. TENNESSEE

BIG ISLAND

27

Access Points ▲
Paved Road ——————
Unpaved Road ••••••••••••
County Line —·—·—·—
Railroad +++++++++++
Dam ◖

ANGEL
FALLS

New Haven

Oneida

A

LEATHERWOOD FORD

Rendered from topographical map; distances proportional,
but not drawn to a standard scale.

SECTION: Parmleysville to confluence with Big South Fork (Wayne Co., McCreary Co.)

USGS QUADS: Bell Farm, Coopersville, Nevelsville

LEVEL OF DIFFICULTY International Class I-II Numerical Points 8

SUITABLE FOR: Cruising **GRADIENT** (feet per mile): 3.60

APPROPRIATE FOR: Advanced Beginners, Intermediates, Advanced

VELOCITY (mph): 2.6-5.0 **AVERAGE WIDTH** (ft): 35-55

MONTHS RUNNABLE: November to mid-May

RUNNABLE WATER LEVEL (cfs) Minimum **200**
Maximum **Up to flood stage**

MEAN WATER TEMPERATURE (°F)

Jan. 40	Feb. 41	Mar. 44	Apr. 51	May 67	Jun. 79
Jul. 81	Aug. 80	Sep. 73	Oct. 63	Nov. 46	Dec. 41

SOURCE OF ADDITIONAL INFORMATION ON WATER CONDITIONS
USGS (606) 549-2406

HAZARDS: Deadfalls, flash floods

RESCUE INDEX: B
A Extremely remote; evacuation only with expert help—6 hours to secure assistance
B Remote; 3-6 hours to secure assistance
C Accessible but difficult; up to 3 hours to secure assistance—evacuation difficult
D Accessible; up to 1 hour to secure assistance, evacuation not difficult

PORTAGES: None required

SCOUTING: None required

INTEREST HIGHLIGHTS: Scenery, wildlife, geology, mild white water

SCENERY: Beautiful to exceptionally beautiful

ACCESS POINT	ACCESS CODE	KEY
A	1 3 5 7	1 Paved Road
B	2 3 5 7	2 Unpaved Road
C	2 3 5 7	3 Short Carry
D	2 3 5 7	4 Long Carry
E	1 3 5 7	5 Easy Grade
		6 Steep Grade
		7 Clear Trail
		8 Brush and Trees
		9 Private Property, Permission Needed
		10 Launching Fee Charged
		11 No Access—For Reference Only

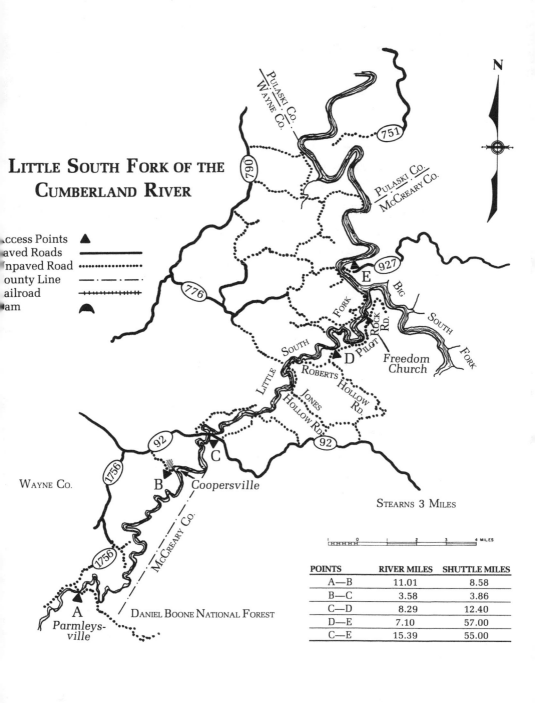

LITTLE SOUTH FORK OF THE CUMBERLAND RIVER

N

Access Points ▲
Paved Roads ――――
Unpaved Road ●●●●●●●
County Line ―・―・―
Railroad ―++++++―
Dam ◗

PULASKI CO.
WAYNE CO.

790

751

PULASKI CO.
McCREARY CO.

927

E

BIG

FORK

SOUTH

PILOT ROCK RD.

776

SOUTH

D

Freedom
Church

FORK

LITTLE

ROBERTS HOLLOW RD.

JONES HOLLOW RD.

92

92

C

WAYNE CO.

1756

B

Coopersville

McCREARY CO.

STEARNS 3 MILES

1756

A
Parmleys-
ville

DANIEL BOONE NATIONAL FOREST

0   2   3   4 MILES

POINTS	RIVER MILES	SHUTTLE MILES
A—B	11.01	8.58
B—C	3.58	3.86
C—D	8.29	12.40
D—E	7.10	57.00
C—E	15.39	55.00

SECTION: White Oak Jct. to Big South Fork of the Cumberland River
(McCreary Co.)

USGS QUADS: Barthell SW, Bell Farm, Barthell

LEVEL OF DIFFICULTY International Class II (IV) Numerical Points   10

SUITABLE FOR: Cruising   **GRADIENT** (feet per mile): 15.01

APPROPRIATE FOR: Advanced Beginners, Intermediates, Advanced

VELOCITY (mph):   5.0+   **AVERAGE WIDTH** (ft): 20-35

MONTHS RUNNABLE: January to April and after heavy rains

RUNNABLE WATER LEVEL (cfs) Minimum 195
Maximum Open: 350   Decked: 400

MEAN WATER TEMPERATURE (°F)

Jan. 40	Feb. 41	Mar. 43	Apr. 52	May 68	Jun. 79
Jul. 80	Aug. 79	Sep. 72	Oct. 63	Nov. 47	Dec. 42

SOURCE OF ADDITIONAL INFORMATION ON WATER CONDITIONS

Big South Fork National Park (615) 879-3625

HAZARDS: Deadfalls, undercut rocks, low bridges, low trees,
flash floods

RESCUE INDEX: D

A Extremely remote; evacuation only with expert help—6 hours to secure assistance
B Remote; 3-6 hours to secure assistance
C Accessible but difficult; up to 3 hours to secure assistance—evacuation difficult
D Accessible; up to 1 hour to secure assistance, evacuation not difficult

PORTAGES: Around low water bridge at Devils Creek Rd., and undercut
rock rapid above Devils Creek Rd.

SCOUTING: At undercut rock rapid

INTEREST HIGHLIGHTS: Scenery, geology, local culture and industry

SCENERY: Pretty to beautiful in spots

ACCESS POINT	ACCESS CODE	KEY
A	1 3 5 7	1 Paved Road
B	1 3 5 7	2 Unpaved Road
C	2 4 6 7	3 Short Carry
		4 Long Carry
		5 Easy Grade
		6 Steep Grade
		7 Clear Trail
		8 Brush and Trees
		9 Private Property, Permission Needed
		10 Launching Fee Charged
		11 No Access—For Reference Only

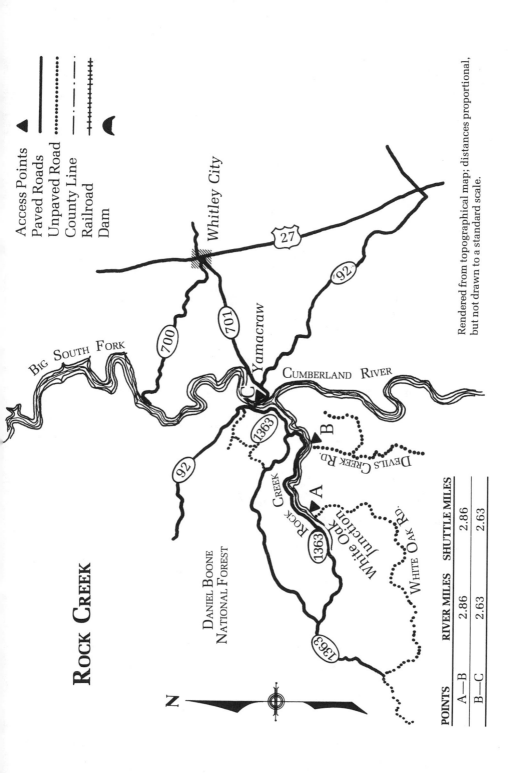

ROCK CREEK

Rendered from topographical map; distances proportional, but not drawn to a standard scale.

POINTS	RIVER MILES	SHUTTLE MILES
A—B	2.86	2.86
B—C	2.63	2.63

Legend

Access Points	◄
Paved Roads	••••••••
Unpaved Road	– • – • –
County Line	+++++++
Railroad	
Dam	◖

Whitley City

Big South Fork

Yamacraw

Cumberland River

Daniel Boone National Forest

Rock Creek

Devils Creek Rd.

White Oak Rd.

White Oak Junction

27

92

701

700

1363

SECTION: Wolf Creek Dam to Tennessee (Russell Co., Cumberland Co., Monroe Co.)

USGS QUADS: Wolf Creek Dam, Burkesville, Waterview, Blacks Ferry, Vernon, Celina

LEVEL OF DIFFICULTY International Class I   Numerical Points   5

SUITABLE FOR: Cruising   **GRADIENT** (feet per mile): 0.60

APPROPRIATE FOR: Families, Beginners, Intermediates, Advanced

VELOCITY (mph): 0-2.5 (2.6-5.0)   **AVERAGE WIDTH** (ft): 160-290

MONTHS RUNNABLE: All when dam is releasing

RUNNABLE WATER LEVEL (cfs) Minimum 300
Maximum Up to flood stage

MEAN WATER TEMPERATURE (°F)

Jan. 45	Feb. 45	Mar. 46	Apr. 49	May 53	Jun. 67
Jul. 67	Aug. 65	Sep. 64	Oct. 66	Nov. 51	Dec. 43

SOURCE OF ADDITIONAL INFORMATION ON WATER CONDITIONS

Corps of Engineers (502) 343-4708
(606) 679-5655

HAZARDS: None

RESCUE INDEX: C
A Extremely remote; evacuation only with expert help—6 hours to secure assistance
B Remote; 3-6 hours to secure assistance
C Accessible but difficult; up to 3 hours to secure assistance—evacuation difficult
D Accessible; up to 1 hour to secure assistance, evacuation not difficult

PORTAGES: None required

SCOUTING: None required

INTEREST HIGHLIGHTS: Scenery, geology

SCENERY: Pretty to beautiful in spots

ACCESS POINT	ACCESS CODE	KEY
A	1 3 5 7	1 Paved Road
B	1 3 5 7	2 Unpaved Road
C	1 3 5 7	3 Short Carry
D	1 3 5 7	4 Long Carry
E	(11)	5 Easy Grade
F	1 4 6 8	6 Steep Grade
G	2 3 5 7	7 Clear Trail
H	1 3 5 7	8 Brush and Trees
I	1 3 5 7	9 Private Property, Permission Needed
		10 Launching Fee Charged
		11 No Access—For Reference Only

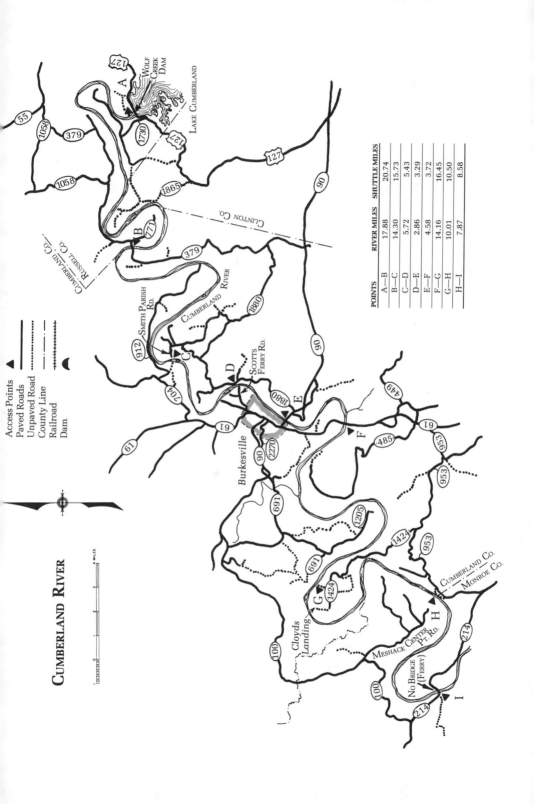

CUMBERLAND RIVER

POINTS	RIVER MILES	SHUTTLE MILES
A–B	17.88	20.74
B–C	14.30	15.73
C–D	5.72	5.43
D–E	2.86	3.29
E–F	4.58	3.72
F–G	14.16	16.45
G–H	10.01	10.50
H–I	7.87	8.58

Access Points
Paved Roads
Unpaved Road
County Line
Railroad
Dam

0 1 2 3 4 MILES

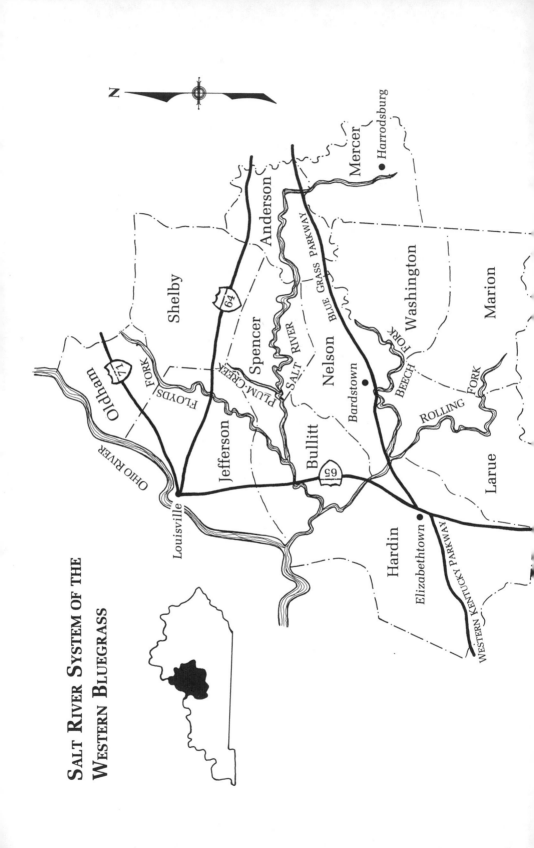

SALT RIVER SYSTEM OF THE WESTERN BLUEGRASS

5

THE SALT RIVER SYSTEM
OF THE WESTERN BLUEGRASS

SALT RIVER

Originating in Boyle County near Danville, the Salt River flows north and then west draining the Bluegrass counties of Mercer, Anderson, Spencer, and Bullitt before disappearing into the Fort Knox Military Reservation en route to emptying into the Ohio River near West Point. Runnable downstream of KY 1160 from late fall to late spring, and downstream of Taylorsville almost all year, the Salt is a winding, sycamore-lined stream often bordered by medium-sized hills and ridges on one bank and by broad fields or grazing land on the other. Running over a bottom of sandy mud, the Salt is dotted with dozens of small islands. Banks in the upper sections incline gently, but below Taylorsville become increasingly steep and muddy. The level of difficulty is Class I+ in most sections with some tight maneuvering occasionally required to navigate around the islands. Deadfalls and logjams are numerous and constitute the primary hazards to paddlers. (There is also a five-foot dam at McBrayer that must be portaged). Frequent small rapids, ledges, and waves enliven the paddling but should pose no problems. Current is usually swift, particularly in the winter and spring; access is generally good. The Salt can be paddled into the military reservation. Since, however, the stream runs through some artillery ranges, it behooves would-be trippers to call ahead (to the Post Information Officer or to the Range Control Officer) and announce their coming.

PLUM CREEK

Plum Creek originates in southwestern Shelby County and flows south through Spencer County before emptying into the

Salt River west of Taylorsville. Only runnable after heavy rains, the Plum rollercoasters over a seemingly continuous series of ledges ranging from several inches to three feet in height. Flowing over a rock bed between high, well-defined banks of varying steepness, Plum Creek is unique among high-water streams (that is, streams that can only be run after exceptionally heavy rains). First, there are practically no deadfalls and the channel is almost uniformly unobstructed. Second, the geology of the riverbed limits lateral erosion and keeps the stream neatly within the confines of its banks even at very high levels.

Plum Creek can be run from the Hochstrasser Road at the Shelby–Spencer county line all the way to its mouth at the Salt River. Above KY 155, however, numerous fences spanning the stream make paddling both dangerous and bothersome. Below KY 155 about a third of a mile, is a low-water bridge followed by a barbed-wire fence across the creek—these can portaged together. Several hundred yards farther down, a single strand of fence wire stretches across the stream. At most levels its is easy to duck under, but it is sometimes very hard to see. Beyond this point the river is normally clear of strainers (man-made or otherwise).

The run is a good, solid Class II with an average gradient of 25.7 feet per mile and would have to be upgraded to Class III at higher water levels (above three feet on the gauge on the upstream side of the KY 155 bridge). The whitewater is challenging but not particularly technical, consisting of nearly continuous waves, small holes, and lots of vertical drops. At higher levels, eddies are few and far between. There are several major rapids between the KY 1319 bridge and the KY 44 bridge that can be easily scouted from KY 1060, which runs parallel to the stream. The principal attraction of Plum Creek is its whitewater and its proximity to Louisville (35 miles). Scenery along the creek is only passable at best, with habitation all along its banks and less-than-average vegetation. Surrounding countyside consists of rolling terrain spotted with small farms. Dangers to navigation, in addition to those mentioned, include several low-water fords and small dams. Since the nature (and difficulty) of the run varies markedly at different water levels, thorough scouting is advised.

FLOYDS FORK OF THE SALT RIVER

A main tributary of the Salt River, Floyds Fork flows southwest along the Oldham–Shelby county line, across western Jefferson County and into Bullitt County where it joins the Salt River near Shepherdsville. Runnable downstream of KY 1408 from mid-fall through the spring, Floyds Fork rolls alternately beneath steep hills and ridges, and fields and pasture land. Current is swift and the stream is punctuated with small ledges, shoals, and rapids as well as with many brush islands. The stream's level of difficulty is Class I+ with good paddling techniques necessary to navigate around many of the islands. Dangers to navigation include numerous deadfalls and logjams. Access is good, especially in Jefferson and Shelby counties where the banks are not particularly steep.

ROLLING FORK OF THE SALT RIVER

Flowing northwest out of Casey County, the Rolling Fork of the Salt River drains portions of Marion, Larue, Nelson, Bullitt, and Hardin counties before joining the Salt River deep inside the Fort Knox Military Reservation. Running over a mud and rock bottom and between wall-like mud banks carved by lateral erosion, the Rolling Fork is runnable downstream of the U.S. 68 bridge from November to May. By and large, the Rolling Fork meanders along beside broad fields on one side of the stream and rolling hills (usually grazing land) on the other. Above the mud walls that contain the river, the banks are brushy and treelined. Grass and brush islands are common in the stream. The most scenic section of the Rolling Fork is between the Marion County line and New Haven (in Nelson County) where the river temporarily departs the farm plains and winds beneath the tall, rugged knobs (a "knob" is larger than a big hill and smaller than a mountain and is so named because of characteristically steep sides and rounded top) of southern Nelson and northern Larue counties. In this area the precipitous hillsides are densely forested and some exposed rock is visible both in the river gorge and high on the ridges. Emerging from the knobs near New Haven, the Rolling Fork continues through hilly farmland until it disappears among the wooded, rolling hills of Fort Knox. Its level of difficulty is Class I+ between U.S. 68 and the confluence with the Salt River. Navigational dangers are limited to deadfalls, logjams, and several brush islands that necessitate good boat control. Unfortuntely, you can survive all the navigational dangers and still be wiped out by an artillery shell as you float through the tank and gunnery ranges on the Fort Knox Military Reservation. If you want to run this section, be sure to secure permission from the Fort Knox Range Control Officer in advance.

BEECH FORK OF THE ROLLING FORK OF THE SALT RIVER

Beech Fork originates in eastern Marion County, flows northwest into Washington County where it joins the Chaplin River, and then turns southwest through Nelson County before finally emptying into the Rolling Fork of the Salt River near Boston, Kentucky. An extremely winding river, the Beech Fork is runnable from November to early June from KY 49 to its mouth. Treelined and having mud banks of varying steepness while flowing over a mud bottom, the Beech Fork (in its runnable section) snakes through the modest knobs of central Nelson County, past the distilleries on the southern edge of Bardstown, and on to the broad, gently rolling farm plains of Boston. Its level of difficulty is Class I with the exception of a man-made Class III+ (a collapsed boulder dam) one-quarter mile upstream of the U.S. 31E bridge. The overall drop here is about five feet. This rapid can be safely run but changes incredibly with varying water levels and should always be scouted. The rapid is dominated by a vault-sized boulder right in the middle of the river at the bottom of a four-foot drop. To its left (as you look downstream) is a mean hole, particularly at higher water levels. When the water is up there is a nice route on the far left, otherwise, choose your own poison or carry around. Other hazards to navigation include numerous brush islands, deadfalls, and some logjams.

Russell Fork of the Levisa Fork of the Big Sandy River   Photograph courtesy of the Commonwealth of Kentucky, Department of Public Information

SECTION: KY 1160 bridge to Glensboro (Mercer Co., Anderson Co.)

USGS QUADS: Cornishville, McBrayer, Lawrenceburg, Glensboro

LEVEL OF DIFFICULTY International Class I+   Numerical Points **6**

SUITABLE FOR: Cruising   **GRADIENT** (feet per mile): **2.04**

APPROPRIATE FOR: Beginners, Intermediates, Advanced

VELOCITY (mph): 2.6-5.0   **AVERAGE WIDTH** (ft): 35-60

MONTHS RUNNABLE: November to mid-May

RUNNABLE WATER LEVEL (cfs) Minimum **200**
   Maximum Up to flood stage

MEAN WATER TEMPERATURE (°F)

Jan. 43	Feb. 43	Mar. 46	Apr. 53	May 67	Jun. 75
Jul. 77	Aug. 75	Sep. 68	Oct. 60	Nov. 46	Dec. 42

SOURCE OF ADDITIONAL INFORMATION ON WATER CONDITIONS
   Corps of Engineers (502) 477-8606

HAZARDS: Dams, deadfalls, low bridges, low trees

RESCUE INDEX: C
   A Extremely remote; evacuation only with expert help—6 hours to secure assistance
   B Remote; 3-6 hours to secure assistance
   C Accessible but difficult; up to 3 hours to secure assistance—evacuation difficult
   D Accessible; up to 1 hour to secure assistance, evacuation not difficult

PORTAGES: Dam at McBrayer, above KY 513

SCOUTING: At blind turns for deadfalls

INTEREST HIGHLIGHTS: Scenery, local culture and industry

SCENERY: Pretty to pretty in spots

ACCESS POINT	ACCESS CODE	KEY
A	1 3 5 7	1 Paved Road
B	1 3 5 8	2 Unpaved Road
C	1 3 5 8	3 Short Carry
D	1 3 5 7	4 Long Carry
E	1 3 5 8	5 Easy Grade
F	1 3 6 7	6 Steep Grade
G	1 3 5 7	7 Clear Trail
H	1 3 5 7	8 Brush and Trees
I	1 3 5 7	9 Private Property, Permission Needed
J	1 3 5 7	10 Launching Fee Charged
K	1 3 5 7 9	11 No Access—For Reference Only

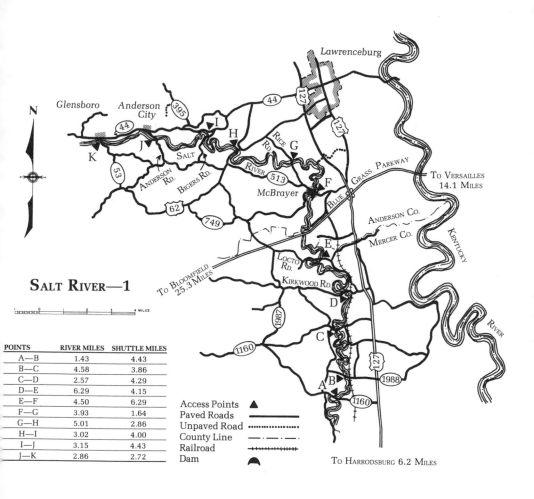

SALT RIVER—1

POINTS	RIVER MILES	SHUTTLE MILES
A—B	1.43	4.43
B—C	4.58	3.86
C—D	2.57	4.29
D—E	6.29	4.15
E—F	4.50	6.29
F—G	3.93	1.64
G—H	5.01	2.86
H—I	3.02	4.00
I—J	3.15	4.43
J—K	2.86	2.72

Access Points ▲
Paved Roads ——————
Unpaved Road ••••••••••••
County Line —•—•—•—
Railroad ┼┼┼┼┼┼┼┼
Dam ◗

To Harrodsburg 6.2 Miles

SECTION: Glensboro to Taylorsville (Anderson Co., Spencer Co.)

USGS QUADS: Glensboro, Ashbrook, Chaplin, Bloomfield, Taylorsville

LEVEL OF DIFFICULTY International Class I+   Numerical Points **6**

SUITABLE FOR: Cruising   **GRADIENT** (feet per mile): **2.32**

APPROPRIATE FOR: Beginners, Intermediates, Advanced

VELOCITY (mph): 2.6-5.0   **AVERAGE WIDTH** (ft): 45-65

MONTHS RUNNABLE: November to mid-May

RUNNABLE WATER LEVEL (cfs) Minimum **200**
Maximum Up to flood stage

MEAN WATER TEMPERATURE (°F)

Jan.	43	Feb.	43	Mar.	46	Apr.	53	May	67	Jun.	75
Jul.	77	Aug.	75	Sep.	68	Oct.	60	Nov.	46	Dec.	42

SOURCE OF ADDITIONAL INFORMATION ON WATER CONDITIONS
Corps of Engineers (502) 477-8606

HAZARDS: Deadfalls, low bridges, low trees

RESCUE INDEX: C
A Extremely remote; evacuation only with expert help—6 hours to secure assistance
B Remote; 3-6 hours to secure assistance
C Accessible but difficult; up to 3 hours to secure assistance—evacuation difficult
D Accessible; up to 1 hour to secure assistance, evacuation not difficult

PORTAGES: None required

SCOUTING: At blind turns for deadfalls

INTEREST HIGHLIGHTS: Scenery, local culture and industry

SCENERY: Pretty to pretty in spots

ACCESS POINT	ACCESS CODE	KEY
K	1 3 5 7 9	1 Paved Road
L	1 3 5 8	2 Unpaved Road
M	2 3 6 8	3 Short Carry
N	1 3 5 8	4 Long Carry
		5 Easy Grade
		6 Steep Grade
		7 Clear Trail
		8 Brush and Trees
		9 Private Property, Permission Needed
		10 Launching Fee Charged
		11 No Access—For Reference Only

SALT RIVER—2

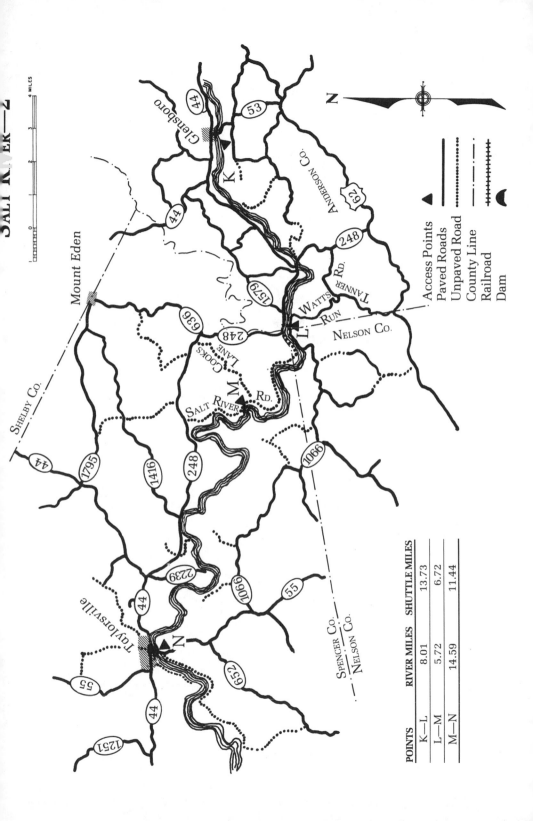

POINTS	RIVER MILES	SHUTTLE MILES
K–L	8.01	13.73
L–M	5.72	6.72
M–N	14.59	11.44

Access Points
Paved Roads
Unpaved Road
County Line
Railroad
Dam

SECTION: Taylorsville to Shepherdsville (Spencer Co., Bullitt Co.)

USGS QUADS: Taylorsville, Waterford, Mt. Washington, Brooks, Shepherdsville

LEVEL OF DIFFICULTY International Class I   Numerical Points 5

SUITABLE FOR: Cruising   **GRADIENT** (feet per mile): 1.86

APPROPRIATE FOR: Families, Beginners, Intermediates, Advanced

VELOCITY (mph): 0-2.5   **AVERAGE WIDTH** (ft): 55-75

MONTHS RUNNABLE: All

RUNNABLE WATER LEVEL (cfs) Minimum 220
    Maximum Up to flood stage

MEAN WATER TEMPERATURE (°F)

Jan.	42	Feb.	42	Mar.	45	Apr.	54	May	68	Jun.	76
Jul.	78	Aug.	78	Sep.	69	Oct.	61	Nov.	46	Dec.	43

SOURCE OF ADDITIONAL INFORMATION ON WATER CONDITIONS
    Corps of Engineers (502) 477-8606

HAZARDS: Deadfalls

RESCUE INDEX: C-D
  A Extremely remote; evacuation only with expert help—6 hours to secure assistance
  B Remote; 3-6 hours to secure assistance
  C Accessible but difficult; up to 3 hours to secure assistance—evacuation difficult
  D Accessible; up to 1 hour to secure assistance, evacuation not difficult

PORTAGES: None required

SCOUTING: None required

INTEREST HIGHLIGHTS: Scenery, local culture and industry

SCENERY: Pleasant to pretty in spots

ACCESS POINT	ACCESS CODE	KEY
N	1 3 5 8	1 Paved Road
O	1 3 5 7	2 Unpaved Road
P	(11)	3 Short Carry
Q	2 4 6 8	4 Long Carry
R	2 3 6 7	5 Easy Grade
		6 Steep Grade
		7 Clear Trail
		8 Brush and Trees
		9 Private Property, Permission Needed
		10 Launching Fee Charged
		11 No Access—For Reference Only

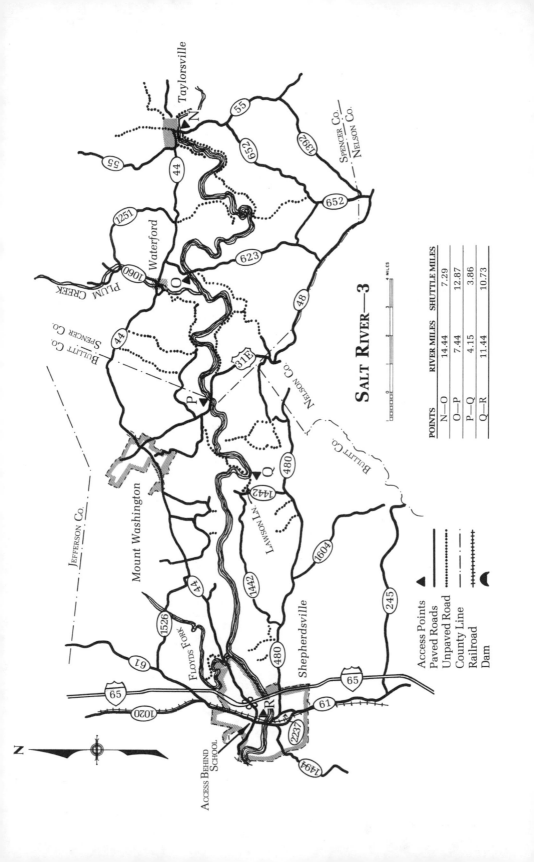

SALT RIVER—3

POINTS	RIVER MILES	SHUTTLE MILES
N—O	14.44	7.29
O—P	7.44	12.87
P—Q	4.15	3.86
Q—R	11.44	10.73

Access Points ▲
Paved Roads ••••••••
Unpaved Road —•—•—
County Line —•••—•••—
Railroad ┼┼┼┼┼┼
Dam ◖

Taylorsville

Waterford

PLUM CREEK

SPENCER CO.
NELSON CO.

BULLITT CO.
SPENCER CO.

JEFFERSON CO.

NELSON CO.

BULLITT CO.

Mount Washington

LAWSON LN.

Shepherdsville

FLOYDS FORK

ACCESS BEHIND
SCHOOL

0 1 2 3 4 MILES

SECTION: Shepherdsville to Ohio River (Bullitt Co., Hardin Co.)

USGS QUADS: Shepherdsville, Pitts Point, Fort Knox, Kosmosdale

LEVEL OF DIFFICULTY International Class I   Numerical Points **5**

SUITABLE FOR: Cruising   **GRADIENT** (feet per mile): 1.66

APPROPRIATE FOR: Families, Beginners, Intermediates, Advanced

VELOCITY (mph): 0-2.5   **AVERAGE WIDTH** (ft): 60-90

MONTHS RUNNABLE: All

RUNNABLE WATER LEVEL (cfs) Minimum **220**
Maximum Up to flood stage

MEAN WATER TEMPERATURE (°F)

Jan.	42	Feb.	42	Mar.	45	Apr.	54	May	68	Jun.	76
Jul.	78	Aug.	78	Sep.	69	Oct.	61	Nov.	46	Dec.	43

SOURCE OF ADDITIONAL INFORMATION ON WATER CONDITIONS
Corps of Engineers (502) 477-8606

HAZARDS: Deadfalls, Fort Knox Artillery Range

RESCUE INDEX: B-C
A Extremely remote; evacuation only with expert help—6 hours to secure assistance
B Remote; 3-6 hours to secure assistance
C Accessible but difficult; up to 3 hours to secure assistance—evacuation difficult
D Accessible; up to 1 hour to secure assistance, evacuation not difficult

PORTAGES: None Required

SCOUTING: None required

INTEREST HIGHLIGHTS: Scenery, local culture and industry

SCENERY: Pleasant to pretty in spots

ACCESS POINT	ACCESS CODE	KEY
R	2 3 6 7	1 Paved Road
S	(11)	2 Unpaved Road
T	2 3 6 8	3 Short Carry
U	2 3 6 8	4 Long Carry
		5 Easy Grade
		6 Steep Grade
		7 Clear Trail
		8 Brush and Trees
		9 Private Property, Permission Needed
		10 Launching Fee Charged
		11 No Access—For Reference Only

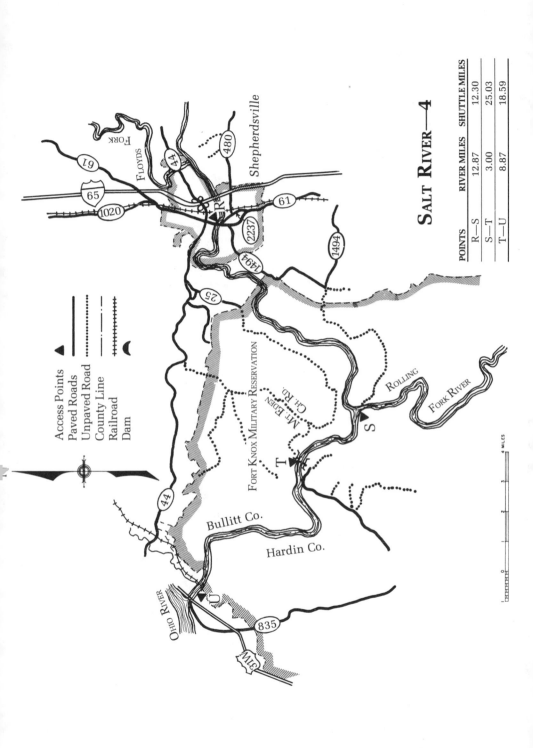

SALT RIVER—4

POINTS	RIVER MILES	SHUTTLE MILES
R–S	12.87	12.30
S–T	3.00	25.03
T–U	8.87	18.59

SECTION: Wilsonville to Salt River* (Spencer Co.)

USGS QUADS: Fisherville, Waterford

LEVEL OF DIFFICULTY International Class II(III) Numerical Points 14

SUITABLE FOR: Cruising   **GRADIENT** (feet per mile): 25.7

APPROPRIATE FOR: Intermediates, Advanced

VELOCITY (mph): 5.0+   **AVERAGE WIDTH** (ft): 35-60

MONTHS RUNNABLE: Early spring and after heavy rains

RUNNABLE WATER LEVEL (cfs) Minimum 300
Maximum Open - 650

MEAN WATER TEMPERATURE (°F)

Jan. 41	Feb. 42	Mar. 44	Apr. 51	May 66	Jun. 76
Jul. 78	Aug. 76	Sep. 66	Oct. 60	Nov. 45	Dec. 42

SOURCE OF ADDITIONAL INFORMATION ON WATER CONDITIONS
Spencer Co. Sheriff Dept. (502) 477-5533

HAZARDS: Dams, low bridges, fences, keeper hydraulics,[†] difficult rapids, scarcity of eddy

RESCUE INDEX: D
A Extremely remote; evacuation only with expert help—6 hours to secure assistance
B Remote; 3-6 hours to secure assistance
C Accessible but difficult; up to 3 hours to secure assistance—evacuation difficult
D Accessible; up to 1 hour to secure assistance, evacuation not difficult

PORTAGES: Low water bridge and barbed-wire fence one-third mile below KY 155

SCOUTING: Section along KY 1060 from road

INTEREST HIGHLIGHTS: Whitewater

SCENERY: Pretty in spots

ACCESS POINT	ACCESS CODE	KEY
A	1 3 5 7	1 Paved Road
B	1 3 5 7	2 Unpaved Road
C	1 3 5 7	3 Short Carry
		4 Long Carry
		5 Easy Grade
		6 Steep Grade
		7 Clear Trail
		8 Brush and Trees
		9 Private Property, Permission Needed
		10 Launching Fee Charged
		11 No Access—For Reference Only

*See map "Salt River—3"
[†]Rare, but can form below several vertical ledges at one or two specific water levels

PLUM CREEK

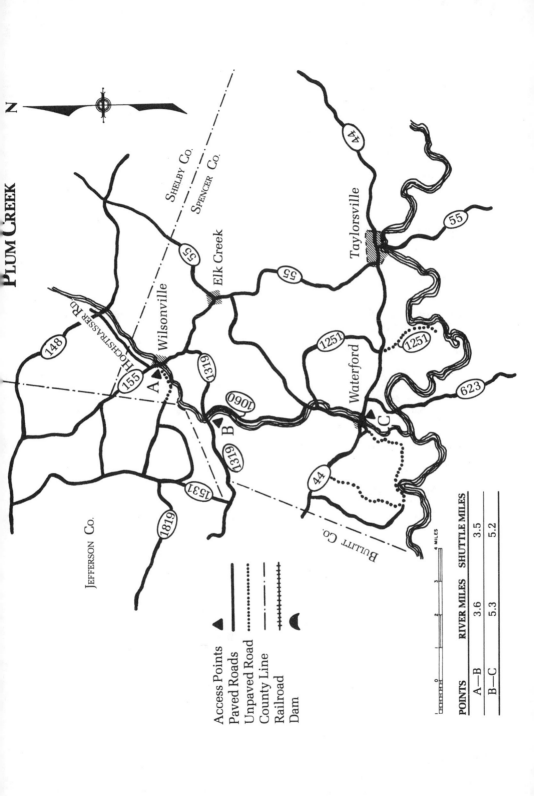

N

JEFFERSON CO.

148

HOCHSTRASSER RD.

155

A

Wilsonville

55

SHELBY CO.
SPENCER CO.

Elk Creek

55

1319

1060

B

1319

1531

1819

BULLITT CO.

44

1251

Waterford

C

1251

623

Taylorsville

44

55

Access Points
Paved Roads
Unpaved Road
County Line
Railroad
Dam

POINTS	RIVER MILES	SHUTTLE MILES
A—B	3.6	3.5
B—C	5.3	5.2

0   1   2   3   4 MILES

SECTION: KY 1408 bridge to U.S. 31E bridge (Oldham Co., Shelby Co., Jefferson Co.)

USGS QUADS: Crestwood, Fisherville, Jeffersontown, Mt. Washington

LEVEL OF DIFFICULTY International Class I+   Numerical Points **6**

SUITABLE FOR: Cruising   **GRADIENT** (feet per mile): **4.47**

APPROPRIATE FOR: Beginners, Intermediates, Advanced

VELOCITY (mph): 2.6-5.0   **AVERAGE WIDTH** (ft): **35-55**

MONTHS RUNNABLE: November to mid-May

RUNNABLE WATER LEVEL (cfs) Minimum **200**
   Maximum   Up to flood stage

MEAN WATER TEMPERATURE (°F)

Jan. 42	Feb. 43	Mar. 45	Apr. 52	May 66	Jun. 75
Jul. 76	Aug. 76	Sep. 66	Oct. 60	Nov. 46	Dec. 42

SOURCE OF ADDITIONAL INFORMATION ON WATER CONDITIONS
   Mount Washington Police Dept. (502) 543-7075

HAZARDS: Deadfalls, low bridges, low trees

RESCUE INDEX: D
   A Extremely remote; evacuation only with expert help—6 hours to secure assistance
   B Remote; 3-6 hours to secure assistance
   C Accessible but difficult; up to 3 hours to secure assistance—evacuation difficult
   D Accessible; up to 1 hour to secure assistance, evacuation not difficult

PORTAGES: Around deadfalls

SCOUTING: None required

INTEREST HIGHLIGHTS: Scenery, local culture and industry

SCENERY: Pretty to pretty in spots

ACCESS POINT	ACCESS CODE	KEY
A	1 3 5 7	1 Paved Road
B	1 3 5 7	2 Unpaved Road
C	1 3 5 7	3 Short Carry
D	1 3 5 7	4 Long Carry
E	1 3 5 7	5 Easy Grade
F	1 3 5 7	6 Steep Grade
G	1 3 5 7	7 Clear Trail
H	1 3 5 7	8 Brush and Trees
I	1 3 5 7 9	9 Private Property, Permission Needed
J	1 3 5 7	10 Launching Fee Charged
K	1 3 6 8	11 No Access—For Reference Only

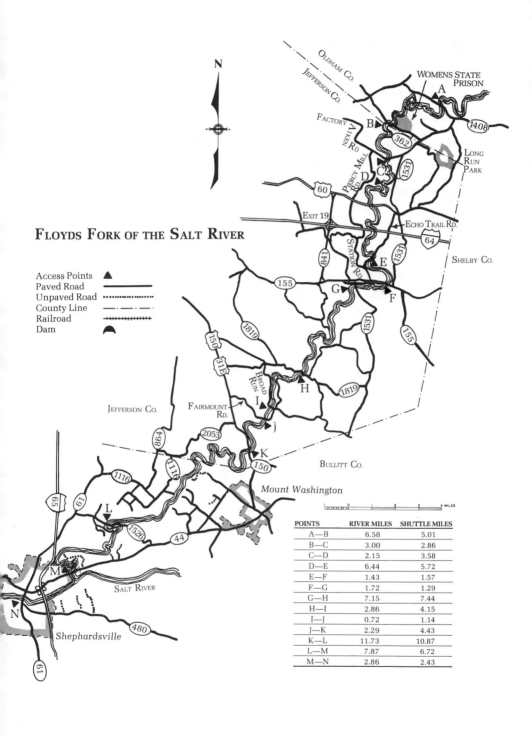

FLOYDS FORK OF THE SALT RIVER

WOMENS STATE PRISON

Access Points ▲
Paved Road
Unpaved Road
County Line
Railroad
Dam

POINTS	RIVER MILES	SHUTTLE MILES
A—B	6.58	5.01
B—C	3.00	2.86
C—D	2.15	3.58
D—E	6.44	5.72
E—F	1.43	1.57
F—G	1.72	1.29
G—H	7.15	7.44
H—I	2.86	4.15
I—J	0.72	1.14
J—K	2.29	4.43
K—L	11.73	10.87
L—M	7.87	6.72
M—N	2.86	2.43

SECTION: U.S. 31E bridge to Shepherdsville (Jefferson Co., Bullitt Co.)

USGS QUADS: Crestwood, Fisherville, Jeffersontown, Mt. Washington

LEVEL OF DIFFICULTY International Class I+   Numerical Points **6**

SUITABLE FOR: Cruising   **GRADIENT** (feet per mile): 3.87

APPROPRIATE FOR: Beginners, Intermediates, Advanced

VELOCITY (mph): 2.6-5.0   **AVERAGE WIDTH** (ft): 45-65

MONTHS RUNNABLE: November to mid-May

RUNNABLE WATER LEVEL (cfs) Minimum **200**
   Maximum Up to flood stage

MEAN WATER TEMPERATURE (°F)

Jan. 42	Feb. 43	Mar. 45	Apr. 52	May 66	Jun. 75
Jul. 76	Aug. 76	Sep. 66	Oct. 60	Nov. 46	Dec. 42

SOURCE OF ADDITIONAL INFORMATION ON WATER CONDITIONS
   Mount Washington Police Dept. (502) 543-7075

HAZARDS: Deadfalls, low trees

RESCUE INDEX: D
   A Extremely remote; evacuation only with expert help—6 hours to secure assistance
   B Remote; 3-6 hours to secure assistance
   C Accessible but difficult; up to 3 hours to secure assistance—evacuation difficult
   D Accessible; up to 1 hour to secure assistance, evacuation not difficult

PORTAGES: Around deadfalls

SCOUTING: None required

INTEREST HIGHLIGHTS: Scenery, local culture and industry

SCENERY: Pretty to pretty in spots

ACCESS POINT	ACCESS CODE	KEY
K	1 3 6 8	1 Paved Road
L	1 4 6 7	2 Unpaved Road
M	1 3 6 8	3 Short Carry
N	2 3 6 7	4 Long Carry
		5 Easy Grade
		6 Steep Grade
		7 Clear Trail
		8 Brush and Trees
		9 Private Property, Permission Needed
		10 Launching Fee Charged
		11 No Access—For Reference Only

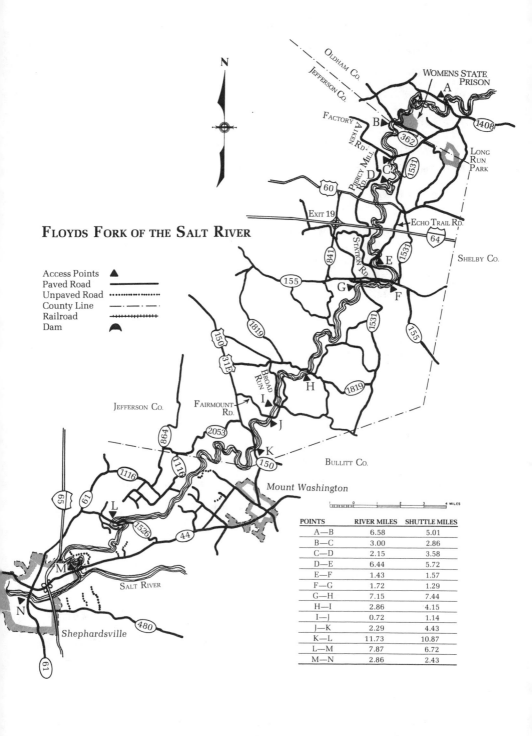

FLOYDS FORK OF THE SALT RIVER

N

WOMENS STATE PRISON

A

B

FACTORY RD.

AIKEN RD.

PERCY MILL RD.

D C

1408

LONG RUN PARK

362

1531

60

EXIT 19

ECHO TRAIL RD.

64

SHELBY CO.

STATION RD.

E

1531

844

155

G

F

1531

155

150

1819

31E

BROAD RUN

H

1819

JEFFERSON CO.

FAIRMOUNT RD.

I

864

2053

J

K

150

BULLITT CO.

1116

1116

Mount Washington

65

91

L

1526

44

M

SALT RIVER

N

480

Shephardsville

61

OLDHAM CO.

JEFFERSON CO.

Access Points ▲
Paved Road ───────
Unpaved Road ••••••••••
County Line ─ · ─ · ─
Railroad ┼┼┼┼┼┼┼┼
Dam

POINTS	RIVER MILES	SHUTTLE MILES
A—B	6.58	5.01
B—C	3.00	2.86
C—D	2.15	3.58
D—E	6.44	5.72
E—F	1.43	1.57
F—G	1.72	1.29
G—H	7.15	7.44
H—I	2.86	4.15
I—J	0.72	1.14
J—K	2.29	4.43
K—L	11.73	10.87
L—M	7.87	6.72
M—N	2.86	2.43

SECTION: U.S. 68 bridge to KY 52 bridge near New Haven (Marion Co., Nelson Co.)

USGS QUADS: Lebanon West, Raywick, Howardstown, New Haven

LEVEL OF DIFFICULTY International Class I+   Numerical Points **4**

SUITABLE FOR: Cruising   **GRADIENT** (feet per mile): **2.22**

APPROPRIATE FOR: Families, Beginners, Intermediates, Advanced

VELOCITY (mph): 2.6-5.0   **AVERAGE WIDTH** (ft): 35-50

MONTHS RUNNABLE: November to May

RUNNABLE WATER LEVEL (cfs) Minimum **200**
   Maximum **Up to flood stage**

MEAN WATER TEMPERATURE ($^{\circ}$F)

Jan. 43	Feb. 43	Mar. 45	Apr. 53	May 66	Jun. 76
Jul. 77	Aug. 76	Sep. 66	Oct. 61	Nov. 46	Dec. 43

SOURCE OF ADDITIONAL INFORMATION ON WATER CONDITIONS
   None available

HAZARDS: Deadfalls, low bridges

RESCUE INDEX: C
   A Extremely remote; evacuation only with expert help—6 hours to secure assistance
   B Remote; 3-6 hours to secure assistance
   C Accessible but difficult; up to 3 hours to secure assistance—evacuation difficult
   D Accessible; up to 1 hour to secure assistance, evacuation not difficult

PORTAGES: At small, concrete fords

SCOUTING: None required

INTEREST HIGHLIGHTS: Scenery, history, local culture and industry

SCENERY: Pleasant to pretty in spots (Points A-E); pretty to beautiful in spots (E-K)

ACCESS POINT	ACCESS CODE	KEY
A	1 3 6 8	1 Paved Road
B	1 3 5 7	2 Unpaved Road
C	1 3 6 8	3 Short Carry
D	1 3 5 7 9	4 Long Carry
E	1 3 6 7	5 Easy Grade
F	1 3 5 7 9	6 Steep Grade
G	2 3 5 7	7 Clear Trail
H	1 3 5 7	8 Brush and Trees
I	1 3 5 8 9	9 Private Property, Permission Needed
J	1 3 5 8	10 Launching Fee Charged
K	1 3 5 7	11 No Access—For Reference Only

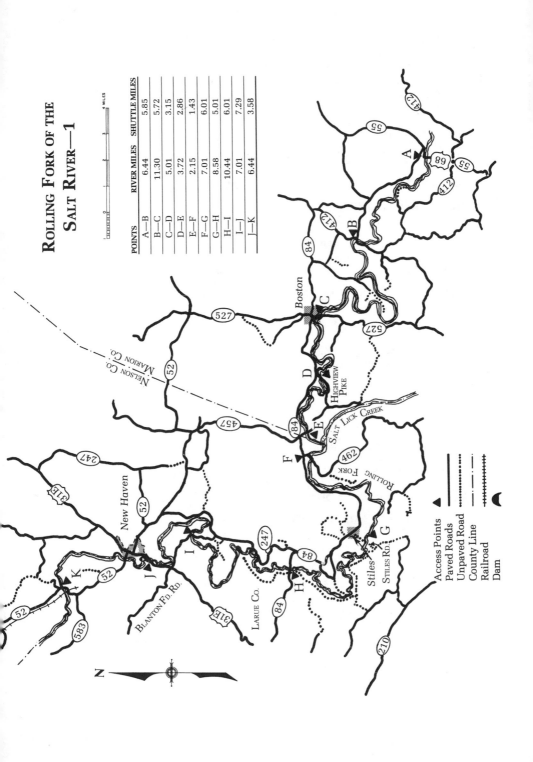

ROLLING FORK OF THE SALT RIVER—1

POINTS	RIVER MILES	SHUTTLE MILES
A–B	6.44	5.85
B–C	11.30	5.72
C–D	5.01	3.15
D–E	3.72	2.86
E–F	2.15	1.43
F–G	7.01	6.01
G–H	8.58	5.01
H–I	10.44	6.01
I–J	7.01	7.29
J–K	6.44	3.58

Access Points
Paved Roads
Unpaved Road
County Line
Railroad
Dam

SECTION: KY 52 bridge near New Haven to the Salt River (Nelson Co., Larue Co., Hardin Co., Bullitt Co.)

USGS QUADS: New Haven, Nelsonville, Lebanon Jct.

LEVEL OF DIFFICULTY International Class I   Numerical Points **4**

SUITABLE FOR: Cruising   **GRADIENT** (feet per mile): **2.07**

APPROPRIATE FOR: Families, Beginners, Intermediates, Advanced

VELOCITY (mph): 2.6-5.0   **AVERAGE WIDTH** (ft): 45-65

MONTHS RUNNABLE: November to May

RUNNABLE WATER LEVEL (cfs) Minimum **200**
Maximum Up to flood stage

MEAN WATER TEMPERATURE (°F)

Jan. 43	Feb. 43	Mar. 45	Apr. 53	May 66	Jun. 76
Jul. 77	Aug. 76	Sep. 66	Oct. 61	Nov. 46	Dec. 43

SOURCE OF ADDITIONAL INFORMATION ON WATER CONDITIONS
None available

HAZARDS: Deadfalls, low bridges, Fort Knox Artillery Range

RESCUE INDEX: C
A   Extremely remote; evacuation only with expert help—6 hours to secure assistance
B   Remote; 3-6 hours to secure assistance
C   Accessible but difficult; up to 3 hours to secure assistance—evacuation difficult
D   Accessible; up to 1 hour to secure assistance, evacuation not difficult

PORTAGES: At small, concrete fords

SCOUTING: None required

INTEREST HIGHLIGHTS: Scenery, history, local culture and industry

SCENERY: Pleasant to pretty in spots

ACCESS POINT	ACCESS CODE	KEY
K	1 3 5 7	1 Paved Road
L	1 4 6 8	2 Unpaved Road
M	1 3 6 8	3 Short Carry
N	2 3 6 8	4 Long Carry
O	2 3 6 8	5 Easy Grade
		6 Steep Grade
		7 Clear Trail
		8 Brush and Trees
		9 Private Property, Permission Needed
		10 Launching Fee Charged
		11 No Access—For Reference Only

ROLLING FORK OF THE SALT RIVER—2

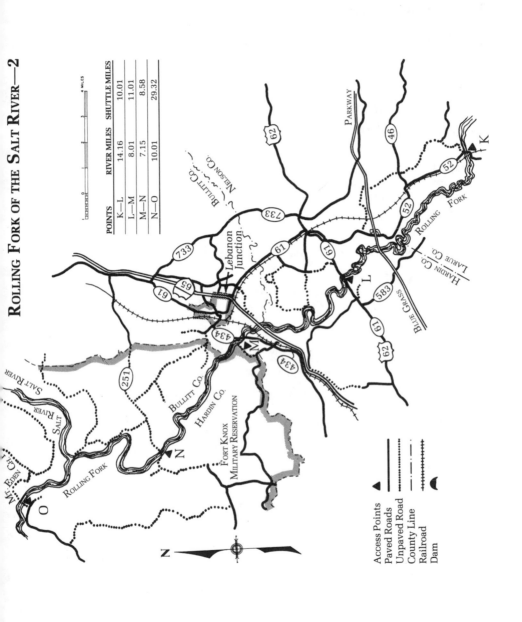

POINTS	RIVER MILES	SHUTTLE MILES
K—L	14.16	10.01
L—M	8.01	11.01
M—N	7.15	8.58
N—O	10.01	29.32

Access Points
Paved Roads
Unpaved Road
County Line
Railroad
Dam

SECTION: KY 49 to the Rolling Fork of the Salt River (Nelson Co.)

USGS QUADS: Bardstown, Cravens, Lebanon Junction

LEVEL OF DIFFICULTY International Class I*   Numerical Points 4

SUITABLE FOR: Cruising   **GRADIENT** (feet per mile): 1.43

APPROPRIATE FOR: Beginners, Intermediates, Advanced

VELOCITY (mph): 2.6-5.0   **AVERAGE WIDTH** (ft): 30-70

MONTHS RUNNABLE: November to early June

RUNNABLE WATER LEVEL (cfs) Minimum 200
  Maximum N/A

MEAN WATER TEMPERATURE (°F)

Jan. 42	Feb. 43	Mar. 46	Apr. 54	May 66	Jun. 76
Jul. 77	Aug. 77	Sep. 65	Oct. 60	Nov. 45	Dec. 43

SOURCE OF ADDITIONAL INFORMATION ON WATER CONDITIONS
  None available

HAZARDS: Deadfalls, low trees, man-made rapid

RESCUE INDEX: C
  A Extremely remote; evacuation only with expert help—6 hours to secure assistance
  B Remote; 3-6 hours to secure assistance
  C Accessible but difficult; up to 3 hours to secure assistance—evacuation difficult
  D Accessible; up to 1 hour to secure assistance, evacuation not difficult

PORTAGES: At man-made rapid at low water levels

SCOUTING: Man-made rapid ¼ mile above U.S. 31E bridge

INTEREST HIGHLIGHTS: Scenery, history, local culture and industry

SCENERY: Pleasant to pretty in spots

ACCESS POINT	ACCESS CODE	KEY
A	1 3 6 8	1 Paved Road
B	1 3 6 7	2 Unpaved Road
C	1 3 6 8	3 Short Carry
D	1 4 6 8	4 Long Carry
		5 Easy Grade
		6 Steep Grade
		7 Clear Trail
		8 Brush and Trees
		9 Private Property, Permission Needed
		10 Launching Fee Charged
		11 No Access—For Reference Only

*One man-made Class III (7 points); advanced paddlers only

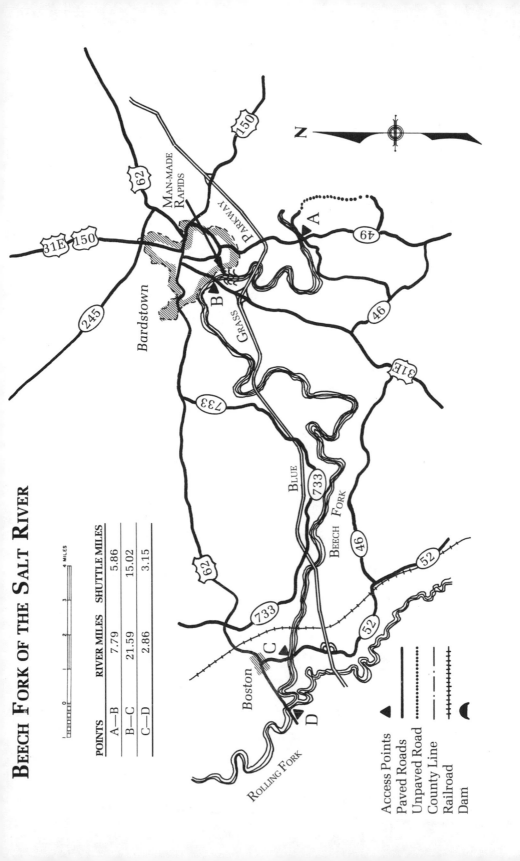

BEECH FORK OF THE SALT RIVER

POINTS	RIVER MILES	SHUTTLE MILES
A—B	7.79	5.86
B—C	21.59	15.02
C—D	2.86	3.15

Bardstown

MAN-MADE RAPIDS

PARKWAY

GRASS

Boston

BLUE

BEECH FORK

ROLLING FORK

Access Points
Paved Roads
Unpaved Road
County Line
Railroad
Dam

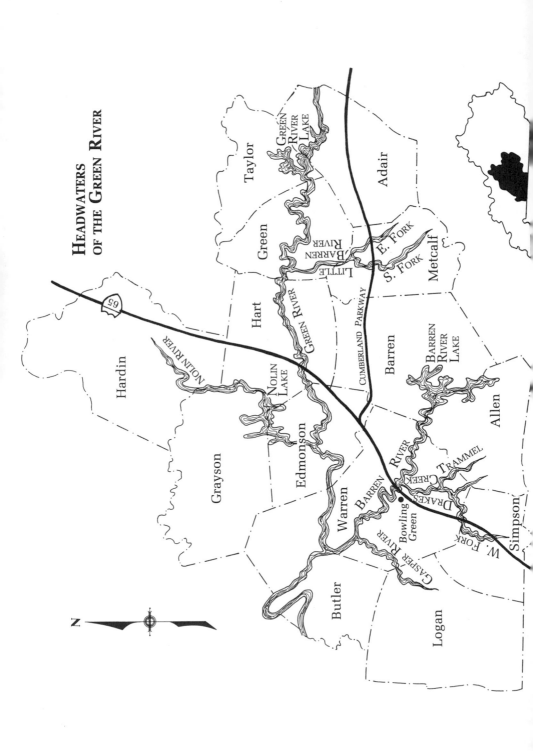

HEADWATERS OF THE GREEN RIVER

Taylor

Green

Hart

Hardin

NOLIN RIVER

65

GREEN RIVER LAKE

Adair

LITTLE BARREN RIVER

E. FORK

S. FORK

Metcalf

GREEN RIVER

CUMBERLAND PARKWAY

Barren

BARREN RIVER LAKE

NOLIN LAKE

Edmonson

Grayson

Warren

BARREN RIVER

DRAKES CREEK

TRAMMEL

Allen

Bowling Green

W. FORK

Simpson

CASPER RIVER

Butler

Logan

N

6

HEADWATERS OF THE GREEN RIVER

GREEN RIVER

The Green River is one of Kentucky's largest, longest, and most navigable rivers. Originating in southwestern Lincoln County, the Green River flows west creating Green River Lake and draining twelve counties before emptying into the Ohio River across from Evansville, Indiana.

While most of the Green River is canoeable all year, certain sections are far more inviting than others. For this reason, the river has been divided into seven sections. (The fifth to seventh sections, from Houchins Ferry at Livermore to the mouth of the Green River at the Rough River, are found in Section 7, "Streams of the Western Coal Fields.")

LIBERTY TO GREEN RIVER LAKE. This upper section of the Green is not often paddled but is very pleasant. Running through farmland and along some steep, wooded hills, the river is tree-lined and flows swiftly. Banks are of mud and vary in steepness. At low water, sandbars and brush islands are common. Although farms line the floodplain, the river itself is fairly secluded and signs of human habitation are surprisingly few. Some modest but interesting exposed rock formations combine with rippling, playful Class-I+ water to keep the paddling interesting. Access is good in most places and navigational hazards are limited to deadfalls and occasional logjams. This section is runnable from November through mid-June. Private property limits canoe camping possibilities on the river, but campers will find several options available by continuing on to Green River Lake.

GREEN RIVER LAKE DAM TO MUNFORDVILLE. This is a popular canoeing section and several trip combinations are available. Flow in this section depends on releases from the Green River Lake Dam (for the past three years the U.S. Army Corps of Engineers has provided adequate water during warm weather months for canoeing). More exposed rock is visible in this section, surrounding terrain is a bit more rugged, and the river is more secluded than in the previous section. Averaging 60 feet in width below the dam, the river widens perceptibly to 100 to 110 feet by the time it reaches Munfordville. Riffles and small rapids enliven the paddling but do not exceed Class I+. Access is good. Deadfalls and an occasional brush jam are the only navigational hazards at normal water levels. A canoe rental and shuttle service is available at the American Legion Park in Greensburg (see Appendix) where paddlers can camp.

MUNFORDVILLE TO HOUCHINS FERRY. This section of the Green River is also extremely popular, running in large part through the Mammoth Cave National Park. Scenery remains essentially the same as for the river section described above, except that beautiful forests supplant the cornfields once the Green River enters the park, and less exposed rock is evident. Wildlife is abundant in this area with great variety visible to the careful observer. Channelled by the steep surrounding hills, the river averages 70 to 100 feet wide until it reaches Mammoth Ferry where it broadens to 130 feet as it encounters the backwater pool of the Brownsville Dam. This point also marks the end of any current or riffles for this section. Needless to say, the Green River here runs through cave country, and at least two caves can be scouted at water's edge. A small cave located a half mile downstream of Dennison's Ferry on the left bank can actually be paddled into for approximately 40 feet. Further downstream, about a mile beyond Mammoth Ferry and 200 feet off the river to the left, is a small cave with a beautiful, clear pool of icy water. Canoe camping is allowed throughout the park, but a backcountry fire and camping permit must be obtained from the park rangers (at no charge). Access to the river is good but some adjoining roads are potholed and torturous and winding. Deadfalls are the only navigational hazards. This section is runnable all year, when the dam is releasing.

BARREN RIVER

The Barren River is one of Kentucky's big rivers. Originating in southern Monroe and Allen counties near the Tennessee border southeast of Bowling Green, it comprises the main drainage system for a large, four-county area, and finally empties into the Green River southeast of Morgantown. It could be very effectively argued that Kentucky's longest and largest river should indeed be the Barren and not the Green. At their confluence, the Barren is easily the larger of the two rivers. Downstream from the mouth of Jennings Creek, the Barren is a huge river, definitely navigable but not particularly appealing for canoeists. Between the mouth of Drakes Creek and Jennings Creek the Barren River is still wide but a little more scenic and interesting for paddling. Running over sand, rock, and clay banks through a deep bed, the river averages from 90 to 150 feet in width. Upstream from the mouth of Drakes Creek, the Barren River is especially nice and averages 40 to 60 feet in width. Along banks of varying steepness, tree roots are exposed by lateral erosion, and the river is more winding. Islands suitable for canoe camping at medium to low water levels are not uncommon. Vegetation is often lush and many hardwoods are in evidence. Occasionally the banks rise steeply with some exposed rock. Below Barren River Dam the river can be run all year with easy access at several points. Deadfalls, occasional sandbars at low water, and a Class-II, man-made rapid on the loop of the river passing through downtown Bowling Green are the only hazards to navigation.

DRAKES CREEK

Drakes Creek, along with its three feeder forks, comprises the drainage system for the area directly south of Bowling Green between U.S. 31W on the west and U.S. 231 on the east. Originating near the Tennessee border in Simpson and Allen counties, Drakes Creek finally empties into the Barren River just outside Bowling Green. Running through deep, rolling farmland and wooded terrain, almost the entire system provides excellent paddling opportunities. Two of the three forks, the West Fork and the Trammel Fork are suitable for canoeing, as is Drakes Creek itself below the confluence of the forks. Running over a sand, rock, and clay bottom, the main creek and the two navigable forks follow a deep bed overhung by various hardwoods. Just enough riffles and current are found to make the paddling interesting and they are interspaced with some very simple (Class I+) shoals and rapids. The water quality is good and very little trash is found near the stream. The width of the stream varies from 30 to 45 feet on the forks to 90 feet below the confluence. Deadfalls are not uncommon on the forks but usually do not block the entire stream. Islands, some of which are suitable for canoe camping, can be found below the confluence. Access is excellent with an unusually great number of paved county roads interlacing the entire area. Drakes Creek is runnable most of the year although an occasional sandbar may have to be portaged during late summer and early fall. Banks vary in steepness and sometimes approach the appearance of a gorge on the West Fork where there are some vertical rock walls.

GASPER RIVER

The Gasper River is a tributary of the Barren River and drains the area between Russellville and Bowling Green. Running over a rock, sand, and clay bottom, the Gasper is one of Western Kentucky's most beautiful rivers. Runnable from mid-November to mid-May, the Gasper flows around medium-sized boulders through a small gorge with steep, exposed rock walls rising almost vertically from the river's edge. The Gasper can be paddled from the Bucksville Road bridge to its mouth at the Barren. Rated Class II, the Gasper sports a few interesting, small rapids and a fairly swift current. Most of the river is very compact, with its width not exceeding 40 feet until just upstream of the KY 626 bridge where the stream broadens to 60 to 80 feet. The upper, more narrow sections (above KY 626) are potentially dangerous at high water levels due to frequent strainers (deadfalls) and the lack of eddies. Access from intersecting bridges is not always easy but it is possible.

LITTLE BARREN RIVER

The Little Barren River, with its east and south forks, drains most of Metcalfe County and the western portion of Green County before emptying into the Green River west of Greensburg. In the upper sections, both forks are runnable. The South Fork is partially spring fed and can be run from late October through June downstream of the Beechville Road Ford. The East Fork can be run from late fall through the spring below the Mell–Cork Road bridge. Both of the forks are intimate and scenic, running between steep hills over rock and mud bottoms. Of the two, the West Fork is the more interesting run with small rapids and ledges occurring frequently (Class I+). Both forks average 30 to 40 feet in width. Access is good and navigational hazards are limited to deadfalls. Below the confluence of the two forks (north of Sulphur Well) the valley deepens, more exposed rock is visible, and the river widens to an average of 50 to 60 feet. Banks are 20 feet high here and are generally steep. As the Little Barren approaches its mouth at the Green River, sandbars become more numerous and the steeper terrain of southern Green and northern Metcalfe counties gives way to more gently rolling farm- and woodland. Access below the confluence of the forks is fair to good (so rated because of a rather difficult access point at the KY 88 bridge). Deadfalls are the primary hazards to navigation. The level of difficulty continues to be Class I.

NOLIN RIVER

The Nolin River winds out of the hilly farm country of Hardin County and flows south along the Grayson–Hart county line to empty into Nolin River Lake. Below the Nolin Dam in Edmonson County, the Nolin River continues south to its confluence with the Green River in Mammoth Cave National Park. An attractive treelined river averaging 35 to 50 feet wide, the Nolin flows between steep banks over a rock and mud bottom. Throughout the upper sections in Hardin County, the terrain is gently rolling with farms adjoining the river. South of Star Mills, the river valley deepens with steep hills rising from time to time along the west bank. From this point to the headwaters of the lake, the stream is interrupted four times by the remnants of dams from a once-flourishing mill industry. Although signs of human habitation are common, regal hardwoods (mostly old growth) overhanging the stream help keep the beauty and the tranquil atmosphere of the stream intact.

The Nolin River is runnable from late fall to mid-summer from the Gilead Church–Star Mills Road bridge to Wheelers Mill. From Wheelers Mill to the headwaters of the lake, the Nolin is runnable all year long. Access for all runs above the lake is good except at Star Mills where access is possible but difficult. Because the stream is bordered without exception by private property, canoe camping is only recommended within the confines of Nolin River Lake. The level of difficulty is Class I, although small shoals and riffles and a good current keep the paddling from becoming tedious. Dangers in these upper sections include deadfalls, and, as mentioned, dams. All of the dams can be portaged without difficulty except at extremely high water levels. With the exception of the dam at Star Mills, all of the dams are extremely dangerous and should not be run for any reason. At Star Mills, however, the dam has collapsed in two places creating artificial Class-II+ (borderline Class-III) rapids. These rapids are runnable but should be scouted anew at every different water level.

From the tailwater of the Nolin River Dam to the mouth of the Nolin at the Green River, the stream flows through the backcountry woodlands of Mammoth Cave National Park. This section of the Nolin is especially scenic with high, exposed bluffs and plentiful wildlife, particularly deer and ducks. This section is only nine miles long (including an easy two-mile paddle upstream on the Green to the take-out at Houchins Ferry) but affords some beautiful camping spots for those with a short way to go and a long time to get there. Once again, the level of difficulty is Class I, but with a good current. The lower section of the Nolin River is usually runnable all year but is entirely dependent on releases at the dam for adequate flow. Navigational hazards are limited to deadfalls. The average stream width is 50 to 80 feet. Access is good.

Big South Fork of the Cumberland River   Photograph courtesy of the Commonwealth of Kentucky, Department of Public Information

SECTION: Liberty to Green River Lake (Casey Co., Adair Co.)

USGS QUADS: Liberty, Phil, Dunnville, Knifley

LEVEL OF DIFFICULTY International Class I+   Numerical Points 6

SUITABLE FOR: Cruising   **GRADIENT** (feet per mile): 3.81

APPROPRIATE FOR: Families, Beginners, Intermediates, Advanced

VELOCITY (mph): 2.6-5.0   **AVERAGE WIDTH** (ft): 50-75

MONTHS RUNNABLE: November to mid-June

RUNNABLE WATER LEVEL (cfs) Minimum 220
    Maximum   Up to flood stage

MEAN WATER TEMPERATURE (°F)

Jan. 44	Feb. 45	Mar. 47	Apr. 53	May 65	Jun. 73
Jul. 75	Aug. 75	Sep. 68	Oct. 61	Nov. 49	Dec. 43

SOURCE OF ADDITIONAL INFORMATION ON WATER CONDITIONS
  Corps of Engineers (502) 465-4463

HAZARDS: Deadfalls, low bridges, low trees

RESCUE INDEX: D
  A Extremely remote; evacuation only with expert help—6 hours to secure assistance
  B Remote; 3-6 hours to secure assistance
  C Accessible but difficult; up to 3 hours to secure assistance—evacuation difficult
  D Accessible; up to 1 hour to secure assistance, evacuation not difficult

PORTAGES: Over concrete ford at low water

SCOUTING: None required

INTEREST HIGHLIGHTS: Scenery, local culture and industry

SCENERY: Pretty to pretty in spots

ACCESS POINT	ACCESS CODE	KEY
A	1 3 6 8	1 Paved Road
B	2 3 5 7	2 Unpaved Road
C	1 3 5 7	3 Short Carry
D	1 3 6 8	4 Long Carry
E	1 3 6 7	5 Easy Grade
F	1 3 5 7	6 Steep Grade
		7 Clear Trail
		8 Brush and Trees
		9 Private Property, Permission Needed
		10 Launching Fee Charged
		11 No Access—For Reference Only

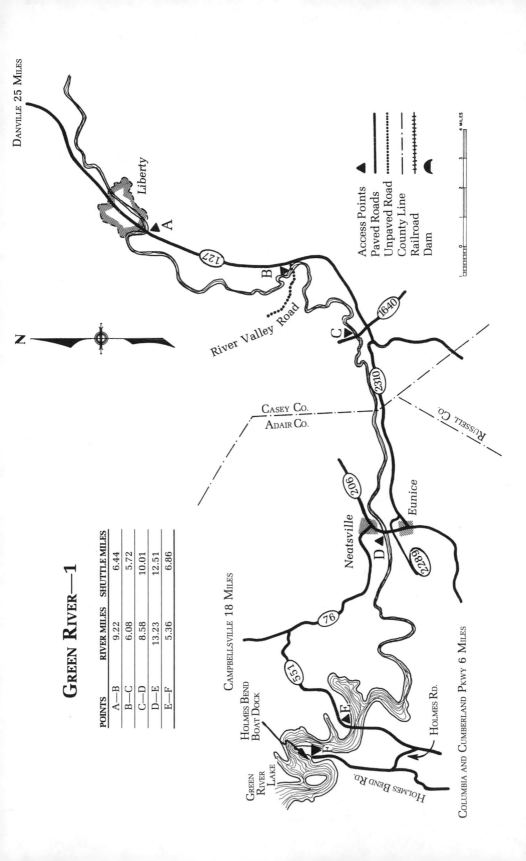

GREEN RIVER—1

POINTS	RIVER MILES	SHUTTLE MILES
A—B	9.22	6.44
B—C	6.08	5.72
C—D	8.58	10.01
D—E	13.23	12.51
E—F	5.36	6.86

DANVILLE 25 MILES

Liberty

N

River Valley Road

Access Points
Paved Roads
Unpaved Road
County Line
Railroad
Dam

4 MILES

CASEY CO.
ADAIR CO.

RUSSELL CO.

Neatsville

Eunice

CAMPBELLSVILLE 18 MILES

HOLMES BEND BOAT DOCK

GREEN RIVER LAKE

HOLMES RD.

HOLMES BEND RD.

COLUMBIA AND CUMBERLAND PKWY 6 MILES

127

1640

2310

206

2288

76

551

SECTION: Bend Rd. boat ramp to KY 88 bridge (Adair Co., Taylor Co., Green Co.)

USGS QUADS: Knifley, Cane Valley, Gresham, Greensburg, Summersville, Hudgins

LEVEL OF DIFFICULTY International Class I+   Numerical Points **6**

SUITABLE FOR: Cruising, camping **GRADIENT** (feet per mile): **1.01**

APPROPRIATE FOR: Families, Beginners, Intermediates, Advanced

VELOCITY (mph): **2.6-5.0**   **AVERAGE WIDTH** (ft): **55-80**

MONTHS RUNNABLE: All when dam is releasing

RUNNABLE WATER LEVEL (cfs) Minimum **220**
Maximum **Up to flood stage**

MEAN WATER TEMPERATURE (°F)

Jan. 45	Feb. 45	Mar. 48	Apr. 54	May 65	Jun. 72
Jul. 74	Aug. 74	Sep. 67	Oct. 58	Nov. 47	Dec. 43

SOURCE OF ADDITIONAL INFORMATION ON WATER CONDITIONS
Corps of Engineers (502) 465-4463

HAZARDS: Deadfalls

RESCUE INDEX: C-D
A Extremely remote; evacuation only with expert help—6 hours to secure assistance
B Remote; 3-6 hours to secure assistance
C Accessible but difficult; up to 3 hours to secure assistance—evacuation difficult
D Accessible; up to 1 hour to secure assistance, evacuation not difficult

PORTAGES: Green River Dam

SCOUTING: None required

INTEREST HIGHLIGHTS: Scenery, wildlife

SCENERY: Pretty to beautiful in spots

ACCESS POINT	ACCESS CODE	KEY
F	1 3 5 7	1 Paved Road
G	1 3 5 7	2 Unpaved Road
H	2 3 5 7	3 Short Carry
I	1 3 5 7	4 Long Carry
J	1 3 6 8	5 Easy Grade
K	(11)	6 Steep Grade
		7 Clear Trail
		8 Brush and Trees
		9 Private Property, Permission Needed
		10 Launching Fee Charged
		11 No Access—For Reference Only

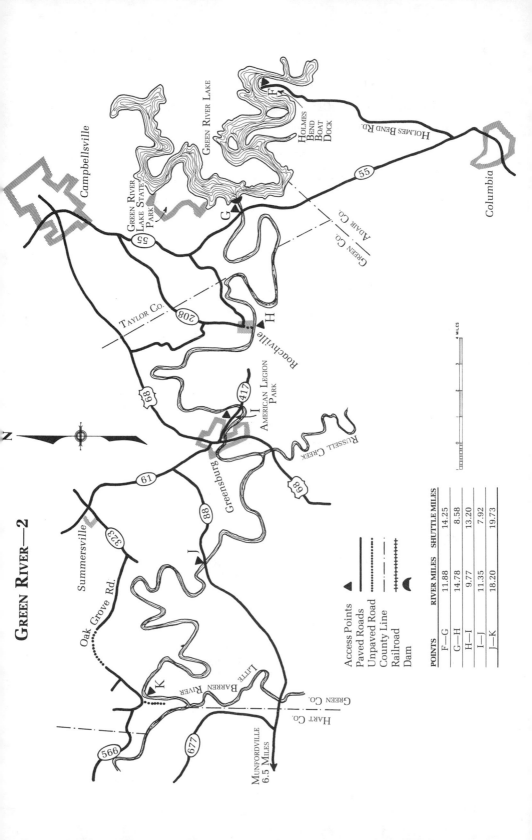

GREEN RIVER—2

POINTS	RIVER MILES	SHUTTLE MILES
F–G	11.88	14.25
G–H	14.78	8.58
H–I	9.77	13.20
I–J	11.35	7.92
J–K	18.20	19.73

Access Points ▲
Paved Roads
Unpaved Road
County Line
Railroad
Dam ◗

Campbellsville

Green River Lake

Green River Lake State Park

Holmes Bend Boat Dock

Holmes Bend Rd.

55

Columbia

Green Co. / Adair Co.

G

Taylor Co.

208

H

Roachville

68

417

American Legion Park

I

Russell Creek

68

Greensburg

61

88

J

Summersville

323

Oak Grove Rd.

Little Barren River

K

Green Co. / Hart Co.

566

677

Munfordville 6.5 Miles

N

MILES

SECTION: KY 88 bridge to Dennisons Ferry (Green Co., Hart Co., Edmonson Co.)

USGS QUADS: Hudgins, Center, Canmer, Munfordville, Cub Run, Mammoth Cave

LEVEL OF DIFFICULTY International Class I+   Numerical Points **6**

SUITABLE FOR: Cruising, camping **GRADIENT** (feet per mile): **1.01**

APPROPRIATE FOR: Families, Beginners, Intermediates, Advanced

VELOCITY (mph): 2.6-5.0   **AVERAGE WIDTH** (ft): 55-80

MONTHS RUNNABLE: All when dam is releasing

RUNNABLE WATER LEVEL (cfs) Minimum **220**
Maximum Up to flood stage

MEAN WATER TEMPERATURE ($^{\circ}$F)

Jan.	45	Feb.	45	Mar.	48	Apr.	54	May	65	Jun.	72
Jul.	74	Aug.	74	Sep.	67	Oct.	58	Nov.	47	Dec.	43

SOURCE OF ADDITIONAL INFORMATION ON WATER CONDITIONS
Corps of Engineers (502) 465-4463

HAZARDS: Deadfalls

RESCUE INDEX: C-D
A Extremely remote; evacuation only with expert help—6 hours to secure assistance
B Remote; 3-6 hours to secure assistance
C Accessible but difficult; up to 3 hours to secure assistance—evacuation difficult
D Accessible; up to 1 hour to secure assistance, evacuation not difficult

PORTAGES: None required

SCOUTING: None required

INTEREST HIGHLIGHTS: Scenery, wildlife

SCENERY: Pretty to beautiful in spots

ACCESS POINT	ACCESS CODE	KEY
J	1 3 6 8	1 Paved Road
K	(11)	2 Unpaved Road
L	2 3 5 7	3 Short Carry
M	1 3 5 7	4 Long Carry
N	2 3 6 7	5 Easy Grade
		6 Steep Grade
		7 Clear Trail
		8 Brush and Trees
		9 Private Property, Permission Needed
		10 Launching Fee Charged
		11 No Access—For Reference Only

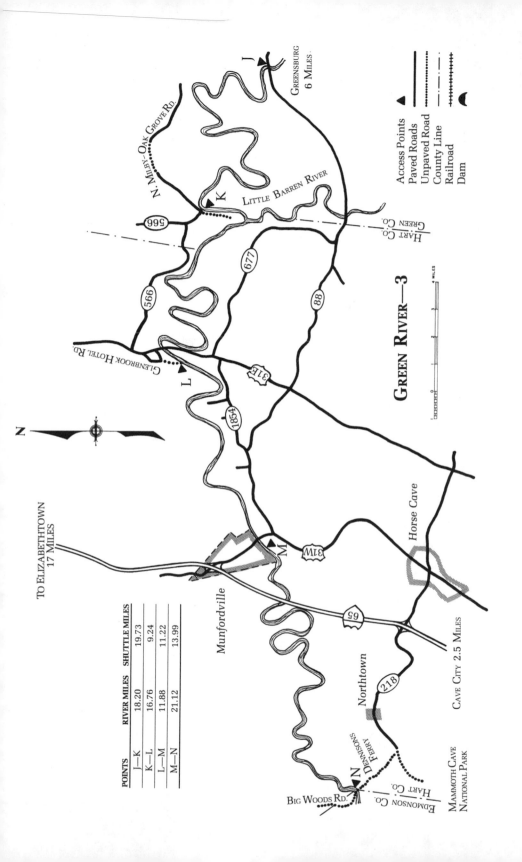

GREENSBURG
6 MILES

N. MILBY–OAK GROVE RD.

566

LITTLE BARREN RIVER

K

566

677

88

HART CO.
GREEN CO.

GLENBROOK HOTEL RD.

L

1854

31E

N

TO ELIZABETHTOWN
17 MILES

Munfordville

Horse Cave

31W

M

65

Northtown

218

Cave City 2.5 Miles

MAMMOTH CAVE
NATIONAL PARK

DENNISONS FERRY

N

EDMONSON CO.
HART CO.

BIG WOODS RD.

POINTS	RIVER MILES	SHUTTLE MILES
J–K	18.20	19.73
K–L	16.76	9.24
L–M	11.88	11.22
M–N	21.12	13.99

GREEN RIVER—3

Access Points
Paved Roads
Unpaved Road
County Line
Railroad
Dam

4 MILES
0 1 2 3 4

SECTION: Munfordville to Houchins Ferry (Hart Co., Edmonson Co.)

USGS QUADS: Munfordville, Horse Cave, Mammoth Cave, Rhoda

LEVEL OF DIFFICULTY International Class I+ Numerical Points 6

SUITABLE FOR: Cruising, camping **GRADIENT** (feet per mile): 1.03

APPROPRIATE FOR: Families, Beginners, Intermediates, Advanced

VELOCITY (mph): 0-5.0 **AVERAGE WIDTH** (ft): 70-105

MONTHS RUNNABLE: All when dam is releasing

RUNNABLE WATER LEVEL (cfs) Minimum 280
Maximum Up to flood stage

MEAN WATER TEMPERATURE (°F)

Jan. 45	Feb. 45	Mar. 48	Apr. 53	May 65	Jun. 72
Jul. 74	Aug. 75	Sep. 67	Oct. 58	Nov. 47	Dec. 44

SOURCE OF ADDITIONAL INFORMATION ON WATER CONDITIONS
Corps of Engineers (502) 465-4463

HAZARDS: Deadfalls

RESCUE INDEX: B
A Extremely remote; evacuation only with expert help—6 hours to secure assistance
B Remote; 3-6 hours to secure assistance
C Accessible but difficult; up to 3 hours to secure assistance—evacuation difficult
D Accessible; up to 1 hour to secure assistance, evacuation not difficult

PORTAGES: None required

SCOUTING: None required

INTEREST HIGHLIGHTS: Scenery, wildlife

SCENERY: Pretty to beautiful in spots

ACCESS POINT	ACCESS CODE	KEY
M	1 3 5 7	1 Paved Road
N	2 3 6 7	2 Unpaved Road
O	1 3 5 7	3 Short Carry
P	2 3 5 7	4 Long Carry
Q	1 3 6 7	5 Easy Grade
		6 Steep Grade
		7 Clear Trail
		8 Brush and Trees
		9 Private Property, Permission Needed
		10 Launching Fee Charged
		11 No Access—For Reference Only

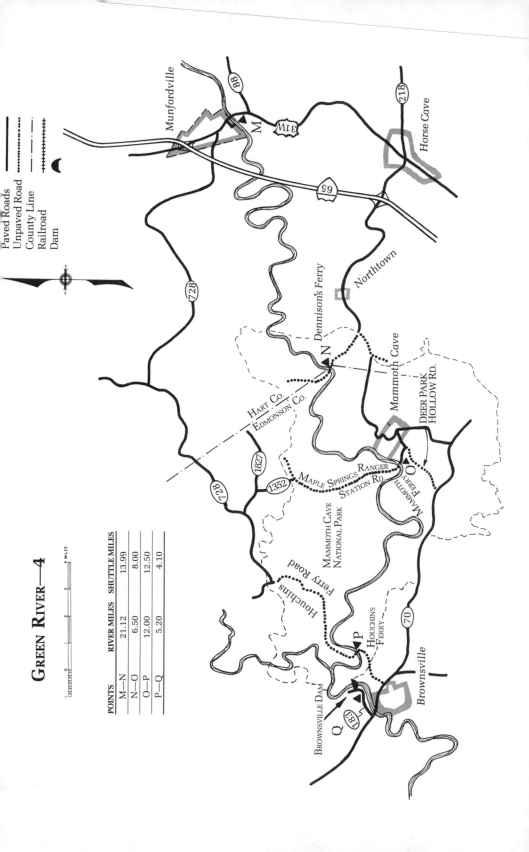

GREEN RIVER—4

POINTS	RIVER MILES	SHUTTLE MILES
M—N	21.12	13.99
N—O	6.50	8.00
O—P	12.00	12.50
P—Q	5.20	4.10

Paved Roads
Unpaved Road
County Line
Railroad
Dam

Munfordville

88

M

31W

65

218

Horse Cave

728

Dennison's Ferry

Northtown

N

Mammoth Cave

DEER PARK
HOLLOW RD.

HART CO.
EDMONSON CO.

1827

1352

728

MAPLE SPRINGS
RANGER
STATION RD.

MAMMOTH
FERRY

O

MAMMOTH CAVE
NATIONAL PARK

Houchins
Ferry Road

P

HOUCHINS
FERRY

70

Brownsville

BROWNSVILLE DAM

183

Q

SECTION: Dam to mouth of Drakes Creek (Barren Co., Allen Co., Warren Co.)

USGS QUADS: Lucas, Meador, Polkville, Bowling Green South

LEVEL OF DIFFICULTY International Class I   Numerical Points **6**

SUITABLE FOR: Cruising, camping **GRADIENT** (feet per mile): **1.33**

APPROPRIATE FOR: Families, Beginners, Intermediates, Advanced

VELOCITY (mph): 0-2.5 (2.6-5.0)   **AVERAGE WIDTH** (ft): 40-60

MONTHS RUNNABLE: All when dam is releasing

RUNNABLE WATER LEVEL (cfs) Minimum   **170**
   Maximum   Up to flood stage

MEAN WATER TEMPERATURE (°F)

Jan. 45	Feb. 46	Mar. 50	Apr. 56	May 66	Jun. 74
Jul. 76	Aug. 76	Sep. 69	Oct. 60	Nov. 48	Dec. 44

SOURCE OF ADDITIONAL INFORMATION ON WATER CONDITIONS
   Corps of Engineers (502) 646-2055

HAZARDS: Deadfalls

RESCUE INDEX: C
   A Extremely remote; evacuation only with expert help—6 hours to secure assistance
   B Remote; 3-6 hours to secure assistance
   C Accessible but difficult; up to 3 hours to secure assistance—evacuation difficult
   D Accessible; up to 1 hour to secure assistance, evacuation not difficult

PORTAGES: None required

SCOUTING: None required

INTEREST HIGHLIGHTS: Scenery

SCENERY: Pretty to pretty in spots

ACCESS POINT	ACCESS CODE	KEY
A	1 3 5 7	1 Paved Road
B	1 3 6 7	2 Unpaved Road
C *	1 3 6 8	3 Short Carry
D	1 4 6 7	4 Long Carry
E†	1 3 6 8	5 Easy Grade
F	1 3 5 7	6 Steep Grade
		7 Clear Trail
		8 Brush and Trees
		9 Private Property, Permission Needed
		10 Launching Fee Charged
		11 No Access—For Reference Only

*Put-in only at Bays Fork
†Put-in only at Drakes Creek

Barren River—1

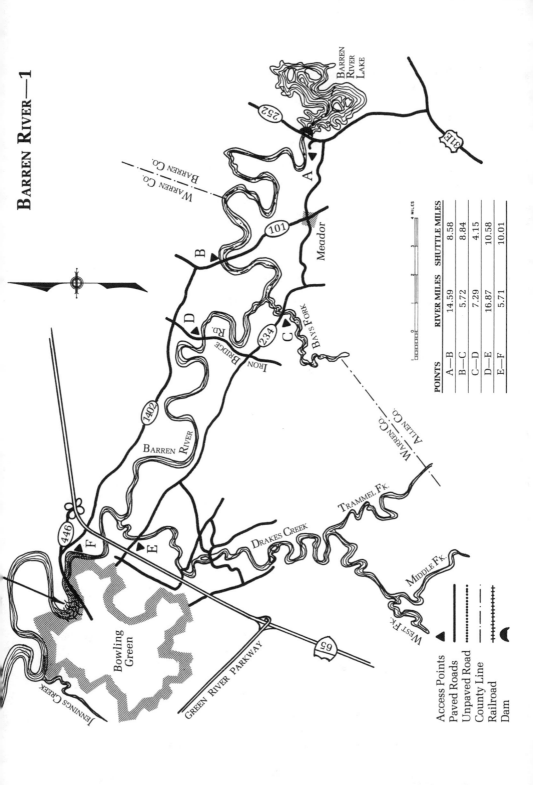

POINTS	RIVER MILES	SHUTTLE MILES
A—B	14.59	8.58
B—C	5.72	8.84
C—D	7.29	4.15
D—E	16.87	10.58
E—F	5.71	10.01

Access Points

Paved Roads

Unpaved Road

County Line

Railroad

Dam

SECTION: Mouth of Drakes Creek to Green River (Butler Co., Warren Co.)

USGS QUADS: Bowling Green South, Bowling Green North, Hadley, Riverside

LEVEL OF DIFFICULTY International Class I (II) Numerical Points 4

SUITABLE FOR: Cruising, camping **GRADIENT** (feet per mile): 0.66

APPROPRIATE FOR: Families, Beginners, Intermediates, Advanced

VELOCITY (mph): 0-2.5 **AVERAGE WIDTH** (ft): 90-150

MONTHS RUNNABLE: All

RUNNABLE WATER LEVEL (cfs) Minimum 400
   Maximum Up to flood stage

MEAN WATER TEMPERATURE ($^\circ$F)

Jan. 46	Feb. 47	Mar. 51	Apr. 57	May 67	Jun. 75
Jul. 77	Aug. 76	Sep. 70	Oct. 61	Nov. 48	Dec. 44

SOURCE OF ADDITIONAL INFORMATION ON WATER CONDITIONS
   Corps of Engineers (502) 646-2055

HAZARDS: Dams, deadfalls, powerboats, man-made rapid at Bowling Green

RESCUE INDEX: C
   A Extremely remote; evacuation only with expert help—6 hours to secure assistance
   B Remote; 3-6 hours to secure assistance
   C Accessible but difficult; up to 3 hours to secure assistance—evacuation difficult
   D Accessible; up to 1 hour to secure assistance, evacuation not difficult

PORTAGES: Lock No. 1 at Greencastle and possibly man-made rapid in Bowling Green

SCOUTING: At rapid

INTEREST HIGHLIGHTS: Scenery, local culture and industry

SCENERY: Pleasant to pretty

ACCESS POINT	ACCESS CODE	KEY
F	1 3 5 7	1 Paved Road
G	1 3 5 7	2 Unpaved Road
H	1 3 5 7	3 Short Carry
I	1 3 5 7	4 Long Carry
J†	1 3 6 7	5 Easy Grade
K‡	1 3 5 7	6 Steep Grade
		7 Clear Trail
		8 Brush and Trees
		9 Private Property, Permission Needed
		10 Launching Fee Charged
		11 No Access—For Reference Only

†Put-in or take-out on Gasper River
‡Take-out only on Green River

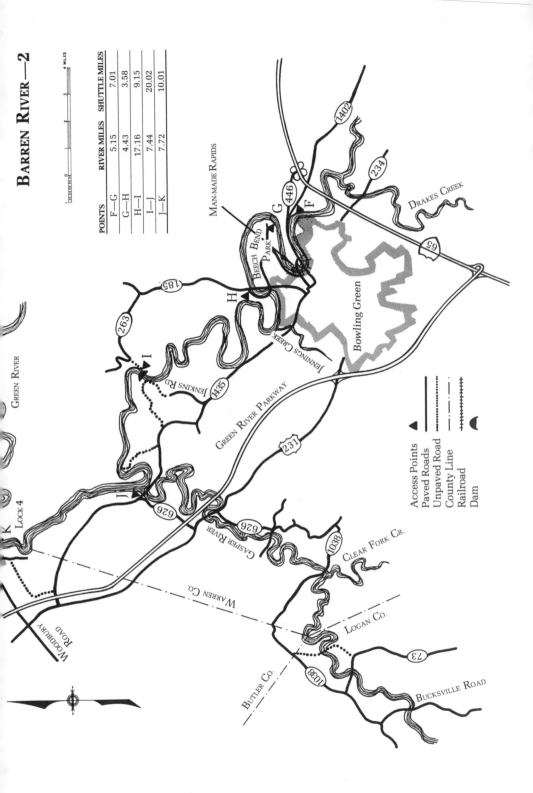

BARREN RIVER—2

POINTS	RIVER MILES	SHUTTLE MILES
F–G	5.15	7.01
G–H	4.43	3.58
H–I	17.16	9.15
I–J	7.44	20.02
J–K	7.72	10.01

MAN-MADE RAPIDS

BEECH BEND PARK

DRAKES CREEK

Bowling Green

JENNINGS CREEK

GREEN RIVER PARKWAY

GREEN RIVER

JENKINS RD.

LOCK 4

GASPER RIVER

CLEAR FORK CR.

WARREN CO.

LOGAN CO.

BUTLER CO.

WOODBURY ROAD

BUCKSVILLE ROAD

Access Points
Paved Roads
Unpaved Road
County Line
Railroad
Dam

SECTION: KY 240 on Trammel Fork, and West Fork to Barren River (Warren Co.)

USGS QUADS: Drake, Allen Springs, Polkville, Bowling Green South

LEVEL OF DIFFICULTY International Class I+ Numerical Points 6

SUITABLE FOR: Cruising   **GRADIENT** (feet per mile): 2.36

APPROPRIATE FOR: Families, Beginners, Intermediates, Advanced

VELOCITY (mph): 2.6-5.0   **AVERAGE WIDTH** (ft): 40-90

MONTHS RUNNABLE: November to mid-June (to forks);
November to July (below forks)

RUNNABLE WATER LEVEL (cfs) Minimum 160
Maximum Up to flood stage

MEAN WATER TEMPERATURE (°F)

Jan. 46	Feb. 46	Mar. 51	Apr. 58	May 68	Jun. 76
Jul. 78	Aug. 78	Sep. 70	Oct. 61	Nov. 49	Dec. 45

SOURCE OF ADDITIONAL INFORMATION ON WATER CONDITIONS

Warren Co. Sheriff Dept. (502) 842-1633

HAZARDS: Deadfalls, low trees

RESCUE INDEX: C
A Extremely remote; evacuation only with expert help—6 hours to secure assistance
B Remote; 3-6 hours to secure assistance
C Accessible but difficult; up to 3 hours to secure assistance—evacuation difficult
D Accessible; up to 1 hour to secure assistance, evacuation not difficult

PORTAGES: None required

SCOUTING: None required

INTEREST HIGHLIGHTS: Scenery

SCENERY: Pretty

ACCESS POINT	ACCESS CODE	KEY
A A	1 3 5 7	1 Paved Road
AAA	1 3 5 7	2 Unpaved Road
BB	1 3 5 7	3 Short Carry
CC	1 3 6 7	4 Long Carry
DD	1 3 6 8	5 Easy Grade
EE	1 3 6 7	6 Steep Grade
FF	1 3 6 8	7 Clear Trail
E	1 3 6 8	8 Brush and Trees
		9 Private Property, Permission Needed
		10 Launching Fee Charged
		11 No Access—For Reference Only

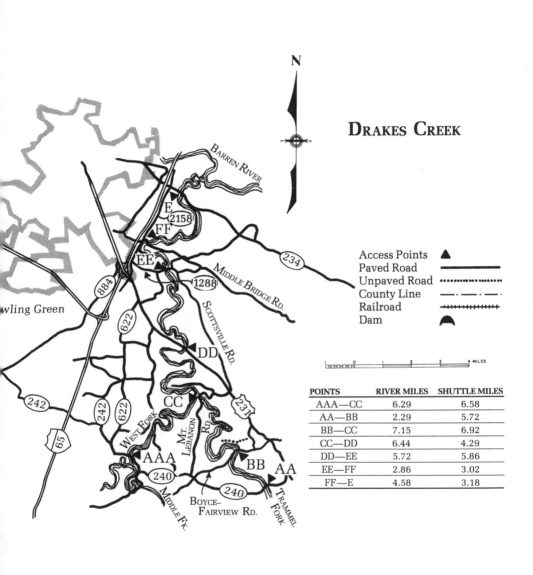

N

DRAKES CREEK

BARREN RIVER

E
2158
FF

EE
1288

234

MIDDLE BRIDGE RD.

SCOTTSVILLE RD.

884

622

wling Green

DD

242

622

242

CC

231

65

WEST FORK

MT. LEBANON RD.

AAA
240

BB

AA

240

BOYCE-
FAIRVIEW RD.

MIDDLE FK.

TRAMMEL FORK

Access Points ▲
Paved Road
Unpaved Road ••••••••••••
County Line — •• — •• —
Railroad +++++++++++
Dam

0   1   2   3   4 MILES

POINTS	RIVER MILES	SHUTTLE MILES
AAA—CC	6.29	6.58
AA—BB	2.29	5.72
BB—CC	7.15	6.92
CC—DD	6.44	4.29
DD—EE	5.72	5.86
EE—FF	2.86	3.02
FF—E	4.58	3.18

SECTION: Bucksville Rd. to Barren River (Logan Co., Warren Co.)

USGS QUADS: South Union, Sugar Grove, Hadley

LEVEL OF DIFFICULTY International Class I-II   Numerical Points 9

SUITABLE FOR: Cruising   **GRADIENT** (feet per mile): 4.81

APPROPRIATE FOR: Beginners, Intermediates, Advanced

VELOCITY (mph): 2.6-5.0   **AVERAGE WIDTH** (ft): 40-60

MONTHS RUNNABLE: Mid-November to mid-May

RUNNABLE WATER LEVEL (cfs) Minimum   210
   Maximum Open: 500   Decked: Up to flood stage

MEAN WATER TEMPERATURE (°F)

Jan. 48	Feb. 48	Mar. 52	Apr. 57	May 66	Jun. 75
Jul. 76	Aug. 77	Sep. 70	Oct. 59	Nov. 48	Dec. 46

SOURCE OF ADDITIONAL INFORMATION ON WATER CONDITIONS
   Logan Co. Sheriff's Dept. (502) 726-2244

HAZARDS: Deadfalls, undercut rocks, low bridges, fences, flash floods

RESCUE INDEX: C
   A Extremely remote; evacuation only with expert help—6 hours to secure assistance
   B Remote; 3-6 hours to secure assistance
   C Accessible but difficult; up to 3 hours to secure assistance—evacuation difficult
   D Accessible; up to 1 hour to secure assistance, evacuation not difficult

PORTAGES: Deadfalls, and concrete ford at Richelieu Rd. at low water

SCOUTING: Occasional blind curves

INTEREST HIGHLIGHTS: Scenery, whitewater

SCENERY: Pretty to beautiful in spots

ACCESS POINT	ACCESS CODE	KEY
A	1 3 6 7	1 Paved Road
B	1 3 6 7	2 Unpaved Road
C	2 3 5 7	3 Short Carry
D	1 3 6 7	4 Long Carry
E	1 3 6 8	5 Easy Grade
F	1 3 6 7	6 Steep Grade
G	1 3 6 7	7 Clear Trail
		8 Brush and Trees
		9 Private Property, Permission Needed
		10 Launching Fee Charged
		11 No Access—For Reference Only

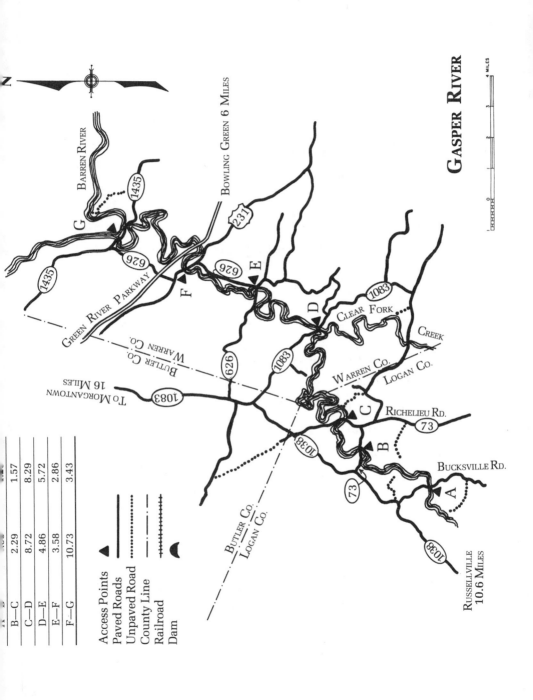

GASPER RIVER

B–C	2.29	1.57
C–D	8.72	8.29
D–E	4.86	5.72
E–F	3.58	2.86
F–G	10.73	3.43

Access Points ▲
Paved Roads ━━━
Unpaved Road •••••••
County Line ━·━·━
Railroad ━┼━┼━
Dam ◗

BARREN RIVER
1435
626
G
1435
GREEN RIVER PARKWAY
626
F
BOWLING GREEN 6 MILES
231
626
E
1083
CLEAR FORK
D
1083
CREEK
BUTLER CO.
WARREN CO.
WARREN CO.
LOGAN CO.
To MORGANTOWN 16 MILES
1083
626
1038
C
RICHELIEU RD.
73
B
1038
73
BUCKSVILLE RD.
A
BUTLER CO.
LOGAN CO.
1038
RUSSELLVILLE
10.6 MILES

N

0   1   2   3   4 MILES

SECTION: So. Fk., Beechville Ford; E. Fk., Mell-Cork Rd. to Green River (Green Co., Metcalfe Co.)

USGS QUADS: Sulphur Well, East Fork, Center

LEVEL OF DIFFICULTY International Class I+   Numerical Points 6

SUITABLE FOR: Cruising   **GRADIENT** (feet per mile): 5.76

APPROPRIATE FOR: Beginners, Intermediates, Advanced

VELOCITY (mph): 2.6-5.0   **AVERAGE WIDTH** (ft): 30-65

MONTHS RUNNABLE: Late October to June (South Fork); November to mid-May (East Fork)

RUNNABLE WATER LEVEL (cfs) Minimum   125 (forks);   220 (below forks)
   Maximum Up to flood stage

MEAN WATER TEMPERATURE (°F)

| Jan. | 45 | Feb. | 46 | Mar. | 48 | Apr. | 53 | May | 65 | Jun. | 73 |
| Jul. | 74 | Aug. | 74 | Sep. | 67 | Oct. | 60 | Nov. | 48 | Dec. | 43 |

SOURCE OF ADDITIONAL INFORMATION ON WATER CONDITIONS

Green Co. Sheriff Dept. (502) 932-5641

HAZARDS: Deadfalls, low trees, fences*

RESCUE INDEX: C

A Extremely remote; evacuation only with expert help—6 hours to secure assistance
B Remote; 3-6 hours to secure assistance
C Accessible but difficult; up to 3 hours to secure assistance—evacuation difficult
D Accessible; up to 1 hour to secure assistance, evacuation not difficult

PORTAGES: None required

SCOUTING: None required

INTEREST HIGHLIGHTS: Scenery, history, geology

SCENERY: Pretty

ACCESS POINT	ACCESS CODE	KEY
A	2 3 5 7	1 Paved Road
B	1 3 5 7	2 Unpaved Road
AA	1 3 6 8	3 Short Carry
BB	1 3 5 7	4 Long Carry
C	2 3 5 7	5 Easy Grade
D	1 4 6 8	6 Steep Grade
		7 Clear Trail
		8 Brush and Trees
		9 Private Property, Permission Needed
		10 Launching Fee Charged
		11 No Access—For Reference Only

*On East Fork

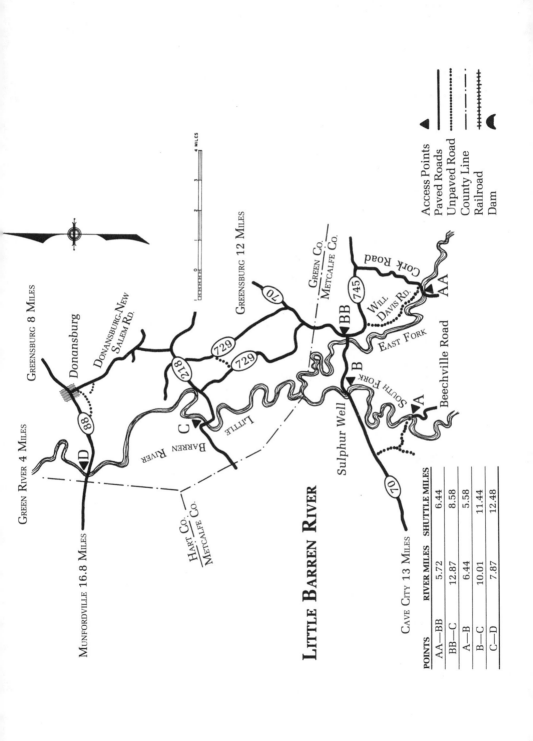

LITTLE BARREN RIVER

POINTS	RIVER MILES	SHUTTLE MILES
AA—BB	5.72	6.44
BB—C	12.87	8.58
A—B	6.44	5.58
B—C	10.01	11.44
C—D	7.87	12.48

GREEN RIVER 4 MILES

GREENSBURG 8 MILES

MUNFORDVILLE 16.8 MILES

GREENSBURG 12 MILES

CAVE CITY 13 MILES

Donansburg

DONANSBURG-NEW SALEM RD.

88

D

C

BARREN RIVER

LITTLE

218

729

729

70

GREEN CO. / METCALFE CO.

HART CO. / METCALFE CO.

BB

745

Cork Road

WILL DAVIS RD.

EAST FORK

AA

Beechville Road

SOUTH FORK

B

A

Sulphur Well

70

4 MILES

0   1   2   3

Access Points

Paved Roads

Unpaved Road

County Line

Railroad

Dam

SECTION: KY 1136 to Nolin River Lake (Hardin Co., Grayson Co., Hart Co.)

USGS QUADS: Sonora, Summit, Millerstown, Cub Run, Nolin Reservoir

LEVEL OF DIFFICULTY International Class I* Numerical Points 5

SUITABLE FOR: Cruising, camping **GRADIENT** (feet per mile): 2.13

APPROPRIATE FOR: Families, Beginners, Intermediates, Advanced

VELOCITY (mph): 0-5.0   **AVERAGE WIDTH** (ft): 45-75

MONTHS RUNNABLE: November to late June

RUNNABLE WATER LEVEL (cfs) Minimum 250
Maximum Up to flood stage

MEAN WATER TEMPERATURE (°F)

Jan. 49	Feb. 48	Mar. 51	Apr. 57	May 64	Jun. 76
Jul. 77	Aug. 76	Sep. 71	Oct. 59	Nov. 49	Dec. 74

SOURCE OF ADDITIONAL INFORMATION ON WATER CONDITIONS
Corps of Engineers (502) 286-4511

HAZARDS: Dams, deadfalls

RESCUE INDEX: C-D
A Extremely remote; evacuation only with expert help—6 hours to secure assistance
B Remote; 3-6 hours to secure assistance
C Accessible but difficult; up to 3 hours to secure assistance—evacuation difficult
D Accessible; up to 1 hour to secure assistance, evacuation not difficult

PORTAGES: Dams at Spurrier, White Mills, and Star Mills; deadfall near Millerstown

SCOUTING: Dam at Star Mills

INTEREST HIGHLIGHTS: Scenery, history

SCENERY: Pretty

ACCESS POINT	ACCESS CODE	KEY
A	1 3 5 8	1 Paved Road
B	1 3 6 8 9	2 Unpaved Road
C	1 3 5 7	3 Short Carry
D	1 3 5 7	4 Long Carry
E	1 3 5 7	5 Easy Grade
F	1 3 6 7	6 Steep Grade
G	1 3 6 7	7 Clear Trail
		8 Brush and Trees
		9 Private Property, Permission Needed
		10 Launching Fee Charged
		11 No Access—For Reference Only

*Partially collapsed dam at Star Mills, Class II+

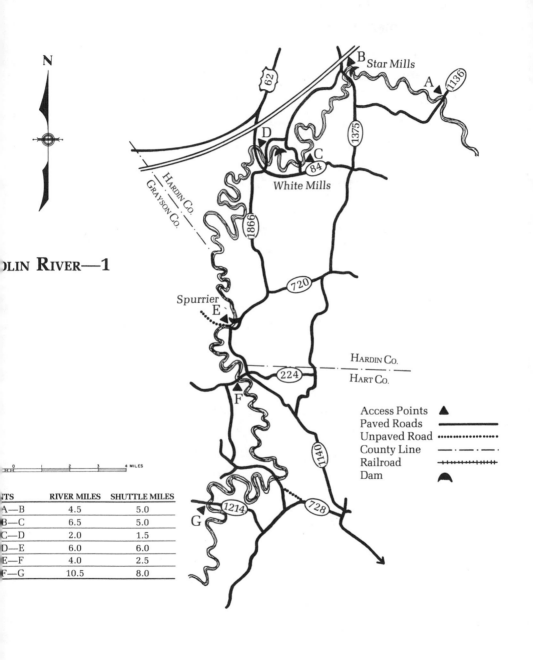

N

B Star Mills

A

1136

62

D

C

84

White Mills

1375

HARDIN CO.

GRAYSON CO.

1866

720

Spurrier
E

OLIN RIVER—1

HARDIN CO.

224

HART CO.

F

Access Points ▲
Paved Roads ——————
Unpaved Road ••••••••••••••
County Line —·—·—·—
Railroad ++++++++++++
Dam

1140

0   1   2   3   4 MILES

1214

728

G

TS	RIVER MILES	SHUTTLE MILES
A—B	4.5	5.0
B—C	6.5	5.0
C—D	2.0	1.5
D—E	6.0	6.0
E—F	4.0	2.5
F—G	10.5	8.0

SECTION: Nolin River Lake to Green River (Edmonson Co.)

USGS QUADS: Nolin Reservoir, Rhoda

LEVEL OF DIFFICULTY International Class I   Numerical Points 5

SUITABLE FOR: Cruising, camping **GRADIENT** (feet per mile): 2.21

APPROPRIATE FOR: Families, Beginners, Intermediates, Advanced

VELOCITY (mph): 0-5.0   **AVERAGE WIDTH** (ft): 45-70

MONTHS RUNNABLE: All when dam is releasing

RUNNABLE WATER LEVEL (cfs) Minimum   **250**
Maximum **Up to flood stage**

MEAN WATER TEMPERATURE (°F)

Jan. 48	Feb. 48	Mar. 51	Apr. 56	May 64	Jun. 75
Jul. 77	Aug. 77	Sep. 70	Oct. 59	Nov. 48	Dec. 44

SOURCE OF ADDITIONAL INFORMATION ON WATER CONDITIONS
Corps of Engineers (502) 286-4511

HAZARDS: Deadfalls

RESCUE INDEX: B-C
  A Extremely remote; evacuation only with expert help—6 hours to secure assistance
  B Remote; 3-6 hours to secure assistance
  C Accessible but difficult; up to 3 hours to secure assistance—evacuation difficult
  D Accessible; up to 1 hour to secure assistance, evacuation not difficult

PORTAGES: None required

SCOUTING: None required

INTEREST HIGHLIGHTS: Scenery, wildlife, geology

SCENERY: Beautiful in spots

ACCESS POINT	ACCESS CODE	KEY
G	1 3 6 7	1 Paved Road
H	1 3 5 7	2 Unpaved Road
I	1 3 5 7	3 Short Carry
J	1 3 5 7	4 Long Carry
K*	2 3 5 7	5 Easy Grade
		6 Steep Grade
		7 Clear Trail
		8 Brush and Trees
		9 Private Property, Permission Needed
		10 Launching Fee Charged
		11 No Access—For Reference Only

*Take-out is upstream on the Green River

NOLIN RIVER—2

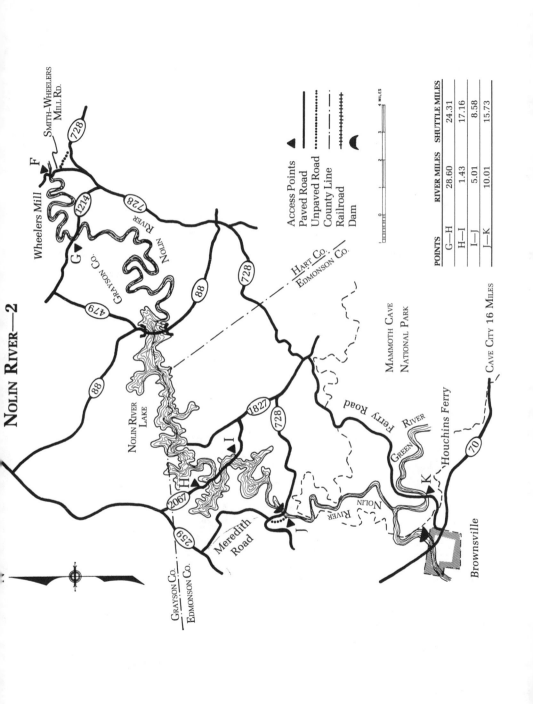

Access Points	▲
Paved Road	● ● ● ●
Unpaved Road	● ● ●
County Line	─ · ─ · ─
Railroad	┼┼┼┼┼
Dam	◗

0 1 2 3 4 MILES

POINTS	RIVER MILES	SHUTTLE MILES
G–H	28.60	24.31
H–I	1.43	17.16
I–J	5.01	8.58
J–K	10.01	15.73

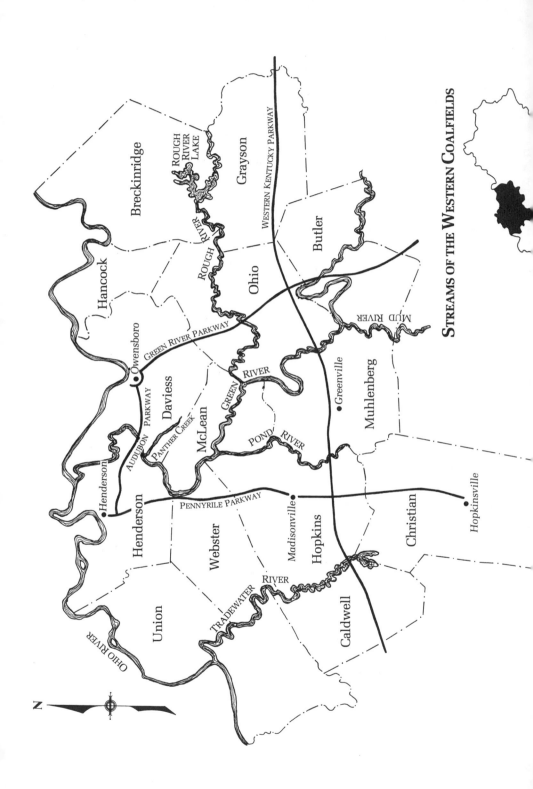

STREAMS OF THE WESTERN COALFIELDS

7
STREAMS OF THE
WESTERN COAL FIELDS

TRADEWATER RIVER

Everyone in Western Kentucky knows about the tragedy of the Tradewater River, that sterile, lifeless stream appropriated as a private sewer for the mining industry. The Tradewater River runs north from Christian County and empties into the Ohio River west of Sturgis. Although the water is almost devoid of life, the stream is nevertheless pleasing to the eye. An intimate river, with willow and hardwood completely shading the water, it winds through rolling farm and mining country. The river channel is generally deep, thereby facilitating paddling, and it is not normally cluttered with deadfalls downstream of the KY 120 bridge. The Tradewater River is generally runnable most of the year downstream of the KY 293 bridge, although an occasional shallow may have to be portaged during the late summer and early fall. The bottom and banks of the river are mud and vary markedly in their degree of slope. The gradient is gentle and current is moderate to slow. The river expands from 35 feet in width at the KY 293 bridge to around 110 feet near its mouth. Canoe camping near the stream is possible at low water levels. Access at bridge intersections is fair to good.

POND RIVER

The Pond River is a main tributary of the Green River. Its headwaters are in northern Todd County and its mouth is west of Calhoun on the McLean–Hopkins border. The Pond River and its tributaries, all of which are small, are the main drainage system for eastern Hopkins, western Muhlenberg, northern Christian, and northern Todd Counties. Although, due to some mining discharge, the water quality is not the best, the stream is nevertheless scenic, with birch and willow trees overhanging the water, and has a well-defined, navigable channel. The Pond River is generally runnable all year from the KY 70 bridge to its mouth, although an occasional shallows may have to be portaged in late summer and early fall. The river is generally clear of deadfalls and debris, but some may be encountered upstream of KY 85 bridge, particularly after spring flooding. At the intersection of KY 70, the Pond River is about 25 feet wide. Moving north, it stays small (under 50 feet) up to within ten miles of its mouth where it broadens to 80 to 100 feet. The river flows through gently rolling, flat farmland and occasionally through some woodland and mining country. Its bottom is of mud with generally high, steep banks. Access is fair to good at most bridge crossings. Current is slow (less than two mph), except at high water. Riverside areas for canoe camping are limited (even at low water) by the steep banks and the dense streamside vegetation. It is possible, however, to secure permission (in advance) to camp on the edge of farm fields above the river.

PANTHER CREEK

Panther Creek constitutes the main drainage system for Daviess County and the area around Owensboro. The creek is canoeable but definitely not aesthetically pleasing. It is narrow, resembles a dredged drainage ditch, and has been denuded of all but scrub vegetation fifteen feet from its banks, presumably for the purpose of terracing or constructing a utility road. The Panther runs through flat farmland. Its banks and bottom are of mud, steep, and six to fifteen feet high. Water quality is poor. Access from intersecting bridges is usually not difficult.

ROUGH RIVER

The Rough River is not very rough but extremely canoeable. Running east to west over a rock bottom through wooded hill country and farmland, the Rough River is typically high banked and shaded with willow and various hardwoods. The Rough can be paddled all year from the tailwater of the dam to its mouth at the Green River near Livermore. The most scenic sections are from the tailwater to Falls of the Rough, and from Falls of the Rough to the KY 54 bridge. Both of these sections sport some minor (Class-I+) rapids, ripples, and shoals. At the time of this writing, unfortunately, access to the portage route around the seven-foot dam at Falls of the Rough has been denied paddlers, thus forcing a premature take-out (up a steep bank thick with

242

scrub vegetation) at the KY 110 bridge. Likewise, the road along the north side of the river leading to the bottom of the dam has been posted, thus precluding a put-in below the dam. The dam itself is considered extremely dangerous and should not be run under any circumstances. Moving further downstream, access is very good all the way to Hartford. From Hartford to the mouth of the Rough near Livermore, access is extremely limited (especially since the abandonment of the U.S. Army Corps of Engineers' lock upstream of Livermore.) Upstream of Rough River Lake, there's a nice run from the KY 920 bridge to the Everleigh Boat Ramp on the lake. This section is runnable except in late summer and early fall. Water quality is generally fair to good. Lateral erosion along the steep banks has exposed many tree roots and has caused a substantial number of deadfalls. The river's width averages from 50 to 70 feet throughout.

MUD RIVER

The Mud River is an uninspiring stream originating near Russellville and running north over a mud bottom to empty into the Green River at Rochester. It is runnable from late fall to mid-summer from the KY 949 bridge to its mouth. Access is good at bridge crossings and at the mouth but almost totally lacking in between. The Mud River runs primarily through hilly farmland. Banks are well vegetated and treelined, but the water quality is poor due to mining waste discharge. Its width varies markedly from about 35 feet at the KY 949 bridge to almost 100 feet upstream of the KY 70 bridge. Deadfalls and some trash are in evidence on the more narrow, upstream sections.

GREEN RIVER FROM HOUCHINS
FERRY TO THE OHIO RIVER

[NOTE: The upstream sections of the Green River are found in the preceding section of this guidebook under "Headwaters of the Green River."]

This long, 185-mile section of the Green River is runnable all year and access is plentiful, but unfortunately so are powerboats, barges, locks, and dams. In short, the lower Green River is one of Kentucky's primary commercial waterways, and is not consistently appealing to paddlers. From Houchins Ferry the Green River broadens considerably (increasing in volume) at its confluence with the Nolin River. Two miles farther downstream is the Brownsville Dam—a difficult portage. From the dam to the mouth of the Barren River the scenery remains pleasant, with farms and wooded hills. In this stretch, pleasure boaters still constitute the majority of river traffic. From the confluence of the Barren and Green rivers to the mouth of the Green River at the Ohio River, however, the river belongs to the coal industry. But while coal tipples, rail yards, and barges are frequently in evidence, the lower Green is not totally lacking in charm. As on any big river, the vistas are panoramic (if not often changing), access is excellent by virtue of the many small marinas, and countless trip possibilities exist. Navigational hazards consist almost exclusively of the well-marked locks and dams.

Elkhorn Creek   Photograph courtesy of the Commonwealth of Kentucky, Department of
Public Information

SECTION: KY 70 to Ohio River (Hopkins Co., Webster Co., Union Co.)

USGS QUADS: Dawson Springs, Olney, Dalton, Providence, Blackford, Sturgis, Dekoven

LEVEL OF DIFFICULTY International Class I   Numerical Points 5

SUITABLE FOR: Cruising, camping* **GRADIENT** (feet per mile): 0.70

APPROPRIATE FOR: Families, Beginners, Intermediates, Advanced

VELOCITY (mph): 0-2.5   **AVERAGE WIDTH** (ft): 30-65

MONTHS RUNNABLE: All (except possibly late summer and early fall)

RUNNABLE WATER LEVEL (cfs) Minimum   130
Maximum   Up to flood stage

MEAN WATER TEMPERATURE (°F)

Jan. 41	Feb. 42	Mar. 49	Apr. 54	May 65	Jun. 75
Jul. 77	Aug. 75	Sep. 69	Oct. 60	Nov. 49	Dec. 41

SOURCE OF ADDITIONAL INFORMATION ON WATER CONDITIONS
Providence Police Dept. (502) 667-2022

HAZARDS: Deadfalls, low trees

RESCUE INDEX: C
A Extremely remote; evacuation only with expert help—6 hours to secure assistance
B Remote; 3-6 hours to secure assistance
C Accessible but difficult; up to 3 hours to secure assistance—evacuation difficult
D Accessible; up to 1 hour to secure assistance, evacuation not difficult

PORTAGES: Around deadfalls and extremely low water at times

SCOUTING: None required

INTEREST HIGHLIGHTS: Scenery, local culture and industry

SCENERY: Uninspiring to pretty in spots

ACCESS POINT	ACCESS CODE	KEY
A	1 3 6 8	1 Paved Road
B	1 3 6 8	2 Unpaved Road
C	1 3 6 8	3 Short Carry
D	1 3 6 8	4 Long Carry
E	1 3 6 7	5 Easy Grade
F	1 3 6 7	6 Steep Grade
G	1 4 6 8	7 Clear Trail
H	1 3 6 7	8 Brush and Trees
		9 Private Property, Permission Needed
		10 Launching Fee Charged
		11 No Access—For Reference Only

*At low water levels

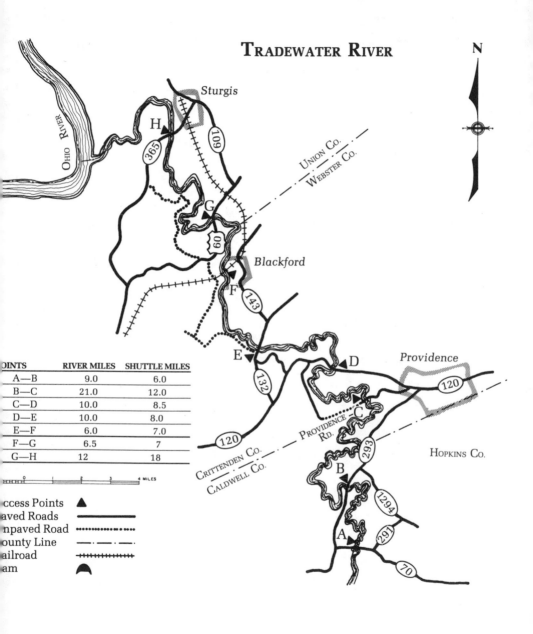

TRADEWATER RIVER

N

OHIO RIVER

Sturgis

H

365

109

UNION CO.
WEBSTER CO.

G

60

Blackford

F

143

E

132

D

Providence

120

120

C

PROVIDENCE RD.

293

HOPKINS CO.

CRITTENDEN CO.
CALDWELL CO.

B

1294

A

291

70

POINTS	RIVER MILES	SHUTTLE MILES
A—B	9.0	6.0
B—C	21.0	12.0
C—D	10.0	8.5
D—E	10.0	8.0
E—F	6.0	7.0
F—G	6.5	7
G—H	12	18

0   1   2   3   4 MILES

Access Points ▲
Paved Roads
Unpaved Road
County Line
Railroad
Dam

SECTION: KY 70 to Green River (Hopkins Co.)

USGS QUADS: Millport, Sacramento, Calhoun

LEVEL OF DIFFICULTY International Class I   Numerical Points 4

SUITABLE FOR: Cruising, camping* **GRADIENT** (feet per mile): 0.76

APPROPRIATE FOR: Families, Beginners, Intermediates, Advanced

VELOCITY (mph): 0-2.5 (2.6-5.0)   **AVERAGE WIDTH** (ft): 35-65

MONTHS RUNNABLE: All

RUNNABLE WATER LEVEL (cfs) Minimum 170
   Maximum Up to flood stage

MEAN WATER TEMPERATURE ($^\circ$F)

Jan. 40	Feb. 42	Mar. 50	Apr. 55	May 65	Jun. 74
Jul. 76	Aug. 75	Sep. 68	Oct. 61	Nov. 49	Dec. 41

SOURCE OF ADDITIONAL INFORMATION ON WATER CONDITIONS
   McClean Co. Sheriff Dept. (502) 273-3276

HAZARDS: Deadfalls, powerboats

RESCUE INDEX: B-C
   A Extremely remote; evacuation only with expert help—6 hours to secure assistance
   B Remote; 3-6 hours to secure assistance
   C Accessible but difficult; up to 3 hours to secure assistance—evacuation difficult
   D Accessible; up to 1 hour to secure assistance, evacuation not difficult

PORTAGES: Around deadfalls in upper sections

SCOUTING: None required

INTEREST HIGHLIGHTS: Scenery, local culture and industry

SCENERY: Uninspiring to pretty in spots

ACCESS POINT	ACCESS CODE	KEY
A	1 3 6 8	1 Paved Road
B	1 3 6 8	2 Unpaved Road
C	1 3 6 7	3 Short Carry
D	1 3 5 7	4 Long Carry
		5 Easy Grade
		6 Steep Grade
		7 Clear Trail
		8 Brush and Trees
		9 Private Property, Permission Needed
		10 Launching Fee Charged
		11 No Access—For Reference Only

*With permission

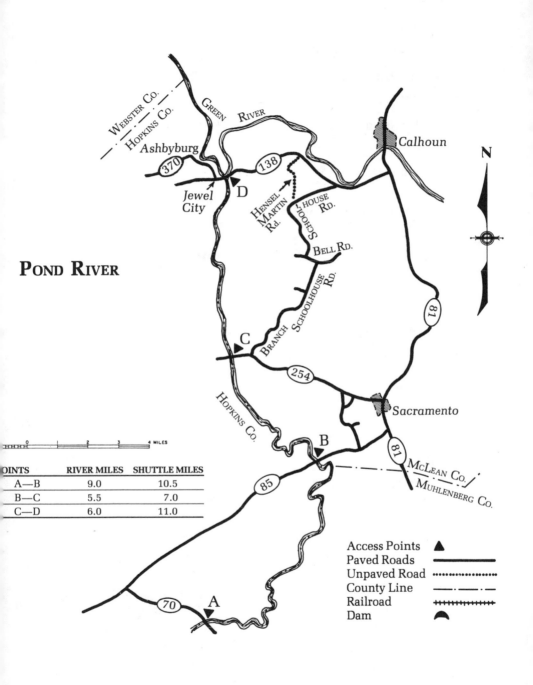

POND RIVER

POINTS	RIVER MILES	SHUTTLE MILES
A—B	9.0	10.5
B—C	5.5	7.0
C—D	6.0	11.0

Access Points ▲
Paved Roads ──────
Unpaved Road ●●●●●●●●●
County Line ─·─·─·─
Railroad ┼┼┼┼┼┼┼┼┼
Dam ⌒

SECTION: KY 81 to Green River (Daviess Co.)

USGS QUADS: Sutherland, Panther, Curdsville

LEVEL OF DIFFICULTY International Class I   Numerical Points 4

SUITABLE FOR: Cruising   **GRADIENT** (feet per mile): 0.61

APPROPRIATE FOR: Dredges

VELOCITY (mph): 0-2.5   **AVERAGE WIDTH** (ft): 25-35

MONTHS RUNNABLE: November to May

RUNNABLE WATER LEVEL (cfs) Minimum 95
Maximum   Up to flood stage

MEAN WATER TEMPERATURE (°F)

Jan. 40	Feb. 41	Mar. 49	Apr. 54	May 66	Jun. 75
Jul. 76	Aug. 76	Sep. 69	Oct. 60	Nov. 49	Dec. 42

SOURCE OF ADDITIONAL INFORMATION ON WATER CONDITIONS
None available

HAZARDS: Deadfalls, flash floods

RESCUE INDEX: C
A Extremely remote; evacuation only with expert help—6 hours to secure assistance
B Remote; 3-6 hours to secure assistance
C Accessible but difficult; up to 3 hours to secure assistance—evacuation difficult
D Accessible; up to 1 hour to secure assistance, evacuation not difficult

PORTAGES: None required

SCOUTING: None required

INTEREST HIGHLIGHTS: None

SCENERY: Unattractive

ACCESS POINT	ACCESS CODE	KEY
A	1 3 6 8	1 Paved Road
B	(at all points)	2 Unpaved Road
		3 Short Carry
		4 Long Carry
		5 Easy Grade
		6 Steep Grade
		7 Clear Trail
		8 Brush and Trees
		9 Private Property, Permission Needed
		10 Launching Fee Charged
		11 No Access—For Reference Only

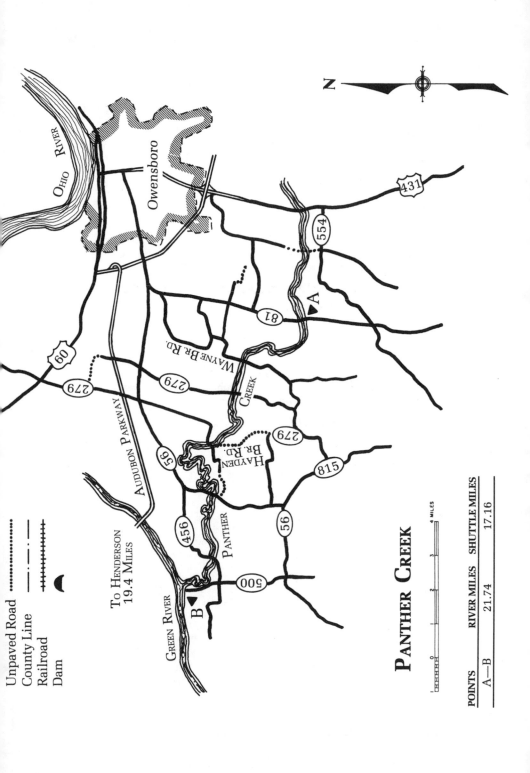

N

Unpaved Road
County Line
Railroad
Dam

Ohio River

Owensboro

431

554

81

Wayne Br. Rd.

Creek

279

279

815

Hayden Br. Rd.

69

279

56

56

456

500

Audubon Parkway

Panther

Green River

To Henderson
19.4 Miles

B

A

Panther Creek

0   1   2   3   4 Miles

POINTS	RIVER MILES	SHUTTLE MILES
A—B	21.74	17.16

SECTION: Rough River Dam to Dundee (Grayson Co., Breckinridge Co., Ohio Co.)

USGS QUADS: McDaniels, Falls of Rough, Olaton, Dundee

LEVEL OF DIFFICULTY International Class I (II) Numerical Points 7

SUITABLE FOR: Cruising   **GRADIENT** (feet per mile): 1.4

APPROPRIATE FOR: Beginners, Intermediates, Advanced

VELOCITY (mph): 0-5.0   **AVERAGE WIDTH** (ft): 45-60

MONTHS RUNNABLE: All

RUNNABLE WATER LEVEL (cfs) Minimum 165
    Maximum   Up to flood stage

MEAN WATER TEMPERATURE (°F)

Jan. 42	Feb. 43	Mar. 48	Apr. 54	May 65	Jun. 74
Jul. 76	Aug. 75	Sep. 68	Oct. 59	Nov. 45	Dec. 41

SOURCE OF ADDITIONAL INFORMATION ON WATER CONDITIONS

Corps of Engineers (502) 257-2061

HAZARDS: Dams, deadfalls

RESCUE INDEX: C
 A Extremely remote; evacuation only with expert help—6 hours to secure assistance
 B Remote; 3-6 hours to secure assistance
 C Accessible but difficult; up to 3 hours to secure assistance—evacuation difficult
 D Accessible; up to 1 hour to secure assistance, evacuation not difficult

PORTAGES: Dam at Falls of Rough

SCOUTING: None required

INTEREST HIGHLIGHTS: Scenery, history, local culture and industry

SCENERY: Pretty

ACCESS POINT	ACCESS CODE	KEY
A	1 3 5 7	1 Paved Road
B	1 4 6 8 9	2 Unpaved Road
C	1 3 5 8	3 Short Carry
D	2 3 5 7	4 Long Carry
E	1 3 6 8	5 Easy Grade
F	2 3 6 8	6 Steep Grade
		7 Clear Trail
		8 Brush and Trees
		9 Private Property, Permission Needed
		10 Launching Fee Charged
		11 No Access—For Reference Only

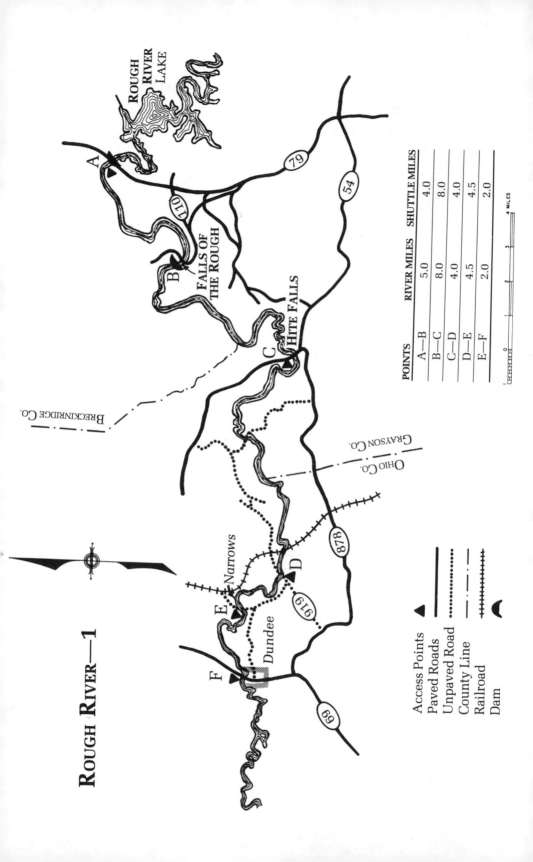

ROUGH RIVER—1

ROUGH RIVER LAKE

FALLS OF THE ROUGH

HITE FALLS

BRECKINRIDGE CO.

GRAYSON CO.

OHIO CO.

Narrows

Dundee

POINTS	RIVER MILES	SHUTTLE MILES
A—B	5.0	4.0
B—C	8.0	8.0
C—D	4.0	4.0
D—E	4.5	4.5
E—F	2.0	2.0

0   1   2   3   4 MILES

Access Points
Paved Roads
Unpaved Road
County Line
Railroad
Dam

SECTION: Dundee to Green River (Ohio Co., McLean Co.)

USGS QUADS: Dundee, Horton, Hartford, Equality

LEVEL OF DIFFICULTY International Class I   Numerical Points **5**

SUITABLE FOR: Cruising   **GRADIENT** (feet per mile): 0.6

APPROPRIATE FOR: Beginners, Intermediates, Advanced

VELOCITY (mph): 0-5.0   **AVERAGE WIDTH** (ft): 55-70

MONTHS RUNNABLE: All

RUNNABLE WATER LEVEL (cfs) Minimum **190**
   Maximum **Up to flood stage**

MEAN WATER TEMPERATURE (°F)
   Jan. 42   Feb. 43   Mar. 48   Apr. 54   May 65   Jun. 74
   Jul. 76   Aug. 75   Sep. 68   Oct. 59   Nov. 45   Dec. 41

SOURCE OF ADDITIONAL INFORMATION ON WATER CONDITIONS
   Corps of Engineers (502) 257-2061

HAZARDS: Dams, deadfalls

RESCUE INDEX: C
   A   Extremely remote; evacuation only with expert help—6 hours to secure assistance
   B   Remote; 3-6 hours to secure assistance
   C   Accessible but difficult; up to 3 hours to secure assistance—evacuation difficult
   D   Accessible; up to 1 hour to secure assistance, evacuation not difficult

PORTAGES: Abandoned lock upstream from Livermore

SCOUTING: None required

INTEREST HIGHLIGHTS: Scenery, local culture and industry

SCENERY: Pleasant to pretty in spots

ACCESS POINT	ACCESS CODE	KEY
F	2 3 6 8	1 Paved Road
G	2 3 6 8	2 Unpaved Road
H	2 3 6 7	3 Short Carry
I	2 3 6 7	4 Long Carry
J	1 3 6 8	5 Easy Grade
		6 Steep Grade
		7 Clear Trail
		8 Brush and Trees
		9 Private Property, Permission Needed
		10 Launching Fee Charged
		11 No Access—For Reference Only

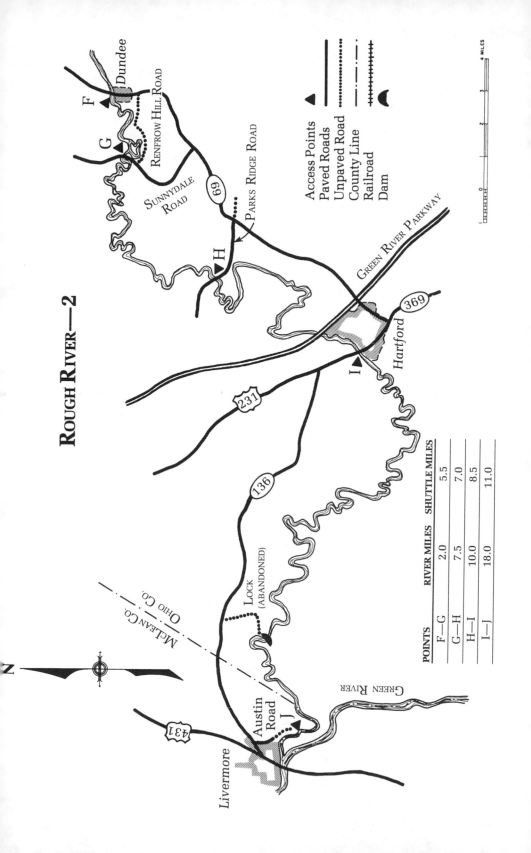

ROUGH RIVER—2

Dundee

F

G

RENFROW HILL ROAD

SUNNYDALE ROAD

69

PARKS RIDGE ROAD

H

GREEN RIVER PARKWAY

369

Hartford

I

231

136

LOCK (ABANDONED)

McLEAN CO.

OHIO CO.

N

431

Austin Road

J

Livermore

GREEN RIVER

Access Points
Paved Roads
Unpaved Road
County Line
Railroad
Dam

4 MILES

POINTS	RIVER MILES	SHUTTLE MILES
F—G	2.0	5.5
G—H	7.5	7.0
H—I	10.0	8.5
I—J	18.0	11.0

SECTION: KY 949 to Rochester (Butler Co.)

USGS QUADS: Dunmor, Rochester

LEVEL OF DIFFICULTY International Class I   Numerical Points 5

SUITABLE FOR: Cruising   **GRADIENT** (feet per mile): 0.56

APPROPRIATE FOR: Beginners, Intermediates, Advanced

VELOCITY (mph): 0-2.5   **AVERAGE WIDTH** (ft): 30-65

MONTHS RUNNABLE: Mid-November to mid-June

RUNNABLE WATER LEVEL (cfs) Minimum 120
   Maximum Up to flood stage

MEAN WATER TEMPERATURE (°F)
Jan. 46	Feb. 45	Mar. 48	Apr. 54	May 65	Jun. 72
Jul. 74	Aug. 73	Sep. 66	Oct. 58	Nov. 47	Dec. 43

SOURCE OF ADDITIONAL INFORMATION ON WATER CONDITIONS
   None available

HAZARDS: Deadfalls, low trees, fences

RESCUE INDEX: C
   A Extremely remote; evacuation only with expert help—6 hours to secure assistance
   B Remote; 3-6 hours to secure assistance
   C Accessible but difficult; up to 3 hours to secure assistance—evacuation difficult
   D Accessible; up to 1 hour to secure assistance, evacuation not difficult

PORTAGES: Around deadfalls and 1 fence

SCOUTING: None required

INTEREST HIGHLIGHTS: None

SCENERY: Pleasant in spots to pleasant

ACCESS POINT	ACCESS CODE	KEY
A	1 3 6 8	1 Paved Road
B	1 3 5 7	2 Unpaved Road
		3 Short Carry
		4 Long Carry
		5 Easy Grade
		6 Steep Grade
		7 Clear Trail
		8 Brush and Trees
		9 Private Property, Permission Needed
		10 Launching Fee Charged
		11 No Access—For Reference Only

MUD RIVER

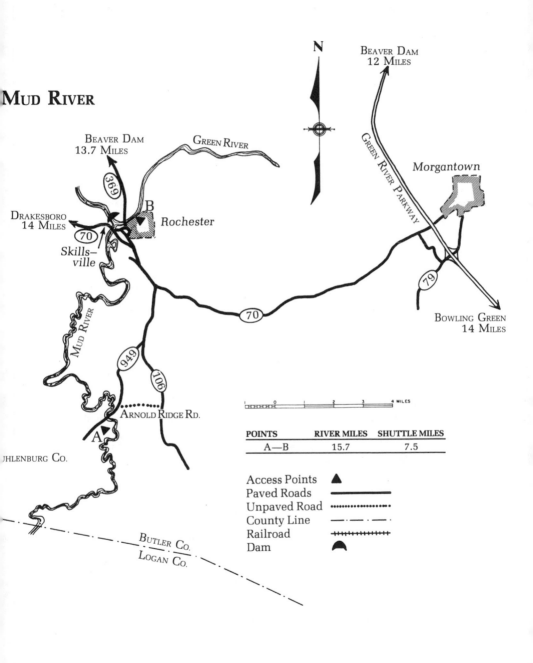

N

BEAVER DAM
12 MILES

BEAVER DAM
13.7 MILES

GREEN RIVER

Morgantown

369

B

Rochester

DRAKESBORO
14 MILES

70

Skills-
ville

GREEN RIVER PARKWAY

79

70

BOWLING GREEN
14 MILES

MUD RIVER

949

106

ARNOLD RIDGE RD.

A

MUHLENBURG CO.

BUTLER CO.

LOGAN CO.

| | | 0 | | 1 | | 2 | 3 | 4 MILES |

POINTS	RIVER MILES	SHUTTLE MILES
A—B	15.7	7.5

Access Points	▲
Paved Roads	▬▬▬▬
Unpaved Road	··············
County Line	—·—·—·
Railroad	++++++++++
Dam	◠

SECTION: Brownsville Dam to Lock No. 3 at Skillsville (Edmonson Co., Butler Co., Warren Co., Muhlenberg Co.)

USGS QUADS: Rhoda, Brownsville, Reedyville, Riverside, Morgantown, Flener, Cromwell, South Hill, Rochester

LEVEL OF DIFFICULTY International Class I   Numerical Points 5

SUITABLE FOR: Cruising   **GRADIENT** (feet per mile): 0.49

APPROPRIATE FOR: Families, Beginners, Intermediates, Advanced

VELOCITY (mph): 0-2.5 (2.6-5.0)   **AVERAGE WIDTH** (ft): 70-100

MONTHS RUNNABLE: All

RUNNABLE WATER LEVEL (cfs) Minimum 340
Maximum Up to flood stage

MEAN WATER TEMPERATURE ($°F$)

Jan. 45	Feb. 46	Mar. 50	Apr. 55	May 67	Jun. 76
Jul. 80	Aug. 79	Sep. 76	Oct. 66	Nov. 56	Dec. 46

SOURCE OF ADDITIONAL INFORMATION ON WATER CONDITIONS

Corps of Engineers (502) 273-3152

HAZARDS: Dams, powerboats

RESCUE INDEX: C-D
  A Extremely remote; evacuation only with expert help—6 hours to secure assistance
  B Remote; 3-6 hours to secure assistance
  C Accessible but difficult; up to 3 hours to secure assistance—evacuation difficult
  D Accessible; up to 1 hour to secure assistance, evacuation not difficult

Portages: Brownsville Dam, Lock Nos. 5 (Naker), and 3 (Skillsville)

SCOUTING: None required

INTEREST HIGHLIGHTS: Scenery, history, local culture and industry

SCENERY: Pretty to pretty in spots

ACCESS POINT	ACCESS CODE	KEY
Q	1 3 6 7	1 Paved Road
R	2 3 5 7	2 Unpaved Road
S	2 3 5 7	3 Short Carry
T	2 3 6 7	4 Long Carry
U	1 3 5 7	5 Easy Grade
V	1 3 5 7	6 Steep Grade
W	1 3 5 7	7 Clear Trail
X	2 3 5 7	8 Brush and Trees
Y	1 3 5 7	9 Private Property, Permission Needed
Z	1 3 5 7	10 Launching Fee Charged
AA	1 3 5 7	11 No Access—For Reference Only
BB	2 3 5 7	

GREEN RIVER—5

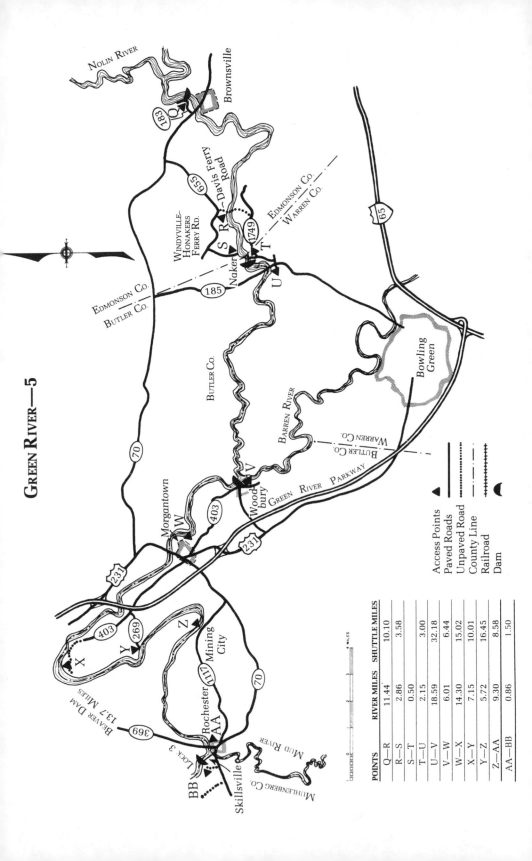

POINTS	RIVER MILES	SHUTTLE MILES
Q–R	11.44	10.10
R–S	2.86	3.58
S–T	0.50	3.00
T–U	2.15	32.18
U–V	18.59	6.44
V–W	6.01	15.02
W–X	14.30	10.01
X–Y	7.15	16.45
Y–Z	5.72	8.58
Z–AA	9.30	1.50
AA–BB	0.86	

Access Points ◄

Paved Roads ———

Unpaved Road ••••••

County Line —··—··—

Railroad ⊢⊢⊢⊢⊢

Dam ◖

SECTION: Rochester to the mouth of the Pond River (Muhlenberg Co., Ohio Co., McLean Co.)

USGS QUADS: Rochester, Paradise, Central City East, Central City West, Equality, Livermore, Glenville, Calhoun

LEVEL OF DIFFICULTY International Class I Numerical Points 5

SUITABLE FOR: Cruising **GRADIENT** (feet per mile): 0.42

APPROPRIATE FOR: Families, Beginners, Intermediates, Advanced

VELOCITY (mph): 0-2.5 (2.6-5.0) **AVERAGE WIDTH** (ft): 110-190

MONTHS RUNNABLE: All

RUNNABLE WATER LEVEL (cfs) Minimum 340
Maximum Up to flood stage

MEAN WATER TEMPERATURE (°F)

Jan. 45	Feb. 46	Mar. 50	Apr. 55	May 67	Jun. 76
Jul. 80	Aug. 79	Sep. 76	Oct. 66	Nov. 56	Dec. 46

SOURCE OF ADDITIONAL INFORMATION ON WATER CONDITIONS

Corps of Engineers, Lock 2 (502) 273-3152

HAZARDS: Powerboats

RESCUE INDEX: C-D
 A Extremely remote; evacuation only with expert help—6 hours to secure assistance
 B Remote; 3-6 hours to secure assistance
 C Accessible but difficult; up to 3 hours to secure assistance—evacuation difficult
 D Accessible; up to 1 hour to secure assistance, evacuation not difficult

PORTAGES: None required

SCOUTING: None required

INTEREST HIGHLIGHTS: Scenery, local culture and industry

SCENERY: Pretty to pretty in spots

ACCESS POINT	ACCESS CODE	KEY
AA	1 3 5 7	1 Paved Road
BB	2 3 5 7	2 Unpaved Road
CC	1 4 6 7	3 Short Carry
DD	2 4 6 7 9	4 Long Carry
EE	2 3 5 7 9	5 Easy Grade
FF	1 3 5 7	6 Steep Grade
GG	1 3 5 7 9	7 Clear Trail
HH	1 3 5 7	8 Brush and Trees
II	1 3 6 7	9 Private Property, Permission Needed
JJ	1 3 5 7	10 Launching Fee Charged
		11 No Access—For Reference Only

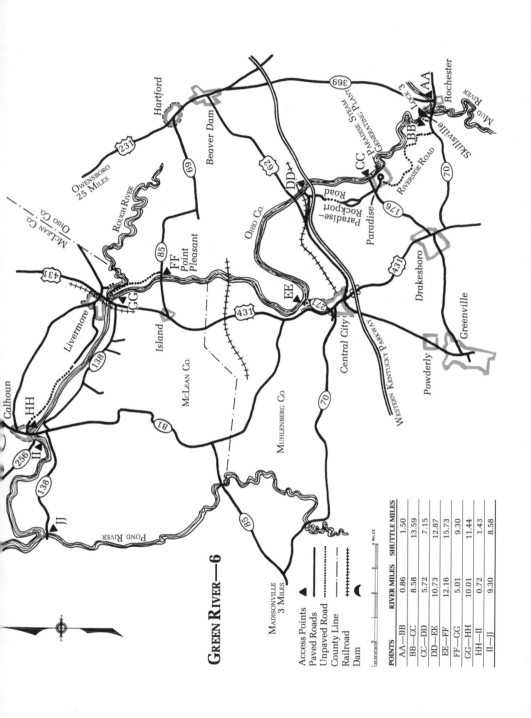

Green River—6

Access Points ▲
Paved Roads ———
Unpaved Road ·········
County Line —·—·—
Railroad ++++++
Dam ◖

POINTS	RIVER MILES	SHUTTLE MILES
AA—BB	0.86	1.50
BB—CC	8.58	13.59
CC—DD	5.72	7.15
DD—EE	10.73	12.87
EE—FF	12.16	15.73
FF—GG	5.01	9.30
GG—HH	10.01	11.44
HH—II	0.72	1.43
II—JJ	9.30	8.58

SECTION: Mouth of Pond River to the Ohio River (Hopkins Co., Webster Co., McLean Co., Henderson Co., Daviess Co.)

USGS QUADS: Calhoun, Beech Grove, Delaware, Curdsville, Reed, Spottsville, Newburgh

LEVEL OF DIFFICULTY International Class I   Numerical Points **4**

SUITABLE FOR: Cruising   **GRADIENT** (feet per mile): **0.40**

APPROPRIATE FOR: Families, Beginners, Intermediates, Advanced

VELOCITY (mph): 2.6-5.0   **AVERAGE WIDTH** (ft): 150-210

MONTHS RUNNABLE: All

RUNNABLE WATER LEVEL (cfs) Minimum **600**
Maximum Up to flood stage

MEAN WATER TEMPERATURE (°F)

Jan. 46	Feb. 46	Mar. 50	Apr. 55	May 68	Jun. 77
Jul. 80	Aug. 79	Sep. 76	Oct. 67	Nov. 56	Dec. 45

SOURCE OF ADDITIONAL INFORMATION ON WATER CONDITIONS

Corps of Engineers, Lock 2 (502) 273-3152

HAZARDS: Dams, powerboats

RESCUE INDEX: C-D
A Extremely remote; evacuation only with expert help—6 hours to secure assistance
B Remote; 3-6 hours to secure assistance
C Accessible but difficult; up to 3 hours to secure assistance—evacuation difficult
D Accessible; up to 1 hour to secure assistance, evacuation not difficult

PORTAGES: Lock Nos. 2(Rumsey), 1(Spottsville)

SCOUTING: None required

INTEREST HIGHLIGHTS: Scenery, history, local culture and industry

SCENERY: Pleasant in spots to pretty in spots

ACCESS POINT	ACCESS CODE	KEY
II	1 3 6 7	1 Paved Road
JJ	1 3 5 7	2 Unpaved Road
KK	1 3 5 7	3 Short Carry
LL	1 3 5 7	4 Long Carry
MM	1 3 5 7	5 Easy Grade
NN	2 3 6 7	6 Steep Grade
OO	2 3 5 7	7 Clear Trail
PP	1 3 5 7	8 Brush and Trees
QQ	2 3 5 7	9 Private Property, Permission Needed
		10 Launching Fee Charged
		11 No Access—For Reference Only

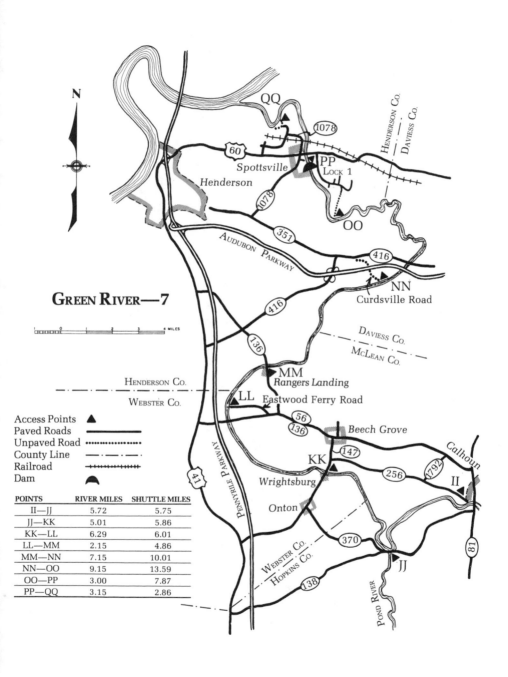

N

QQ

HENDERSON CO.
DAVIESS CO.

1078

60

PP
Spottsville   LOCK 1

Henderson

1078

351   OO

AUDUBON PARKWAY

416

NN
Curdsville Road

GREEN RIVER—7

416

136

DAVIESS CO.
McLEAN CO.

1 0 1 2 3 4 MILES

MM
Rangers Landing

HENDERSON CO.

LL   Eastwood Ferry Road

WEBSTER CO.

56
136

Beech Grove

147

Calhoun

Access Points ▲
Paved Roads
Unpaved Road ••••••••••••
County Line — • • — • •
Railroad +++++++++++
Dam

KK

256   1792

II

Wrightsburg

41

PENNYRILE PARKWAY

Onton

POINTS	RIVER MILES	SHUTTLE MILES
II—JJ	5.72	5.75
JJ—KK	5.01	5.86
KK—LL	6.29	6.01
LL—MM	2.15	4.86
MM—NN	7.15	10.01
NN—OO	9.15	13.59
OO—PP	3.00	7.87
PP—QQ	3.15	2.86

370

WEBSTER CO.
HOPKINS CO.

JJ

81

138

POND RIVER

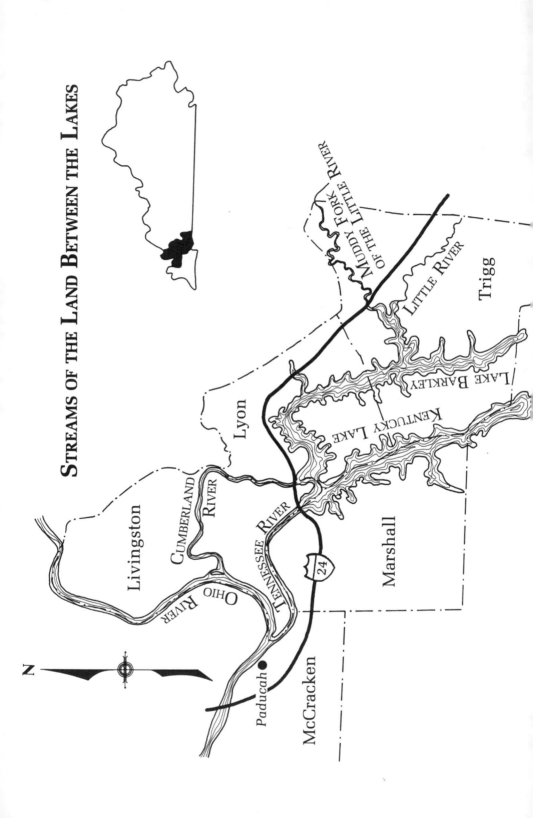

STREAMS OF THE LAND BETWEEN THE LAKES

8
STREAMS OF THE LAND BETWEEN THE LAKES

CUMBERLAND RIVER
NORTH OF LAKE BARKLEY

This section of the Cumberland River flows northwest from the tailwaters of Barkley Dam, through Livingston County, to the Ohio River. Of all the streams scouted in Western Kentucky, this is the only one on which I encountered other paddlers. Pleasant but decidedly unspectacular, the Cumberland River makes long, graceful curves through the hilly farmland east of Paducah. Trees, primarily willow, line the riverside but do not consistently obstruct the paddler's view of surrounding farms, small towns, and occasional businesses. The average width below the dam is 240 feet. Powerboats of all sizes are common. This section of the Cumberland is runnable all year. Access is good (although sometimes a little hard to find). The level of difficulty is Class I with no navigational dangers except powerboats.

TENNESSEE RIVER NORTH OF KENTUCKY LAKE

This 16-mile section of the Tennessee River flowing north along the southern boundary of Livingston County is all that is left of the beautiful Tennessee River in the state of Kentucky. Averaging 200 to 250 feet in width, this section of the Tennessee accommodates almost continuous commercial traffic. Scenery is similar to that of the Cumberland River below Barkley Dam (see above) except that the river valley here is somewhat deeper. Runnable all year, access is good where it exists. The level of difficulty is Class I with powercraft, particularly barges, constituting the major danger to paddlers.

MUDDY FORK OF THE LITTLE RIVER

The Muddy Fork of the Little River originates in western Christian County and flows west to drain northern Trigg County before emptying into Lake Barkley. The Muddy Fork (not to be confused with the Mud River) is in many ways an inviting, intimate stream. The banks are steep, profusely shaded with tall hardwoods, and, from time to time, exposed rock is visible at water's edge. Averaging 35 feet in width, the Muddy Fork can be run from late fall to mid-summer downstream of the John King bridge, and its proximity to Lake Barkley makes canoe camping possible. Scenery streamside consists of rolling farm- and woodland (which you cannot see except in winter because of the dense foliage along the banks). The level of difficulty is Class I throughout with deadfalls (and some flashflooding in the upper sections) being the only hazards to navigation. Steep banks make access fair to difficult.

LITTLE RIVER

The Little River originates in southern Christian County and flows north through Cadiz in Trigg County before emptying into Lake Barkley. A good canoe-camping run, the Little River is runnable below the KY 272 bridge to Cadiz (there is a boat ramp at the U.S. 68 bridge) from November to mid-July, and from Cadiz to Lake Barkley all year long. The upper section is winding and treelined with some giant, virgin timber. Terrain is hilly and rolling. The banks and bed are of mud with thick vegetation near the river's edge. Access is good. Some deadfalls, a fallen bridge, and a small one-foot) dam pose the only difficulties to navigation. From Cadiz downstream there is no current due to the backed-up lake pool. The river broadens from 45 feet in the upper stretches to 60 to 75 feet here. Surrounding hillsides are steeper with some exposed rock visible. There are no real hazards to navigation below Cadiz except an occasional gusty wind coming off the lake. Access is excellent, and runs on the Little River can readily be combined with trips of various length on Lake Barkley.

Elkhorn Creek   Photograph courtesy of the Commonwealth of Kentucky, Department of Public Information

SECTION: Barkley Dam to Ohio River (Livingston Co.)

USGS QUADS: Grand Rivers, Dycusburg, Burna, Smithland

LEVEL OF DIFFICULTY International Class I   Numerical Points 4

SUITABLE FOR: Cruising   **GRADIENT** (feet per mile): 0.36

APPROPRIATE FOR: Families, Beginners, Intermediates, Advanced

VELOCITY (mph): 0-2.5   **AVERAGE WIDTH** (ft): 220-230

MONTHS RUNNABLE: All

RUNNABLE WATER LEVEL (cfs) Minimum   N/A
   Maximum   N/A

MEAN WATER TEMPERATURE (°F)
   Jan. 45   Feb. 47   Mar. 50   Apr. 55   May 65   Jun. 77
   Jul. 80   Aug. 81   Sep. 72   Oct. 70   Nov. 53   Dec. 46

SOURCE OF ADDITIONAL INFORMATION ON WATER CONDITIONS
   Lake Barkley Power Plant and Dam (502) 362-8430

HAZARDS: Powerboats

RESCUE INDEX: D
   A Extremely remote; evacuation only with expert help—6 hours to secure assistance
   B Remote; 3-6 hours to secure assistance
   C Accessible but difficult; up to 3 hours to secure assistance—evacuation difficult
   D Accessible; up to 1 hour to secure assistance, evacuation not difficult

PORTAGES: None required

SCOUTING: None required

INTEREST HIGHLIGHTS: Scenery, local culture and industry

SCENERY: Pleasant to pretty in spots

ACCESS POINT	ACCESS CODE	KEY
A	1 3 5 7	1 Paved Road
B	2 3 5 7	2 Unpaved Road
C	1 3 5 7	3 Short Carry
D	2 3 5 8	4 Long Carry
		5 Easy Grade
		6 Steep Grade
		7 Clear Trail
		8 Brush and Trees
		9 Private Property, Permission Needed
		10 Launching Fee Charged
		11 No Access—For Reference Only

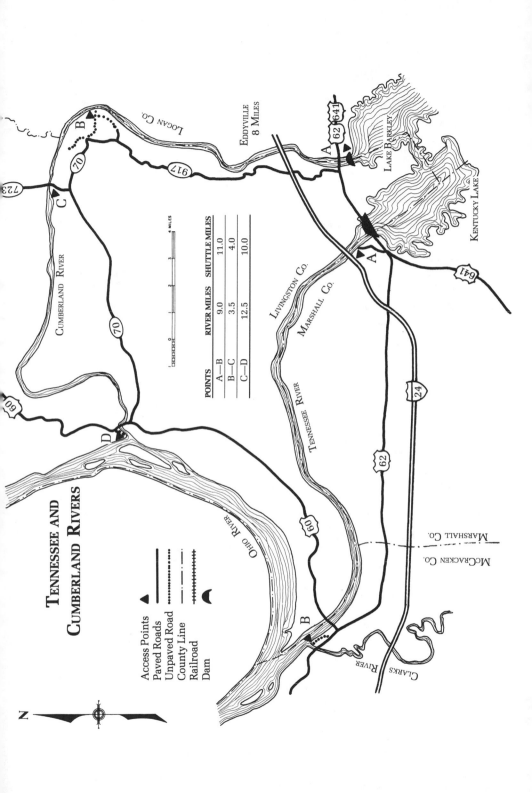

TENNESSEE AND
CUMBERLAND RIVERS

Access Points
Paved Roads
Unpaved Road
County Line
Railroad
Dam

POINTS	RIVER MILES	SHUTTLE MILES
A–B	9.0	11.0
B–C	3.5	4.0
C–D	12.5	10.0

CUMBERLAND RIVER

LOGAN CO.

EDDYVILLE
8 MILES

LAKE BARKLEY

KENTUCKY LAKE

LIVINGSTON CO.

MARSHALL CO.

TENNESSEE RIVER

OHIO RIVER

McCRACKEN CO.
MARSHALL CO.

CLARKS RIVER

N

0   1   2   3   4 MILES

SECTION: Dam to mouth of Clarks River (Marshall Co., McCracken Co.)

USGS QUADS: Calvert City, Little Cypress, Paducah East

LEVEL OF DIFFICULTY International Class I   Numerical Points **5**

SUITABLE FOR: Cruising   **GRADIENT** (feet per mile): 0.27

APPROPRIATE FOR: Beginners, Intermediates, Advanced

VELOCITY (mph): 0-2.5   **AVERAGE WIDTH** (ft): 220-340

MONTHS RUNNABLE: All

RUNNABLE WATER LEVEL (cfs) Minimum N/A
Maximum N/A

MEAN WATER TEMPERATURE (°F)

Jan. 45	Feb. 48	Mar. 50	Apr. 56	May 65	Jun. 76
Jul. 81	Aug. 81	Sep. 73	Oct. 69	Nov. 53	Dec. 46

SOURCE OF ADDITIONAL INFORMATION ON WATER CONDITIONS
Kentucky Lake Locks (502) 362-4221

HAZARDS: Powerboats

RESCUE INDEX: C
A Extremely remote; evacuation only with expert help—6 hours to secure assistance
B Remote; 3-6 hours to secure assistance
C Accessible but difficult; up to 3 hours to secure assistance—evacuation difficult
D Accessible; up to 1 hour to secure assistance, evacuation not difficult

PORTAGES: None required

SCOUTING: None required

INTEREST HIGHLIGHTS: Scenery, local culture and industry

SCENERY: Pleasant to pleasant in spots

ACCESS POINT	ACCESS CODE	KEY
A	1 3 5 7	1 Paved Road
B *	1 3 5 7	2 Unpaved Road
		3 Short Carry
		4 Long Carry
		5 Easy Grade
		6 Steep Grade
		7 Clear Trail
		8 Brush and Trees
		9 Private Property, Permission Needed
		10 Launching Fee Charged
		11 No Access—For Reference Only

*Take-out at boat ramp on Clarks River in Paducah

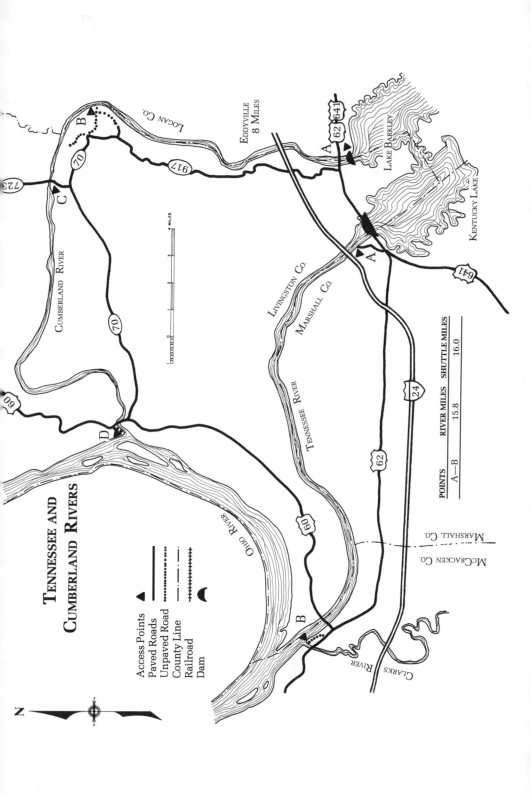

TENNESSEE AND
CUMBERLAND RIVERS

N

Access Points ▲
Paved Roads
Unpaved Road ••••••
County Line —·—·—
Railroad ++++++
Dam ◗

Ohio River

Cumberland River

Tennessee River

Clarks River

Livingston Co.

Marshall Co.

McCracken Co.

Marshall Co.

Lake Barkley

Kentucky Lake

Logan Co.

Eddyville
8 Miles

4 MILES

POINTS	RIVER MILES	SHUTTLE MILES
A – B	15.8	16.0

60
70
917
723
62
641
641
24
62
60

SECTION: John King Rd. bridge to Lake Barkley (Trigg Co.)

USGS QUADS: Cobb, Cadiz, Lamasco, Canton

LEVEL OF DIFFICULTY International Class I+ Numerical Points 6

SUITABLE FOR: Cruising, camping **GRADIENT** (feet per mile): 0.69

APPROPRIATE FOR: Beginners, Intermediates, Advanced

VELOCITY (mph): 0-5.0 **AVERAGE WIDTH** (ft): 35-50

MONTHS RUNNABLE: Late fall to mid-summer

RUNNABLE WATER LEVEL (cfs) Minimum 160
  Maximum Up to flood stage

MEAN WATER TEMPERATURE (°F)
Jan. 46	Feb. 47	Mar. 47	Apr. 55	May 64	Jun. 73
Jul. 75	Aug. 74	Sep. 72	Oct. 62	Nov. 54	Dec. 43

SOURCE OF ADDITIONAL INFORMATION ON WATER CONDITIONS
  Cadiz Police Dept. (502) 522-3305

HAZARDS: Deadfalls, low trees, flash floods

RESCUE INDEX: C
  A Extremely remote; evacuation only with expert help—6 hours to secure assistance
  B Remote; 3-6 hours to secure assistance
  C Accessible but difficult; up to 3 hours to secure assistance—evacuation difficult
  D Accessible; up to 1 hour to secure assistance, evacuation not difficult

PORTAGES: Around deadfalls

SCOUTING: None required

INTEREST HIGHLIGHTS: Scenery

SCENERY: Pretty to pretty in spots

ACCESS POINT	ACCESS CODE	KEY
AA	1 3 6 7	1 Paved Road
BB	1 3 6 8	2 Unpaved Road
CC	1 3 6 8	3 Short Carry
C	1 3 5 7	4 Long Carry
D	1 3 5 7	5 Easy Grade
E	1 3 5 7	6 Steep Grade
		7 Clear Trail
		8 Brush and Trees
		9 Private Property, Permission Needed
		10 Launching Fee Charged
		11 No Access—For Reference Only

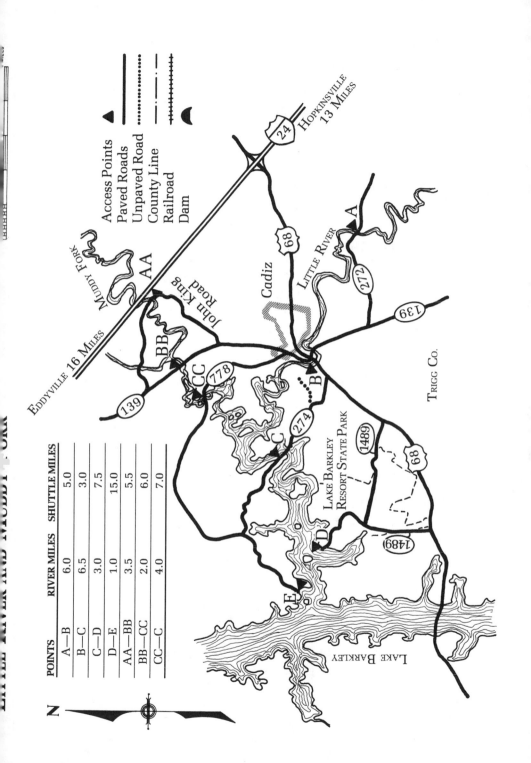

LITTLE RIVER AND MUDDY FORK

POINTS	RIVER MILES	SHUTTLE MILES
A—B	6.0	5.0
B—C	6.5	3.0
C—D	3.0	7.5
D—E	1.0	15.0
AA—BB	3.5	5.5
BB—CC	2.0	6.0
CC—C	4.0	7.0

Access Points
Paved Roads
Unpaved Road
County Line
Railroad
Dam

EDDYVILLE 16 MILES

MUDDY FORK

AA

John King Road

BB

CC

139

778

Cadiz

68

LITTLE RIVER

272

139

TRIGG CO.

24

HOPKINSVILLE 13 MILES

B

274

C

1489

68

LAKE BARKLEY RESORT STATE PARK

1489

D

E

LAKE BARKLEY

N

SECTION: KY 272 to Lake Barkley (Trigg Co.)

USGS QUADS: Roaring Spring, Caledonia, Cadiz, Cobb, Lamasco, Canton

LEVEL OF DIFFICULTY International Class I+   Numerical Points   7

SUITABLE FOR: Cruising, camping **GRADIENT** (feet per mile):   0.98

APPROPRIATE FOR: Families, Beginners, Intermediates, Advanced

VELOCITY (mph):   0-5.0   **AVERAGE WIDTH** (ft):   55-70

MONTHS RUNNABLE: November to mid-July*; all†

RUNNABLE WATER LEVEL (cfs) Minimum   200
   Maximum   Up to flood stage

MEAN WATER TEMPERATURE ($^\circ$F)
Jan. 46	Feb. 46	Mar. 47	Apr. 54	May 64	Jun. 73
Jul. 74	Aug. 74	Sep. 71	Oct. 62	Nov. 54	Dec. 44

SOURCE OF ADDITIONAL INFORMATION ON WATER CONDITIONS

Cadiz Police Dept. (502)   522-3305

HAZARDS: Dams, deadfalls, powerboats below Cadiz

RESCUE INDEX: C
   A Extremely remote; evacuation only with expert help—6 hours to secure assistance
   B Remote; 3-6 hours to secure assistance
   C Accessible but difficult; up to 3 hours to secure assistance—evacuation difficult
   D Accessible; up to 1 hour to secure assistance, evacuation not difficult

PORTAGES: Deadfalls and small dam 1 mile below KY 272 bridge

SCOUTING: None required

INTEREST HIGHLIGHTS: Scenery

SCENERY: Pretty to beautiful in spots

ACCESS POINT	ACCESS CODE	KEY
A	1 3 6 7	1 Paved Road
B	1 3 5 7	2 Unpaved Road
C	1 3 5 7	3 Short Carry
D	1 3 5 7	4 Long Carry
E	1 3 5 7	5 Easy Grade
		6 Steep Grade
		7 Clear Trail
		8 Brush and Trees
		9 Private Property, Permission Needed
		10 Launching Fee Charged
		11 No Access—For Reference Only

*KY 272 to Cadiz
†Cadiz to Lake Barkley

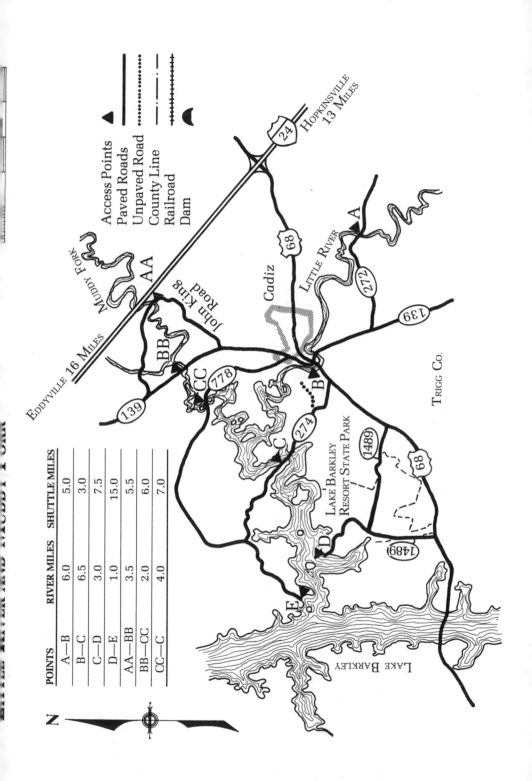

N

POINTS	**RIVER MILES**	**SHUTTLE MILES**
A–B	6.0	5.0
B–C	6.5	3.0
C–D	3.0	7.5
D–E	1.0	15.0
AA–BB	3.5	5.5
BB–CC	2.0	6.0
CC–C	4.0	7.0

Access Points
Paved Roads
Unpaved Road
County Line
Railroad
Dam

Eddyville 16 Miles

Muddy Fork

John King Road

AA

BB

CC

778

139

Cadiz

274

C

D

E

Lake Barkley Resort State Park

1489

1489

68

Lake Barkley

24

Hopkinsville 13 Miles

68

Little River

A

272

139

Trigg Co.

B

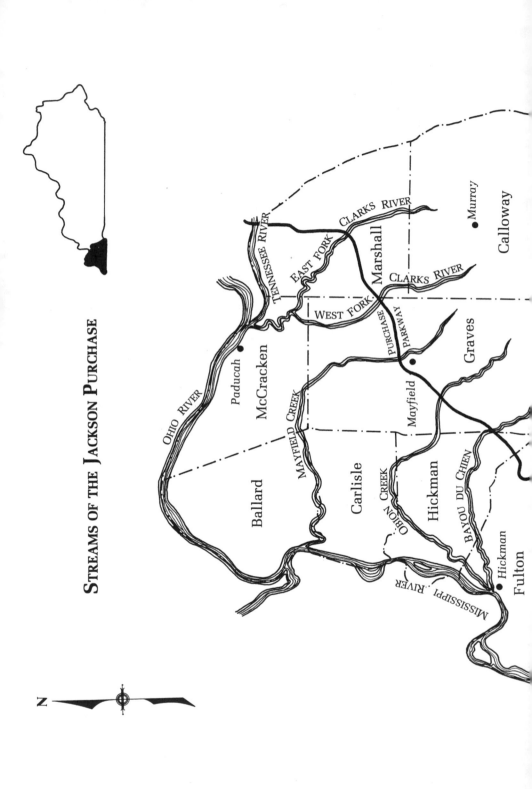

STREAMS OF THE JACKSON PURCHASE

9

STREAMS OF THE JACKSON PURCHASE

BAYOU DU CHIEN

The Bayou du Chien is a diminutive, willow- and cypress-canopied stream that flows west out of Graves County draining southern Hickman and northern Fulton counties before emptying into the Mississippi River. Although artificially channelled (dredged) at one time, nature has fought back over the years to reoccupy the banks with vegetation. The result is a beautiful, almost primeval little bayou that has a generally unobstructed, navigable channel. Bayou du Chien runs over a mud bottom within the confines of five-foot banks through flat farmland. At high water, the Bayou broadens from its normal 30 feet to more than a half mile in certain places creating an immense, lowland swamp and making it difficult to stay on course. Runnable downstream of the KY 307 bridge from late fall through June, access is generally good. The level of difficulty is Class I. Dangers consist of numerous deadfalls, droves of mosquitoes, and the possibility of getting lost at higher water. The most scenic section of Bayou du Chien lies between KY 307 and KY 239. In this section particularly, wildlife abounds.

OBION CREEK

Obion Creek drains the south central portion of the Jackson Purchase area in far Western Kentucky. Originating at the bottom of Graves County, the creek flows over a mud bottom into Hickman and Carlisle Counties before heading southwest to empty into the Mississippi River. Averaging 30 feet in width, Obion

Creek is a dense tangle of cypress trees and deadfalls. Recommended only to those adventurous souls who don't mind paddling in a cloud of mosquitoes or portaging every 200 feet, Obion Creek offers the utmost in flatwater paddling hardship. Banks are from five to eight feet high and broaden onto wide, flat floodplains forested with oak and hickory trees. The creek itself is dense with scrub vegetation and almost completely overhung with trees, primarily willows. Obion Creek is runnable (has sufficient water) from U.S. 51 to its mouth from November to mid-June. Access is difficult at best. Deadfalls and flashflooding present the greatest hazards to navigation.

MAYFIELD CREEK

Mayfield Creek originates in Calloway County and flows northwest through Graves and McCracken counties before becoming the Ballard–Carlisle county line and emptying into the Mississippi River south of Cairo, Illinois. Only runnable north of the city of Mayfield, the creek is distinguished by the purity of its water and the abundance of wildlife along its banks. Flowing through flat farmland, over a sand and clay bottom, beneath steep ten-foot banks, Mayfield Creek is serenely enclosed by cypress, willow, and sycamore trees, and by thick scrub vegetation. The level of difficulty is Class I throughout, but sandbars and the twisting nature of the stream make paddling interesting. Averaging 35 to 55 feet in width, the creek can be run from just east of Hickory (north of Mayfield) downstream from late fall to early summer. Access is generally good. Dangers consist of deadfalls, beaver dams, and flashflooding that turns the floodplain into a large swamp. Paddlers who may canoe the Mayfield during hunting season are advised to wear bright clothing and to attach an orange bicycle flag (on a pole) to the bow of the boat since the area is a perennial favorite of hunters. Recommended paddling sections are from east of Hickory to U.S. 62. West of U.S. 62 access is more difficult and the stream not nearly as pristine or beautiful.

CLARKS RIVER

The Clarks River drains Marshall, Graves, and McCracken counties southeast of Paducah. Except for the three or four miles near Paducah, upstream of its mouth at the Tennessee River, the Clarks River is beautiful and engaging. Wildlife, particularly beaver, raccoon, deer, and (during the fall) duck, abounds. If you cruise the river at night, beaver will follow your canoe slapping their tails on the water to scare you away. Running through flat farm- and woodland (and through what, during the rainy season, is swamp), the river flows between steep mud banks crowded with cypress, sycamore, willow, maple, and scrub vegetation. The stream is exceptionally winding and continually loops back on itself. Ox-bow lakes are common and are worth visiting to observe the wildlife. The Clarks River is runnable downstream of the bridge on the Sharpe–Elva Road on the East Fork, to its mouth at the Tennessee River from mid-fall to early summer. The West Fork of the Clarks River is not runnable. The Clarks' average width is 35 to 45 feet on the East Fork and 60 feet below the confluence of the two forks. The level of difficulty is Class I with deadfalls and seasonal flooding posing the major dangers. On the East Fork especially, it is very easy to get lost when the river has overflowed the adjoining floodplain. Current in the upper sections is unexpectedly swift for a low-gradient stream of Western Kentucky, but it halts abruptly about six miles upstream of the mouth where the backwater of the Tennessee River begins. In this same section, some powerboats are encountered and the stream sacrifices much of its attractiveness as it approaches Paducah. Scrub vegetation, insects, and streamside private property limit canoe-camping possibilities. Access is good, but many of the access roads are dirt and gravel and are unmarked.

SECTION: KY 1283 to mouth (Hickman Co., Fulton Co.)

USGS QUADS: Water Valley, Crutchfield, Clinton, Cayce, Hickman

LEVEL OF DIFFICULTY International Class I   Numerical Points **4**

SUITABLE FOR: Cruising   **GRADIENT** (feet per mile): 2.72

APPROPRIATE FOR: Families, Beginners, Intermediates, Advanced

VELOCITY (mph): 0-2.5   **AVERAGE WIDTH** (ft): 20-35

MONTHS RUNNABLE: November to June

RUNNABLE WATER LEVEL (cfs) Minimum **100**
Maximum   N/A

MEAN WATER TEMPERATURE (°F)
Jan.	45	Feb.	44	Mar.	47	Apr.	56	May	66	Jun.	74
Jul.	77	Aug.	75	Sep.	73	Oct.	63	Nov.	53	Dec.	46

SOURCE OF ADDITIONAL INFORMATION ON WATER CONDITIONS
Hickman Police Dept. (502) 236-2529

HAZARDS: Deadfalls, low trees, flash floods

RESCUE INDEX: C
A Extremely remote; evacuation only with expert help—6 hours to secure assistance
B Remote; 3-6 hours to secure assistance
C Accessible but difficult; up to 3 hours to secure assistance—evacuation difficult
D Accessible; up to 1 hour to secure assistance, evacuation not difficult

PORTAGES: Around deadfalls

SCOUTING: None required

INTEREST HIGHLIGHTS: Scenery, wildlife

SCENERY: Pretty to beautiful in spots

ACCESS POINT	ACCESS CODE	KEY
A	1 3 5 8	1 Paved Road
B	1 3 5 8	2 Unpaved Road
C	1 3 6 8	3 Short Carry
D	2 3 5 8	4 Long Carry
E	1 3 5 8	5 Easy Grade
F	1 3 5 8	6 Steep Grade
		7 Clear Trail
		8 Brush and Trees
		9 Private Property, Permission Needed
		10 Launching Fee Charged
		11 No Access—For Reference Only

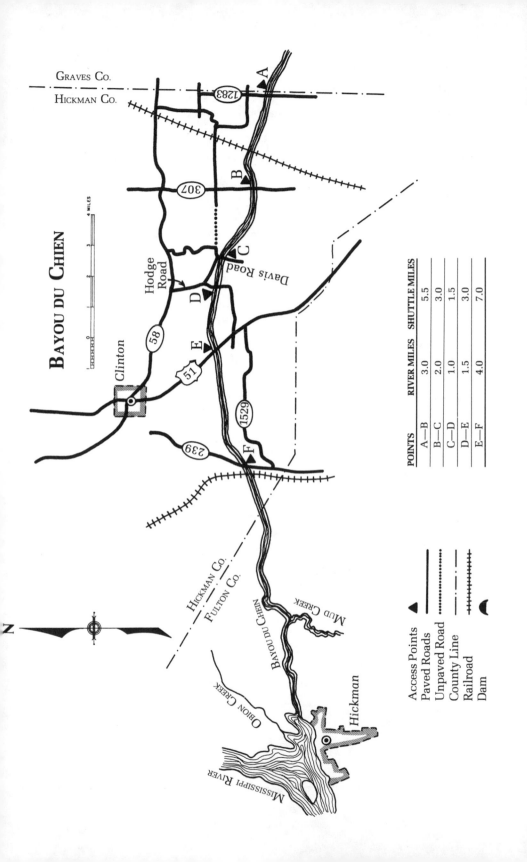

Bayou du Chien

4 MILES

POINTS	RIVER MILES	SHUTTLE MILES
A—B	3.0	5.5
B—C	2.0	3.0
C—D	1.0	1.5
D—E	1.5	3.0
E—F	4.0	7.0

Access Points
Paved Roads
Unpaved Road
County Line
Railroad
Dam

Graves Co.
Hickman Co.

Hodge Road

Davis Road

Clinton

Hickman Co.
Fulton Co.

Bayou du Chien

Mud Creek

Obion Creek

Mississippi River

Hickman

N

SECTION: U.S. 51 to mouth (Hickman Co., Fulton Co.)

USGS QUADS: Oakton, Wolf Island, Hickman

LEVEL OF DIFFICULTY International Class I   Numerical Points 7

SUITABLE FOR: Cruising   **GRADIENT** (feet per mile): 2.48

APPROPRIATE FOR: Intermediates, Advanced

VELOCITY (mph): 0-2.5   **AVERAGE WIDTH** (ft): 25-40

MONTHS RUNNABLE: November to mid-June

RUNNABLE WATER LEVEL (cfs) Minimum   125
Maximum N/A

MEAN WATER TEMPERATURE (°F)

Jan. 45	Feb. 43	Mar. 47	Apr. 57	May 66	Jun. 75
Jul. 77	Aug. 76	Sep. 73	Oct. 61	Nov. 52	Dec. 45

SOURCE OF ADDITIONAL INFORMATION ON WATER CONDITIONS
Hickman Police Dept. (502) 236-2529

HAZARDS: Deadfalls, low trees, flash floods

RESCUE INDEX: C
A Extremely remote; evacuation only with expert help—6 hours to secure assistance
B Remote; 3-6 hours to secure assistance
C Accessible but difficult; up to 3 hours to secure assistance—evacuation difficult
D Accessible; up to 1 hour to secure assistance, evacuation not difficult

PORTAGES: Countless logjams and deadfalls

SCOUTING: None required

INTEREST HIGHLIGHTS: Wildlife

SCENERY: Uninspiring

ACCESS POINT	ACCESS CODE	KEY
A	1 3 6 8	1 Paved Road
B	1 3 6 8	2 Unpaved Road
C	1 3 6 8	3 Short Carry
D	2 3 6 8	4 Long Carry
		5 Easy Grade
		6 Steep Grade
		7 Clear Trail
		8 Brush and Trees
		9 Private Property, Permission Needed
		10 Launching Fee Charged
		11 No Access—For Reference Only

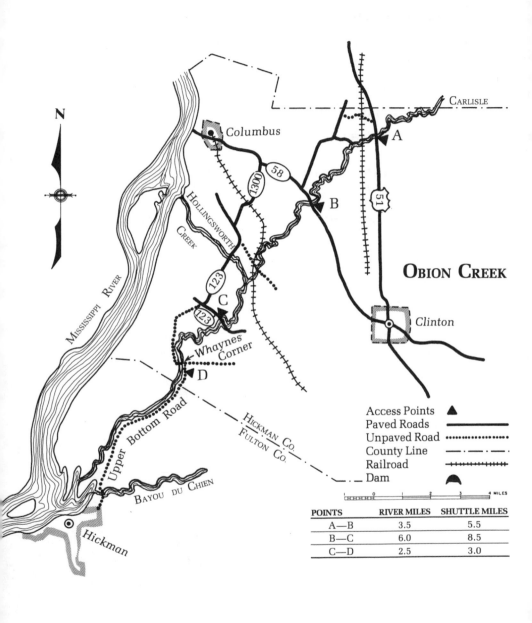

N

CARLISLE

Columbus

1300

58

A

B

51

OBION CREEK

Clinton

HOLLINGSWORTH CREEK

MISSISSIPPI RIVER

123

C

123

Whaynes Corner

D

Upper Bottom Road

HICKMAN CO.
FULTON CO.

BAYOU DU CHIEN

Hickman

Access Points	▲
Paved Roads	——
Unpaved Road	••••••
County Line	—·—·—
Railroad	++++++
Dam	⌒

4 MILES
0   2   3   4 MILES

POINTS	RIVER MILES	SHUTTLE MILES
A—B	3.5	5.5
B—C	6.0	8.5
C—D	2.5	3.0

SECTION: East of Hickory to KY 121 (Graves Co., Carlisle Co., McCracken Co.)

USGS QUADS: Westplains, Hickory, Melber, Lovelaceville, Blandville, Wickcliffe

LEVEL OF DIFFICULTY International Class I   Numerical Points 6

SUITABLE FOR: Cruising   **GRADIENT** (feet per mile): 3.75

APPROPRIATE FOR: Beginners, Intermediates, Advanced

VELOCITY (mph): 0-2.5   **AVERAGE WIDTH** (ft): 40-60

MONTHS RUNNABLE: Late fall to early summer

RUNNABLE WATER LEVEL (cfs) Minimum 160
Maximum N/A

MEAN WATER TEMPERATURE (°F)

Jan. 44	Feb. 43	Mar. 47	Apr. 56	May 65	Jun. 73
Jul. 76	Aug. 76	Sep. 74	Oct. 61	Nov. 53	Dec. 44

SOURCE OF ADDITIONAL INFORMATION ON WATER CONDITIONS
Mayfield City Hall (502) 247-1971

HAZARDS: Deadfalls, low trees, flash floods

RESCUE INDEX: C
A Extremely remote; evacuation only with expert help—6 hours to secure assistance
B Remote; 3-6 hours to secure assistance
C Accessible but difficult; up to 3 hours to secure assistance—evacuation difficult
D Accessible; up to 1 hour to secure assistance, evacuation not difficult

PORTAGES: Around deadfalls

SCOUTING: None required

INTEREST HIGHLIGHTS: Scenery, wildlife

SCENERY: Pretty to beautiful in spots

ACCESS POINT	ACCESS CODE	KEY
A	2 3 6 7	1 Paved Road
B	1 3 6 8	2 Unpaved Road
C	1 3 6 8	3 Short Carry
D	1 3 6 8	4 Long Carry
E	1 3 6 7	5 Easy Grade
F	1 3 6 8	6 Steep Grade
G	1 3 6 8	7 Clear Trail
		8 Brush and Trees
		9 Private Property, Permission Needed
		10 Launching Fee Charged
		11 No Access—For Reference Only

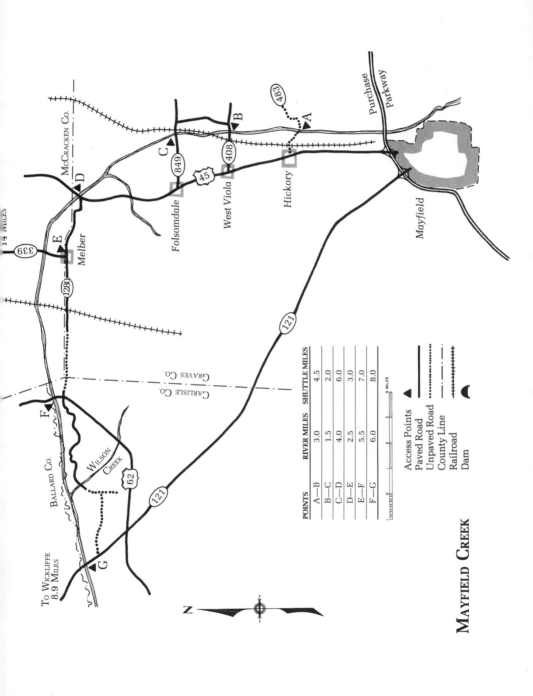

POINTS	RIVER MILES	SHUTTLE MILES
A—B	3.0	4.5
B—C	1.5	2.0
C—D	4.0	6.0
D—E	2.5	3.0
E—F	5.5	7.0
F—G	6.0	8.0

▲ Access Points

•••••• Paved Road

•••••• Unpaved Road

—•—•— County Line

+++++ Railroad

◖ Dam

MAYFIELD CREEK

SECTION: East Fork on Sharpe-Elva Rd. to mouth of Clarks River
(Marshall Co.. McCracken Co., Graves Co.)
USGS QUADS: Elva, Symsonia, Paducah East

LEVEL OF DIFFICULTY International Class I   Numerical Points 5

SUITABLE FOR: Cruising   **GRADIENT** (feet per mile): 1.27

APPROPRIATE FOR: Beginners, Intermediates, Advanced

VELOCITY (mph): 0-2.5   **AVERAGE WIDTH** (ft): 30-65

MONTHS RUNNABLE: Mid-fall to early summer

RUNNABLE WATER LEVEL (cfs) Minimum 150 (E. fork); 165 (Below fork)
Maximum N/A

MEAN WATER TEMPERATURE (°F)

Jan. 45	Feb. 44	Mar. 47	Apr. 54	May 64	Jun. 73
Jul. 75	Aug. 74	Sep. 71	Oct. 63	Nov. 52	Dec. 44

SOURCE OF ADDITIONAL INFORMATION ON WATER CONDITIONS
U.S. Coast Guard (502) 442-1621

HAZARDS: Deadfalls, low trees, flash floods, power boats*

RESCUE INDEX: C
A Extremely remote; evacuation only with expert help—6 hours to secure assistance
B Remote; 3-6 hours to secure assistance
C Accessible but difficult; up to 3 hours to secure assistance—evacuation difficult
D Accessible; up to 1 hour to secure assistance, evacuation not difficult

PORTAGES: Around deadfalls

SCOUTING: None required

INTEREST HIGHLIGHTS: Scenery, wildlife

SCENERY: Pretty to beautiful in spots

ACCESS POINT	ACCESS CODE	KEY
A	2 3 6 7	1 Paved Road
B	1 4 5 8 9	2 Unpaved Road
C	1 3 5 7	3 Short Carry
D	1 3 5 7	4 Long Carry
		5 Easy Grade
		6 Steep Grade
		7 Clear Trail
		8 Brush and Trees
		9 Private Property, Permission Needed
		10 Launching Fee Charged
		11 No Access—For Reference Only

*Near Paducah

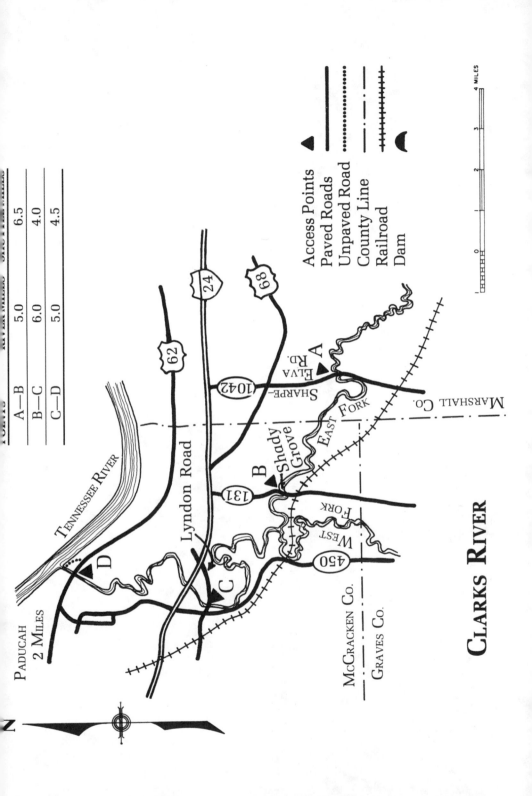

POINTS	RIVER MILES	...
A—B	5.0	6.5
B—C	6.0	4.0
C—D	5.0	4.5

Access Points
Paved Roads
Unpaved Road
County Line
Railroad
Dam

0   1   2   3   4 MILES

TENNESSEE RIVER

62

24

68

1042

SHARPE-ELVA RD.

A

131

Shady Grove

EAST FORK

B

MARSHALL CO.

Lyndon Road

WEST FORK

450

C

D

PADUCAH
2 MILES

McCRACKEN CO.

GRAVES CO.

CLARKS RIVER

N

10
Special Mention

BALLARD WILDLIFE MANAGEMENT AREA

Located in Ballard County in the far northwestern corner of the state along the Ohio River, the Ballard Wildlife Management Area (BWMA) is easily one of the most unusual water resources in the state of Kentucky. Consisting of more than fifteen oxbow lakes and cypress bogs, the refuge–hunting area is home to countless deer, beaver, waterfowl, songbirds, and reptiles. Captivating in its primeval beauty, sometimes ghostly and mysterious with imposing cypress standing guard over a watery carpet of lotus, the BWMA is always alive, always alluring. For the paddler whose canoe allows exploring without restriction, the lakes of the BWMA offer unparalleled serenity and an opportunity to observe firsthand myriad forms of bird, animal, and fish life. Several well-kept, primitive camping areas designated within the BWMA serve as base camps from which the refuge can be explored. Lakes and bogs are generally separated by only a few hundred feet so that portaging from one lake to another is not difficult. All paddling is on lakes with no moving current, and motorboat traffic is light, with BWMA regulations forbidding the use of all but silent electric motors. There are no hazards to navigation. Insects and mosquitoes represent the only potential nuisance.

RED RIVER OF LOGAN COUNTY

Kentucky has two Red Rivers. This Red River is the north fork of the Red River of Tennessee, originating in Simpson County (KY) and flowing west along the Kentucky–Tennessee border through Logan County. Runnable below Prices Mill from early November through mid-June, the Red River meanders through flat and rolling farm country and woodland. The riverbed is of rock, sand, and clay with lushly vegetated banks of varying steepness. The stream is very tranquil, with a slow current and several varieties of trees (including sycamores) shading the water. Access is easy at the KY 591 bridge west of Adairville and also at the TN 161 bridge south of Keysburg. At the KY 591 bridge at Prices Mill, however, access is extremely difficult and permission should be secured from the landowner on the southern (downstream) side of the bridge to put in. The Red River averages 60 to 70 feet in width with no obstructions other than an infrequent deadfall.

OTTER CREEK OF MEADE COUNTY

Otter Creek is a direct tributary of the Ohio River that originates in Hardin County and flows north draining the eastern portion of Meade County. Averaging 30 to 45 feet in width, Otter Creek is a delightful Class-II whitewater run during the winter and spring and following heavy rains. Runnable downstream of the dam near the U.S. 60 bridge on the Fort Knox Military Reservation, the stream bounces along with an abundance of standing waves and small drops. Its gradient is good and the current very swift. Strainers abound and constitute the primary paddling hazard. At the put-in for the upper section (U.S. 60 to KY 1638) is a dam with a 45-degree incline that can be safely run on the left (this may be the fastest you will ever go in a canoe).* Scenery is pleasant with exposed rock ledges and wooded hills (you may even see an army tank).

HARRODS CREEK OF
OLDHAM AND JEFFERSON COUNTIES

Harrods Creek originates in western Henry County and flows southwest through Oldham and Jefferson Counties before emptying into the Ohio River in northeastern Louisville. Runnable from late November to early May downstream of KY 53 (and all year between the bridge at KY 329 and the Ohio River), Harrods Creek is a pleasant Class-I (-II) run that winds between large boulders at the bottom of an intimate, wooded gorge. In spite of its proximity to Louisville, the creek is incredibly secluded and almost pristine in its rugged setting. Rapids never exceed an easy Class II in difficulty (and most wash out at very high water), and dangers are

*This is the one dam out of a thousand that can be safely run. Inclusion of this exception in this guide should not be construed as a contradiction to the general rule of safety that dams and weirs should be portaged.

limited to an occasional deadfall. Access is excellent. After heavy rains there is sometimes sufficient water to paddle Harrods Creek above KY 53. This is neither practicable nor safe, however, due to numerous cattle gates (fences) crossing the stream.

LITTLE KENTUCKY RIVER

The Little Kentucky River originates in Henry County and flows northeast draining portions of Trimble and Carroll counties before emptying into the Ohio River near Carrollton. Treelined, with a rock and mud bottom and banks of varying steepness averaging five feet in height, the Little Kentucky is runnable downstream of KY 157 from mid-November to late April or early May. The most popular section, between Sulphur and U.S. 421, is a bouncy, Class-II, whitewater run when the water is up. Scenery is pleasant with rolling grazingland flanking the stream and some occasional exposed rock cliffs. Dangers to paddlers include numerous deadfalls, a dam (at access point B) that must be portaged, and cattle gates. Access is good for the section recommended.

BIG SOUTH FORK GORGE
OF THE CUMBERLAND RIVER

The Big South Fork Gorge is part of the headwaters of the Big South Fork of the Cumberland River. Although situated entirely in Tennessee, it is worth including in this guide since it is far and away the most popular whitewater run enjoyed by advanced Kentucky paddlers. Consisting of almost continuous Class-III (and IV?) whitewater, the run begins on the Clear Fork (which combines with New River of Tennessee to form the Big South Fork of the Cumberland River) about twelve miles southwest of Oneida and ends at Leatherwood Ford west of Oneida. In all there are thirteen major rapids and several dozen smaller ones. Considered by many to be a decked-boat river, the Big South Fork Gorge has been run successfully on several occasions by both solo and tandem open boaters. The nature of the run varies incredibly with water level, being extremely technical at lower water and big and pushy (much like the New River Gorge in West Virginia) when flowing high. At moderate levels the paddler gets a taste of both worlds with quick, technical water on the Clear Fork and bigger, less technical water below the confluence (of the Clear Fork and the New River). Scenery is magnificent, when you have time to notice it, with boulders lining the banks and canyon walls rising on both sides. For a Class-III (-IV) river, the Big South Fork Gorge is surprisingly free of dangers; deadfalls and logjams are infrequent and the holes are washouts at almost all levels. The drops, however, are huge (several exceeding four feet), and helmets are a must for all paddlers. Also, some of the rapids are extremely long, making rescue difficult (especially at higher water levels). Extra flotation is essential for open canoes and a good roll is definitely recommended for decked boaters. Access at the river is good at both put-in and take-out, but connecting roads are sometimes muddy and slippery. The Big South Fork Gorge is runnable from late fall to mid-May in years of average rainfall.

Big South Fork Gorge of the Cumberland River   Photograph by Dave Moccia

SECTION: Ballard Co.

USGS QUADS: Olmstead, Barlow

LEVEL OF DIFFICULTY International Class N/A   Numerical Points   N/A

SUITABLE FOR: Cruising   **GRADIENT** (feet per mile): 0

APPROPRIATE FOR: Families, Beginners, Intermediates, Advanced

VELOCITY (mph): Lakes   **AVERAGE WIDTH** (ft): 200-900

MONTHS RUNNABLE: March 15 to October 15

RUNNABLE WATER LEVEL (cfs) Minimum N/A
   Maximum   N/A

MEAN WATER TEMPERATURE (°F) (Data not available)

Jan.	Feb.	Mar.	Apr.	May	Jun.
Jul.	Aug.	Sep.	Oct.	Nov.	Dec.

SOURCE OF ADDITIONAL INFORMATION ON WATER CONDITIONS
   BWMA (502) 224-2244

HAZARDS: None

RESCUE INDEX: D
 A Extremely remote; evacuation only with expert help—6 hours to secure assistance
 B Remote; 3-6 hours to secure assistance
 C Accessible but difficult; up to 3 hours to secure assistance—evacuation difficult
 D Accessible; up to 1 hour to secure assistance, evacuation not difficult

PORTAGES: None required

SCOUTING: None required

INTEREST HIGHLIGHTS: Scenery, history, wildlife

SCENERY: Beautiful to exceptionally beautiful

ACCESS POINT	ACCESS CODE	KEY
All	2 3 5 7	1 Paved Road
		2 Unpaved Road
		3 Short Carry
		4 Long Carry
		5 Easy Grade
		6 Steep Grade
		7 Clear Trail
		8 Brush and Trees
		9 Private Property, Permission Needed
		10 Launching Fee Charged
		11 No Access—For Reference Only

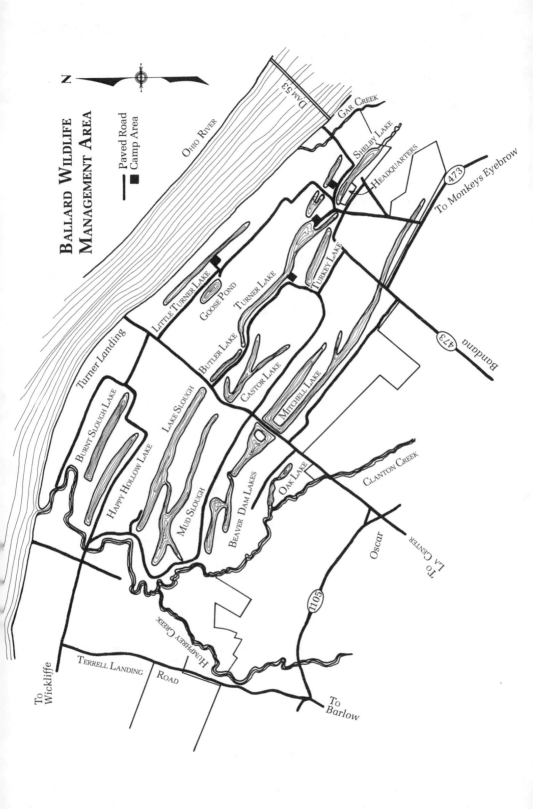

SECTION: Prices Mill to TN 161 bridge (Simpson Co., Logan Co.)

USGS QUADS: Prices Mill, Adairville, Dot, Allensville

LEVEL OF DIFFICULTY International Class I   Numerical Points **4**

SUITABLE FOR: Cruising   **GRADIENT** (feet per mile): **4.28**

APPROPRIATE FOR: Families, Beginners, Intermediates, Advanced

VELOCITY (mph): 2.6-5.0   **AVERAGE WIDTH** (ft): 50-70

MONTHS RUNNABLE: Late November to mid-June

RUNNABLE WATER LEVEL (cfs) Minimum **200**
   Maximum Up to flood stage

MEAN WATER TEMPERATURE (°F)

Jan. 40	Feb. 41	Mar. 45	Apr. 55	May 66	Jun. 77
Jul. 79	Aug. 77	Sep. 67	Oct. 62	Nov. 45	Dec. 41

SOURCE OF ADDITIONAL INFORMATION ON WATER CONDITIONS
   Adairville Police Dept. (502) 539-6131

HAZARDS: Deadfalls, low bridges

RESCUE INDEX: C-D
A Extremely remote; evacuation only with expert help—6 hours to secure assistance
B Remote; 3-6 hours to secure assistance
C Accessible but difficult; up to 3 hours to secure assistance—evacuation difficult
D Accessible; up to 1 hour to secure assistance, evacuation not difficult

PORTAGES: None required

SCOUTING: None required

INTEREST HIGHLIGHTS: Scenery, wildlife, local culture and industry

SCENERY: Pretty

ACCESS POINT	ACCESS CODE	KEY
AA	1 3 6 8 9	1 Paved Road
A	2 3 5 7	2 Unpaved Road
B	1 3 6 7	3 Short Carry
C	1 3 6 8	4 Long Carry
D	1 3 6 8	5 Easy Grade
E	1 3 5 8	6 Steep Grade
F	1 3 5 7	7 Clear Trail
G	1 3 6 8	8 Brush and Trees
H	1 3 6 7	9 Private Property, Permission Needed
		10 Launching Fee Charged
		11 No Access—For Reference Only

RED RIVER OF LOGAN COUNTY

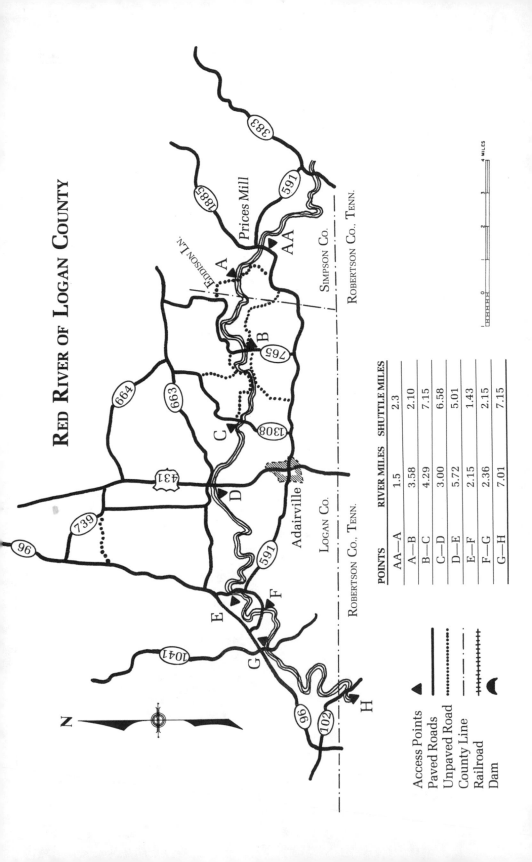

POINTS	RIVER MILES	SHUTTLE MILES
AA—A	1.5	2.3
A–B	3.58	2.10
B–C	4.29	7.15
C–D	3.00	6.58
D–E	5.72	5.01
E–F	2.15	1.43
F–G	2.36	2.15
G–H	7.01	7.15

Access Points
Paved Roads
Unpaved Road
County Line
Railroad
Dam

MILES

SECTION: U.S. 60 to Firetower Road (Meade Co.)

USGS QUADS: Flaherty, Rock Haven

LEVEL OF DIFFICULTY International Class II   Numerical Points **10**

SUITABLE FOR: Cruising   **GRADIENT** (feet per mile): **12.73**

APPROPRIATE FOR: Intermediates, Advanced

VELOCITY (mph): 2.6-5.0+   **AVERAGE WIDTH** (ft): 35-60

MONTHS RUNNABLE: December to mid-April and after heavy rains

RUNNABLE WATER LEVEL (cfs) Minimum **200**
     Maximum   Open: N/A   Decked: All levels

MEAN WATER TEMPERATURE (°F)

Jan. 42	Feb. 43	Mar. 46	Apr. 54	May 65	Jun. 77
Jul. 78	Aug. 78	Sep. 67	Oct. 61	Nov. 46	Dec. 42

SOURCE OF ADDITIONAL INFORMATION ON WATER CONDITIONS

Otter Creek Park (502) 942-3641
           (502) 583-3577

HAZARDS: Deadfalls, low trees

RESCUE INDEX: C-D
 A Extremely remote; evacuation only with expert help—6 hours to secure assistance
 B Remote; 3-6 hours to secure assistance
 C Accessible but difficult; up to 3 hours to secure assistance—evacuation difficult
 D Accessible; up to 1 hour to secure assistance, evacuation not difficult

PORTAGES: None required

SCOUTING: Dam at put-in

INTEREST HIGHLIGHTS: Scenery, local culture and industry

SCENERY: Pleasant to pretty spots

ACCESS POINT	ACCESS CODE	KEY
A	1 4 6 8	1 Paved Road
B	1 3 5 7	2 Unpaved Road
C	2 4 5 8	3 Short Carry
		4 Long Carry
		5 Easy Grade
		6 Steep Grade
		7 Clear Trail
		8 Brush and Trees
		9 Private Property, Permission Needed
		10 Launching Fee Charged
		11 No Access—For Reference Only

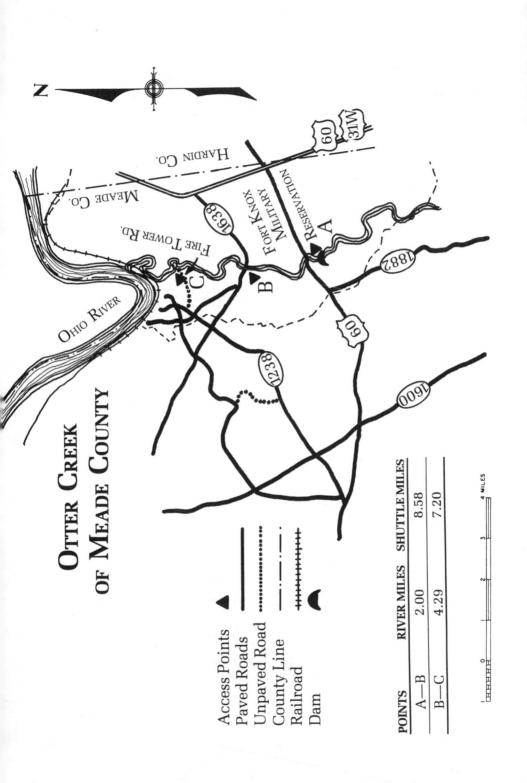

OTTER CREEK
OF MEADE COUNTY

N

OHIO RIVER

MEADE CO.

HARDIN CO.

FIRE TOWER RD.

1638

FORT KNOX MILITARY RESERVATION

C

B

A

1882

60

31W

60

1238

1600

Access Points	▲
Paved Roads	────
Unpaved Road	••••••
County Line	─·─·─
Railroad	─┼┼┼─
Dam	◄

POINTS	RIVER MILES	SHUTTLE MILES
A—B	2.00	8.58
B—C	4.29	7.20

0 1 2 3 4 MILES

SECTION: KY 53 to the Ohio River (Oldham Co., Jefferson Co.)

USGS QUADS: LaGrange, Owen, Anchorage, Jeffersonville

LEVEL OF DIFFICULTY International Class I-II   Numerical Points   7

SUITABLE FOR: Cruising   **GRADIENT** (feet per mile):   11.16

APPROPRIATE FOR: Beginners, Intermediates, Advanced

VELOCITY (mph): 2.6-5.0+   **AVERAGE WIDTH** (ft): 25-40

MONTHS RUNNABLE: November to early May and after heavy rains

RUNNABLE WATER LEVEL (cfs) Minimum   180
   Maximum   Up to flood stage

MEAN WATER TEMPERATURE (°F)

| Jan. 41 | Feb. 42 | Mar. 46 | Apr. 54 | May 66 | Jun. 77 |
| Jul. 77 | Aug. 77 | Sep. 68 | Oct. 61 | Nov. 45 | Dec. 41 |

SOURCE OF ADDITIONAL INFORMATION ON WATER CONDITIONS
   La Grange Police Dept. (502) 222-0111

HAZARDS: Deadfalls

RESCUE INDEX: C-D
A   Extremely remote; evacuation only with expert help—6 hours to secure assistance
B   Remote; 3-6 hours to secure assistance
C   Accessible but difficult; up to 3 hours to secure assistance—evacuation difficult
D   Accessible; up to 1 hour to secure assistance, evacuation not difficult

PORTAGES: None required

SCOUTING: None required

INTEREST HIGHLIGHTS: Scenery

SCENERY: Pretty to beautiful in spots

ACCESS POINT	ACCESS CODE	KEY
A	1 3 5 7	1 Paved Road
B	1 3 5 7	2 Unpaved Road
C	1 3 5 7	3 Short Carry
D	1 3 5 7	4 Long Carry
E	1 3 5 7 (10)	5 Easy Grade
		6 Steep Grade
		7 Clear Trail
		8 Brush and Trees
		9 Private Property, Permission Needed
		10 Launching Fee Charged
		11 No Access—For Reference Only

HARRODS CREEK

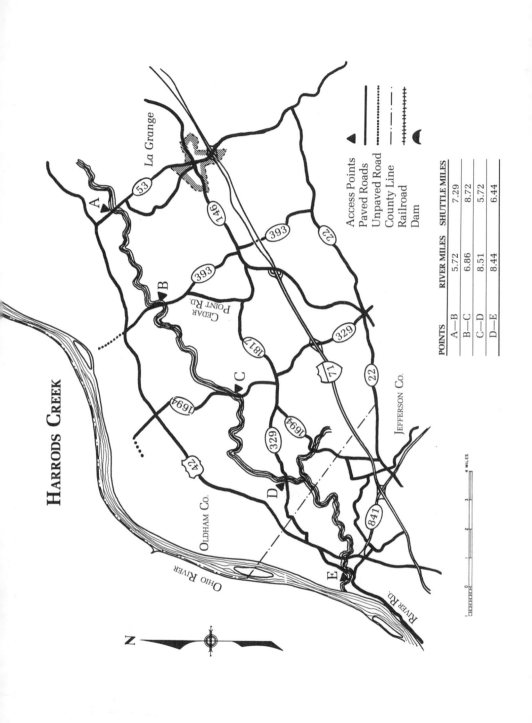

Access Points	◄
Paved Roads	
Unpaved Road	········
County Line	—·—·—
Railroad	+++++++
Dam	◖

POINTS	RIVER MILES	SHUTTLE MILES
A–B	5.72	7.29
B–C	6.86	8.72
C–D	8.51	5.72
D–E	8.44	6.44

SECTION: Sulphur to KY 316 (Henry Co., Trimble Co.)

USGS QUADS: Smithfield, Bedford, Campbellsburg

LEVEL OF DIFFICULTY International Class II   Numerical Points 9

SUITABLE FOR: Cruising   **GRADIENT** (feet per mile): 17.14

APPROPRIATE FOR: Advanced Beginners, Intermediates, Advanced

VELOCITY (mph): 2.6-5.0   **AVERAGE WIDTH** (ft): 35-55

MONTHS RUNNABLE: December to mid-May

RUNNABLE WATER LEVEL (cfs) Minimum   160
   Maximum   Up to high flood stage

MEAN WATER TEMPERATURE (°F)

Jan. 41	Feb. 43	Mar. 45	Apr. 54	May 66	Jun. 77
Jul. 79	Aug. 78	Sep. 66	Oct. 61	Nov. 45	Dec. 41

SOURCE OF ADDITIONAL INFORMATION ON WATER CONDITIONS
   None available

HAZARDS: Dams, deadfalls

RESCUE INDEX: C-D
   A Extremely remote; evacuation only with expert help—6 hours to secure assistance
   B Remote; 3-6 hours to secure assistance
   C Accessible but difficult; up to 3 hours to secure assistance—evacuation difficult
   D Accessible; up to 1 hour to secure assistance, evacuation not difficult

PORTAGES: Dam at point B

SCOUTING: None required

INTEREST HIGHLIGHTS: Scenery

SCENERY: Pleasant to pretty in spots

ACCESS POINT	ACCESS CODE	KEY
A	1 3 5 7	1 Paved Road
B	1 3 5 7	2 Unpaved Road
C	1 3 5 7	3 Short Carry
		4 Long Carry
		5 Easy Grade
		6 Steep Grade
		7 Clear Trail
		8 Brush and Trees
		9 Private Property, Permission Needed
		10 Launching Fee Charged
		11 No Access—For Reference Only

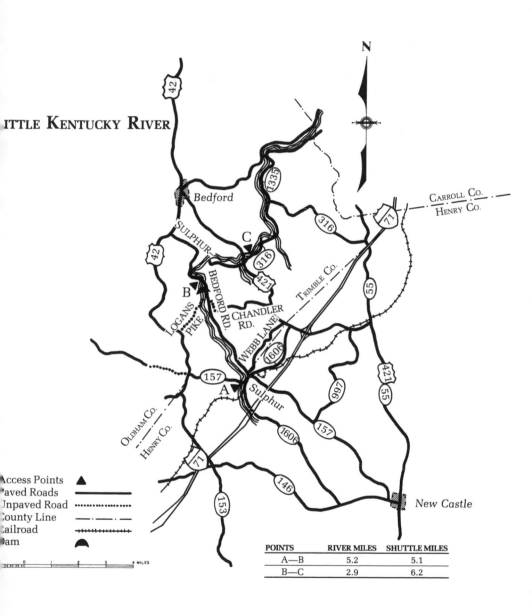

LITTLE KENTUCKY RIVER

N

42

Bedford

CARROLL CO.
HENRY CO.

1335

316

71

SULPHUR

C

42

BEDFORD RD.

316

421

TRIMBLE CO.

55

B

LOGANS PIKE

CHANDLER RD.

WEBB LANE

1606

421
55

157

A

Sulphur

997

OLDHAM CO.

HENRY CO.

1606

157

71

146

New Castle

153

Access Points
Paved Roads
Unpaved Road
County Line
Railroad
Dam

0   1   2   3   4 MILES

POINTS	RIVER MILES	SHUTTLE MILES
A—B	5.2	5.1
B—C	2.9	6.2

SECTION: Burnt Mill bridge to Leatherwood Ford (Scott Co., TN)

USGS QUADS: Oneida South, Honey Creek

LEVEL OF DIFFICULTY International Class III-IV Numerical Points 28

SUITABLE FOR: Cruising **GRADIENT** (feet per mile): 19.44

APPROPRIATE FOR: Open boats: Advanced Decked boats: Intermediates, Advanced

VELOCITY (mph): 2.6-5.0+ **AVERAGE WIDTH** (ft): 35-70

MONTHS RUNNABLE: Late November to early May

RUNNABLE WATER LEVEL (cfs) Minimum 450
  Maximum Open: 1200 Decked: 2000 (Intermediates), 6000 (Advanced)

MEAN WATER TEMPERATURE ($^\circ$F)

Jan. 41	Feb. 43	Mar. 47	Apr. 55	May 67	Jun. 77
Jul. 79	Aug. 79	Sep. 73	Oct. 64	Nov. 48	Dec. 41

SOURCE OF ADDITIONAL INFORMATION ON WATER CONDITIONS
  USGS (606) 549-2406

HAZARDS: Undercut rocks, difficult rapids

RESCUE INDEX: A-B
  A Extremely remote; evacuation only with expert help—6 hours to secure assistance
  B Remote; 3-6 hours to secure assistance
  C Accessible but difficult; up to 3 hours to secure assistance—evacuation difficult
  D Accessible; up to 1 hour to secure assistance, evacuation not difficult

PORTAGES: Routes around major rapids are extremely difficult

SCOUTING: Major rapids

INTEREST HIGHLIGHTS: Scenery, wildlife, geology, whitewater

SCENERY: Spectacular to exceptionally beautiful

ACCESS POINT	ACCESS CODE	KEY
AA	2 3 5 7	1 Paved Road
A	2 3 5 7	2 Unpaved Road
		3 Short Carry
		4 Long Carry
		5 Easy Grade
		6 Steep Grade
		7 Clear Trail
		8 Brush and Trees
		9 Private Property, Permission Needed
		10 Launching Fee Charged
		11 No Access—For Reference Only

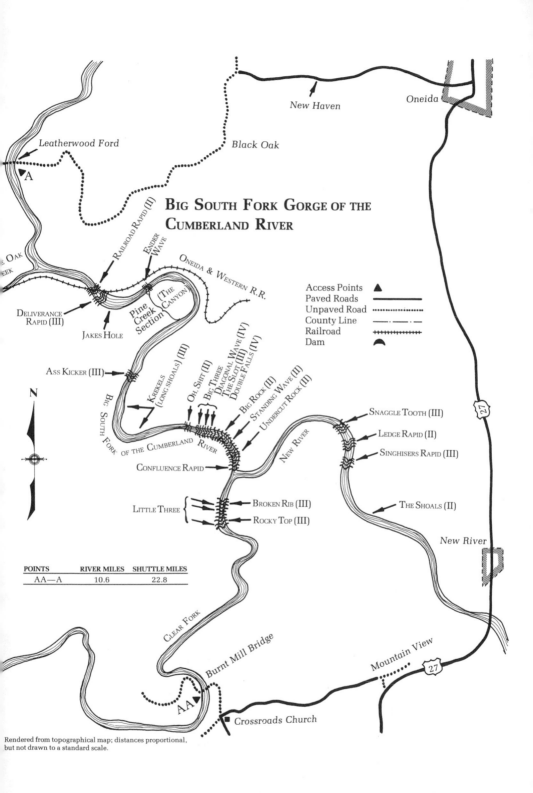

BIG SOUTH FORK GORGE OF THE CUMBERLAND RIVER

Oneida

New Haven

Oneida

Leatherwood Ford

Black Oak

▼A

RAILROAD RAPID (II)

ENDER WAVE

OE OAK CREEK

ONEIDA & WESTERN R.R.

DELIVERANCE RAPID (III)

Pine Creek Section

(THE CANYON)

JAKES HOLE

Access Points ▲
Paved Roads ———
Unpaved Road ••••••••••
County Line —•—•—
Railroad ++++++++
Dam ◠

ASS KICKER (III)

KREKELS (LONG SHOALS) (III)

OH, SHIT (II)

BIG THREE

DIAGONAL WAVE (IV)

THE SLOT (III)

DOUBLE FALLS (IV)

BIG ROCK (II)

STANDING WAVE (II)

UNDERCUT ROCK (II)

SNAGGLE TOOTH (III)

LEDGE RAPID (II)

SINGHISERS RAPID (III)

BIG SOUTH FORK OF THE CUMBERLAND RIVER

N

CONFLUENCE RAPID

NEW RIVER

THE SHOALS (II)

New River

LITTLE THREE {

BROKEN RIB (III)

ROCKY TOP (III)

POINTS	RIVER MILES	SHUTTLE MILES
AA—A	10.6	22.8

CLEAR FORK

Burnt Mill Bridge

Mountain View

27

AA ▼

■ Crossroads Church

Rendered from topographical map; distances proportional,
but not drawn to a standard scale.

SPECIAL SUPPLEMENT
CREEKS of MADISON COUNTY

CREEK DRAINAGES OF
MADISON COUNTY

MADISON COUNTY TRIBUTARIES
OF THE KENTUCKY RIVER

Along Interstate 75, across the Kentucky River and just south of Lexington lies Madison County, a region of limestone hills and numerous creek drainages. The northern border between Madison County and Lexington/Fayette Urban County is formed by twists and turns of the Kentucky River. The creeks that drain Madison County's farmland and small towns flow generally northward, tumbling over exposed limestone ledges on their way to the Kentucky River.

These creeks—Silver, Tates, Muddy, the Main Stem of Otter, the West Fork of Otter, and the East Prong of Otter—are all high-water runs, boatable during and soon after periods of heavy rains, most often from October through March. Many of the 100 or more members of the Bluegrass Wildwater Association live in Richmond, Lexington, Berea, and surrounding areas and have explored the half-dozen or so of the more promising high-water runs in Madison County on rainy evenings after work, or on that rare and fine Saturday morning following a Thursday and Friday of torrential rain.

Rainfall tends to be locally heavy in this region, with one creek drainage experiencing a frog-choker while adjacent drainages get next to none. The amount of rainfall required to bring the creeks up is highly variable, dependent upon water table, upstream development, type and state of foliage, and other factors. But any rainfall in excess of one and one-half inches in a 12-hour period is worth a few phone calls or an hour's drive in search of boating. Rain as measured in backyard rain gauges usually exceeds the "official" amount recorded at Bluegrass Airport in Lexington, so don't rely upon the Weather Service for boating conditions!

TOUR DE MADISON

With the smallest drainage areas, Tates Creek and the East Prong of Otter Creek rise, crest, and fall the most rapidly of Madison County's creeks. Put on Tates and East Prong during or immediately after torrential rains; they're usually runnable for only a couple of hours.

Otter Creek's West Fork and Main Stem rise and fall less rapidly, although the effects of recent (1992-'93) extensive commercial development upstream (K-Mart, WalMart, Richmond Mall and Carriage Gate Shopping Center on KY 876) and a new dam forming Lake Reba at Gibson Bay Golf Course remain to be seen. Run the East Prong or Tates first, then put on the West Fork or the Main Stem.

With a larger drainage area of 63 square miles, Muddy Creek usually has a lag time of 3 hours or more following a heavy rain, and often stays up overnight during the winter. If you are able to run Tates Creek or any of the branches of Otter Creek late one afternoon, check out Muddy the following morning.

Silver Creek, located west of Interstate 75 in the central and southern parts of the county, has the largest watershed of all of Madison County's creeks. With a drainage area of 112 miles, Silver Creek has the biggest water and stays up the longest. Silver usually won't rise for 24 hours following a heavy rain, and sometimes stays runnable for two days. A run on Muddy Creek one afternoon can be followed by a run on Silver the following morning.

The Bluegrass Wildwater Association's Handbook/membership list, available to members, is the best (only) source of local and current information on water levels. Contact the BWA at P.O. Box 4231, Lexington, KY 40504.

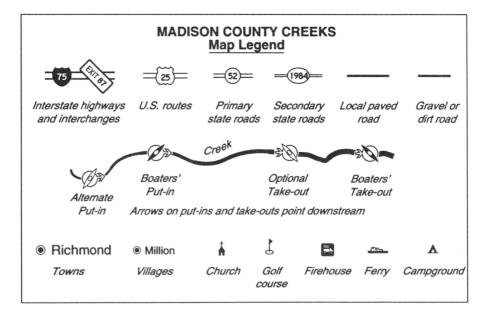

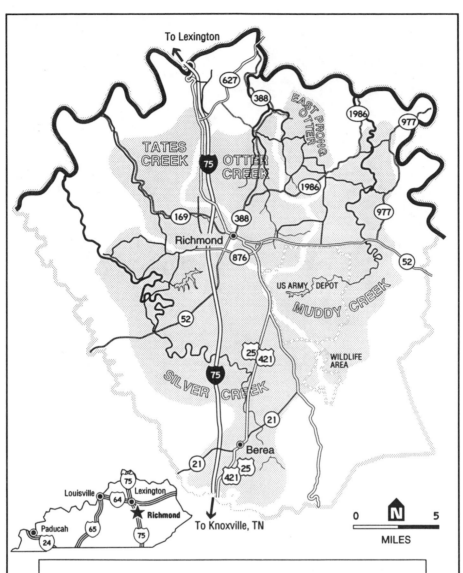

To Lexington

TATES CREEK

EAST PRONG OTTER

OTTER CREEK

Richmond

US ARMY DEPOT

MUDDY CREEK

WILDLIFE AREA

SILVER CREEK

Berea

Louisville   Lexington

Paducah   Richmond

To Knoxville, TN

0   N   5
MILES

Creek Drainages of Madison County, Kentucky

Drainage	Square Miles
Silver Creek	112
Muddy Creek	63
Otter Creek (Main Stem and West Fork)	42
Tates Creek	33
East Prong of Otter Creek	15

Shaded area indicates drainage areas above boaters' take-outs.

Kayaker running Silver Creek Ledge on the day after Christmas. Terry "Dr. Safety" Wyatt/Photo

SILVER CREEK

DESCRIPTION

While considered to be an easy but enjoyable Class II run at normal boatable levels, Silver Creek really rocks-n-rolls when bankfull or out of its banks. During full-on flood conditions, this creek might just be *too much* fun—eight-to-ten-foot waves, a bank-to-bank keeper hydraulic, numerous strainers, and mobile log jams all vie for the boater's attention.

The creek is very scenic, with herons and other bird species present along the way. Recent streambed dredging has detracted somewhat from the quality of the run, as have tornado blowdowns along the best paddling section, but any time spent paddling Silver Creek won't be deducted from the rest of your life.

PUT-IN

The standard put-in is on a tributary of Silver Creek, Taylor Fork, which drains a fishing impoundment called Wilgreen Lake. The put-in is reached from I-75's Exit 87 by heading west on KY 876 (Eastern Bypass or Barnes Mill Road). Turn left off Barnes Mill onto Curtis Pike and follow it to a small, paved road that leads to the dam at Wilgreen

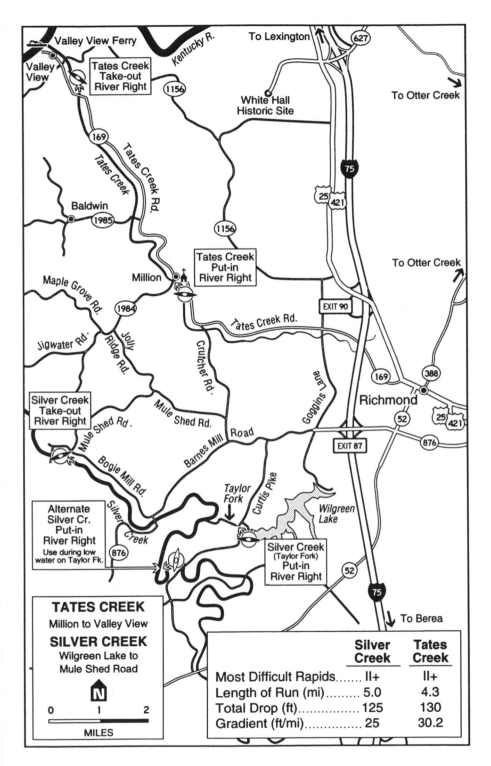

Valley View Ferry

To Lexington

627

Valley View

Tates Creek Take-out River Right

1156

Kentucky R.

To Otter Creek

White Hall Historic Site

169

Tates Creek Rd.

Tates Creek

Baldwin

1985

75

25
421

1156

Million

Tates Creek Put-in River Right

EXIT 90

To Otter Creek

Maple Grove Rd.

1984

Jigwater Rd.

Jolly Ridge Rd.

Crutcher Rd.

Tates Creek Rd.

169

388

Richmond

52

25
421

Silver Creek Take-out River Right

Mule Shed Rd.

Mule Shed Rd.

Barnes Mill Road

Goggins Lane

EXIT 87

876

Bogie Mill Rd.

Silver Creek

Taylor Fork

Curtis Pike

Wilgreen Lake

Alternate Silver Cr. Put-in River Right
Use during low water on Taylor Fk.

876

Silver Creek (Taylor Fork) Put-in River Right

52

75

To Berea

TATES CREEK
Million to Valley View
SILVER CREEK
Wilgreen Lake to Mule Shed Road

N

0	1	2

MILES

	Silver Creek	Tates Creek
Most Difficult Rapids	II+	II+
Length of Run (mi)	5.0	4.3
Total Drop (ft)	125	130
Gradient (ft/mi)	25	30.2

311

Lake. Turn left and park alongside the road. Taylor Fork lies in the woods across Curtis Pike. If Taylor Fork is too low, continue further on Curtis Pike to where a concrete bridge crosses Silver Creek and put in there.

TAKE-OUT

The normal take-out can be reached by following Barnes Mill Road west from the interstate to Bogie Mill Road, which continues straight on river right where Barnes Mill crosses Silver Creek from right to left on a concrete bridge. Follow Bogie Mill along the creek for about 2 miles, and continue on past Mule Shed Road to where a small bridge in poor condition crosses over to farmland. Park take-out vehicles near the bridge, making sure not to block access to it.

GAUGE

On your way to the take-out, stop and look at Silver Creek Ledge, a four-foot, river-wide drop just upstream of the bridge. This drop becomes a keeper at higher levels, and the recirculating boater usually has the company of several trees and utility poles. Use the Ledge as a gauge; what you see is what you get. If it looks like you'll scrape going over the Ledge, get ready for a low-water run. Use discretion when scouting and boating this section, as the land along much of the creek belongs to a single landowner who may not relate to your peaceable intentions.

HAZARDS

Hazards include strainers, brush piles, floating debris, dirty diapers, fences, and swinging bridges swept into the creek during high water. Additional hazards include the high-water keeper at the Ledge, and possibly unfriendly landowners.

TATES CREEK

DESCRIPTION

Tates Creek is the most accessible of Madison County's Creeks, as it flows alongside KY 169 (Tates Creek Road) just a few miles from I-75. It is a fun, quick little Class II stream with several decent drops and many play spots. One of the better stretches is near the concrete bridge where KY 1985 crosses over toward the community of Baldwin. During extreme high-water runs, the crests of the standing waves reach the underside of this bridge!

PUT-IN

To reach the put-in, take Exit 90 off I-75 and travel south on U.S. 25/421 to the yellow blinking light (before the center of Richmond). Turn right onto KY 169 (Tates Creek Road) and drive for several miles to the community of Million, marked by a white church on the left between the creek and the road. Park near the church, unless it's a Sunday morning or Wednesday evening, and put in on either side.

TAKE-OUT
The take-out for Tates Creek is downstream where KY 169 crosses from right to left on a concrete bridge. There is another take-out some distance upstream on a gravel road that tracks down to an old barn.

GAUGE
Check the water level at the Million Church—if it's over the road, you're on your own. If the creek has already crested and is too low, drive up KY 1984 from the church, left on Jolly Ridge Road, right on Mule Shed Road, and left on Bogie Mill Road to check the level on Silver Creek.

HAZARDS
Hazards along Tates Creek include strainers, especially along the section just upstream of the KY 1985 bridge that can't be road scouted. Additional dangers are posed by the activities of a tiny minority of the residents, who insist upon using the creek as a dump, sewage conduit, wrecking yard, and pet cemetery.

MUDDY CREEK

DESCRIPTION
While it lacks any single large drop or difficult rapid, Muddy Creek remains the run of choice on your Tour de Madison. If the Bluegrass Wildwater Association had a brothel, it would be Muddy Creek. Several small waterfalls add to the scenic quality of this run. While an easy Class II run at normal levels, the numerous small ledges form almost nonstop surfing waves and holes. At higher levels, there is a perfect river-wide, four-foot, glassy smooth bow surfing wave about one and one-half miles from the put-in. There is a park-and-surf where Cain Springs Road crosses the creek, and a triple drop/hole just above the take-out.

PUT-IN
The standard put-in is on Oakley Wells Road (a.k.a. Union City-College Hill Road) just downstream of the bridge crossing, where the unpaved section of the road runs along the creek on river left. Reach the put-in from Exit 87 on I-75 by taking KY 876 (Eastern Bypass) east all the way past Eastern Kentucky University, past Richmond Mall, through the intersection with U.S. 25/421, and turning right or east on KY 52. (Note on the map that 52 is first crossed at EKU—go straight through this intersection.) Take KY 52 east to Waco (the yellow blinking light) and turn left (north) onto KY 977 (College Hill Road). Follow College Hill Road for about three miles, to Oakley Wells Road—just

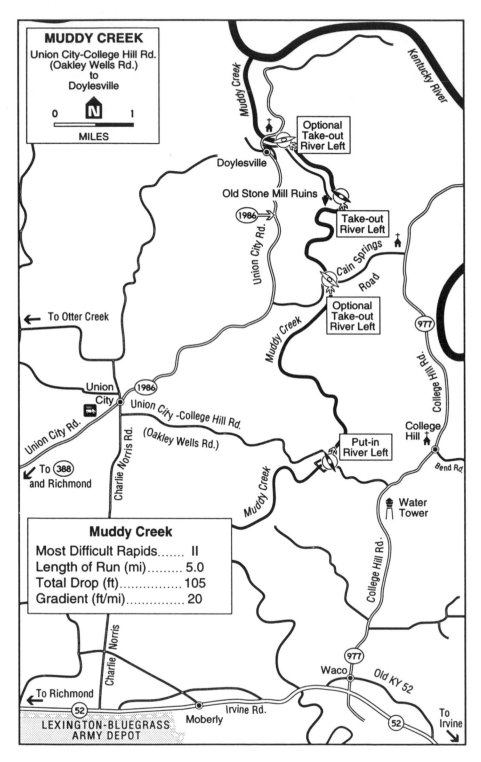

MUDDY CREEK

Union City-College Hill Rd.
(Oakley Wells Rd.)
to
Doylesville

0 _____ 1
MILES

Muddy Creek

Kentucky River

Optional
Take-out
River Left

Doylesville

Old Stone Mill Ruins

Take-out
River Left

1986

Union City Rd.

Cain Springs Road

Optional
Take-out
River Left

To Otter Creek

977

Muddy Creek

College Hill Rd.

Union City

1986

Union City - College Hill Rd.

(Oakley Wells Rd.)

College Hill

Union City Rd.

Charlie Norris Rd.

Put-in
River Left

Bend Rd.

To 388
and Richmond

Muddy Creek

Water
Tower

Muddy Creek

Most Difficult Rapids	II
Length of Run (mi)	5.0
Total Drop (ft)	105
Gradient (ft/mi)	20

College Hill Rd.

Charlie Norris

977

Waco

Old KY 52

To Richmond

52

Irvine Rd.

Moberly

52

To
Irvine

LEXINGTON-BLUEGRASS
ARMY DEPOT

past the water tower—and turn left down the hill towards the creek. Cross the creek and park out of the way on several gravel pull-outs on river left.

TAKE-OUT

The normal take-out can be reached by following Oakley Wells Road around the right-angle turn at the put-in. Don't go straight downstream on the dirt/gravel lane; that's a private drive. Go several miles to Charlie Norris Road and turn right into beautiful downtown Union City. Turn right again at the small market onto KY 1986, the Union City Expressway, and follow it into Doylesville. KY 1986 makes two 90° bends—first right, then left—just before the gravel road to the put-in enters the pavement from the right. If you cross Muddy Creek or reach the Doylesville Church, you've gone too far. Turn right off the paved road onto the gravel road and follow it to the end at the creek crossing near the old stone mill ruins. Park off the single lane road.

An intermediate take-out (or put-in?) can be found at the park-and-surf where Cain Springs Road crosses the creek. From the intersection of College Hill Road (KY 977) and Oakley Wells Road, continue north on KY 977 to Cain Springs Road, at the Cain Springs Primitive Baptist Church. Turn left down the hill to the creek crossing.

GAUGE

On your way to the put-in, look at Muddy Creek from the KY 52 crossing just before Waco. Again, what you see is what you get—if it looks runnable, it is.

HAZARDS

Hazards include the standards: strainers, brush piles, floating debris, disposable diapers, fences, and swinging bridges swept into the creek during high water.

OTTER CREEK (Main Stem and West Fork)

DESCRIPTION

Otter Creek's Main Stem and West Fork run downhill along KY 388 (Red House Road), next to the railroad tracks. Numerous small ledges create surfing spots at normal boatable levels, and keeper hydraulics at higher levels. Of particular interest to boaters on an auto-destruct sequence is Marrea's Hole, just upstream of the take-out.

PUT-IN

The standard put-in for the Main Stem can be reached by taking Exit 90 off of I-75 and heading south on U.S. 25/421 to downtown Richmond. Turn left at the courthouse onto KY 388 (Second Street, Red House Road) and follow KY 388 to Red House. Just before crossing

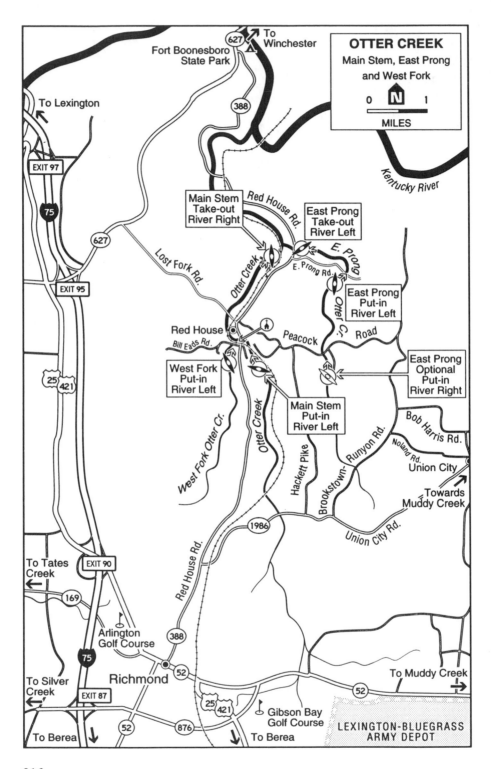

Otter Creek on KY 388, turn right onto a small, poor road that follows the creek back upstream on river left for about one hundred yards. Park out of the way near the creek. There is an additional put-in on the Main Stem where Lost Fork Road crosses as the road approaches Red House.

To boat the short distance down the West Fork before it joins the Main Stem, turn left off KY 388 at the Red House Church, onto Bill Eads Road. Drive several hundred yards upstream on river left and park at a turn-out on your left where Bill Eads turns right, away from the Creek.

TAKE-OUT

The take-out is reached by continuing downstream on KY 388 from Red House to where a small paved road leaves KY 388 on the left down a steep hill at a sharp angle downstream. The takeout is just beyond the uncontrolled railroad crossing, on river right, underneath the bridge crossing Otter Creek. Don't go across the bridge; this is a private drive.

GAUGE

You'll find out if it's runnable when you put on!

HAZARDS

Otter Creek is usually free of strainers above the take-out. Downstream of the take-out there are several large, submerged, brushy islands which present serious dangers to boaters. High water on Otter may produce several keeper hydraulics, generally just upstream of the take-out.

OTTER CREEK (East Prong)

DESCRIPTION

The East Prong of Otter Creek is the steepest of Madison County's creeks, with a gradient of over 35 feet per mile. At medium levels, this creek is a play-boater's fantasy, and at higher levels it's non-stop read and run to the take-out.

PUT-IN

The lower section of the East Prong is most commonly run, putting in where East Prong Road crosses the creek on a small bridge about

	Otter Creek	East Prong
Most Difficult Rapids	II	II+
Length of Run (mi)	5.3	2.8
Total Drop (ft)	120	100
Gradient (ft/mi)	22.6	35.7

one and one-half miles upstream from KY 388.

The put-in for the upper section of the East Prong, which has only been run a couple of times, can be reached by turning east off KY 388 onto Peacock Road in Red House. Follow Peacock Road up the hill to where a small road turns right just after Peacock Road crosses a tributary of the East Prong on a bridge. This road follows this stream for a few hundred yards on river right. Park where convenient and out of the way. *Don't put in further up the East Prong on Peacock Road, as there are several cattle fences that cross the stream, and eddies are not common.*

TAKE-OUT

The take-out for the East Prong is where East Prong Road intersects KY 388.

GAUGE

The only way to gauge this creek is to look at it.

HAZARDS

Hazards along the East Prong include strainers, particularly on the piers of the several small, private bridges crossing to residences on river right. Additional hazards are a scarcity of eddies at high water and steep drops. The upper section of the creek, between East Prong Road and Peacock Road, contains both steep gradient and an abundance of strainers. The upper, upper section along Peacock Road is crossed by several cattle fences and should not be run.

Thanks to the first descent team of Mike "Six Pack" Molnar, Terry "Dr. Safety" Wyatt, Butch "Table Saw" Quire, and Tim Krasnansky. Special thanks to David "I Don't See No Danger" Earle for sharing the hydrological data.

APPENDIX I

OUTFITTERS, CANOE RENTALS, AND GUIDE SERVICES

AMERICAN WHITEWATER, P.O. Box 23559, Columbus, Ohio 43223. Phone: (800) 837-3022. Runs trips on the Russel Fork.

BACKWOODS ADVENTURE, P.O. Box 4037, Oneida, Tennessee 37841. Phone: (615) 569-9573. Runs trips on the Big South Fork of the Cumberland.

CHEROKEE ADVENTURES, Route 1, P.O. Box 605, Erwin, Tennessee 37650. Phone: (800) 445-7238. Runs trips on the Russel Fork.

CUMBERLAND RAPID TRANSIT, Rockcreek Route, Box 200, Jamestown, Tennessee 38556. Phone: (615) 879-4818. Canoe rentals. Guided rafting and canoe trips on the Big South Fork of the Cumberland.

RIVER CREEK INN, 6301 Upper River Road, Harrods Creek, Kentucky 40027. Phone: (502) 228-4857. Canoe rentals on lower Harrods Creek near the Ohio River. No shuttle service, canoes must paddle back to point of departure.

ROCKCASTLE ADVENTURES, P.O. Box 662, London, Kentucky 40741. Phone: (606) 864-9407. Canoe and kayak rentals, new and used canoes and kayaks for sale. Shuttle service for day, weekend, and extended trips on Rockcastle River. Jim Honchell, owner.

RUSSEL FORK WHITEWATER ADVENTURES, P.O. Box 434, Big Rock, Virginia 24603. Phone: (703) 530-7044 or (703) 530-7243. Runs trips on Russel Fork, both full and split (non-canyon) trips. Danny and Darlene Elswick, owners.

SHELTOWEE TRACE OUTFITTERS, P.O. Box 1060, Whitely City, Kentucky 42653. Phone: (800) 541-7238 or (606) 679-5026. Runs trips on the Big South Fork of the Cumberland.

USA RAFT, P.O. Box 277, Rowlesburg, West Virginia 26425. Phone: (800) 872-7238. Runs trips on the Russel Fork.

KENTUCKY PADDLING CLUBS

VIKING CANOE CLUB: The Viking Canoe Club has an active membership of both decked and open boaters. The club runs a varied program consisting of cruises for paddlers of all skill levels, training clinics, and social outings. Business meetings are held on the third Monday of odd-numbered months. Business is usually transacted in short order and is followed by a program and refreshments. Six times a year a club newsletter is published. Individual membership costs $15.00 a year with family memberships included. Further information concerning activities and membership can be obtained by writing Viking Canoe Club, P.O. Box 32263, Louisville, Kentucky 32263.

CANOEING ORGANIZATIONS

NATIONAL

AMERICAN CANOE ASSOCIATION, 4260 East Evans Ave., Denver, CO 80222

AMERICAN WHITE WATER AFFILIATION, P.O. Box 1854, San Bruno, CA 94066

U.S. CANOE ASSOCIATION, P.O. Box 9, Winamac, IN 46996

NEIGHBORING STATES

GEORGIA CANOEING ASSOCIATION, INC., Box 7023, Atlanta, GA 30357

CAROLINA CANOE CLUB, Box 9011, Greensboro, NC 27408

KEEL-HAULERS CANOE CLUB, 1649 Allen Drive, Westlake, OH 44145

Kentucky River   Photograph courtesy of the Commonwealth of Kentucky, Department of Public Information

APPENDIX II

RANGER DISTRICT HEADQUARTERS

DANIEL BOONE NATIONAL FOREST, U.S. FOREST SERVICE, 100 Vaught Road, Winchester, Kentucky 40391.
Phone: (606) 745-3100
MOOREHEAD RANGER DISTRICT HEADQUARTERS, P.O. Box 910, Moorehead, Kentucky 40351.
Phone: (606) 784-5624
STANTON RANGER DISTRICT HEADQUARTERS, Don Fig, 705 W. College Ave., Stanton, Kentucky 40380.
Phone: (606) 663-2852
BEREA RANGER DISTRICT HEADQUARTERS, 1835 Big Hill Road, Berea, Kentucky 40403.
Phone: (606) 986-8434
LONDON RANGER DISTRICT HEADQUARTERS, Highway U.S. 25 South, London, Kentucky 40741.
Phone: (606) 864-4164
SOMERSET RANGER DISTRICT HEADQUARTERS, 156 Realty Ln., Somerset, Kentucky 42501.
Phone: (606) 679-2018
STEARNS RANGER DISTRICT HEADQUARTERS, Highway U.S. 27 (3 miles north of Whitley City), P.O. Box 429, Whitley City, Kentucky 42653.
Phone: (606) 376-5323
REDBIRD RANGER DISTRICT HEADQUARTERS, Garnet Wood, HC 68, P.O. Box 65, Big Creek, Kentucky 40914.
Phone: (606) 598-2192

GLOSSARY OF PADDLING TERMS

BOTTOM. The stream bottoms described in this guide allude to what the paddler sees as opposed to the geological composition of the river bed. From a geologist's perspective, for example, the Kentucky River may flow over a limestone bed. The paddler, however, because of the overlying silt and sediment, perceives the bottom as being mud.

BOW. The front of a boat.

BROACHING. A boat that is sideways to the current and usually out of control or pinned to an obstacle in the stream.

CFS. Cubic feet per second; an accurate method of expressing river flow in terms of function of flow and volume.

C-1. One-person, decked canoe equipped with a spray skirt; frequently mistaken for a kayak. The canoeist kneels in the boat and uses a single-bladed paddle.

C-2. A two-person, decked canoe; frequently mistaken for a two-person kayak.

CHUTE. A clear channel between obstructions that has faster current than the surrounding water.

CURLER. A wave that curls or falls back on itself (upstream).

DEADFALLS. Trees that have fallen into the stream totally or partially obstructing it.

DECKED BOAT. A completely enclosed canoe or kayak fitted with a spray skirt. When the boater is properly in place, this forms a nearly waterproof unit.

DOWNSTREAM FERRY. A technique for moving sideways in the current while facing downstream. Can also be done by "surfing" on a wave.

DOWNWARD EROSION. The wearing away of the bottom of a stream by the current.

DRAINAGE AREA. Officially defined as an area measured in a horizontal plane, enclosed by a topographic divide, from which direct surface runoff from precipitation normally drains by gravity into a stream above a specified point. In other words, this is an area that has provided the water on which you are paddling at any given time. Accordingly, the drainage area increases as you go downstream. The drainage basin of a river is expressed in square miles. (Also known as a "watershed.")

DROP. Paddler's term for **GRADIENT.**

EDDY. The water behind an obstruction in the current or behind a river bend. The water may be relatively calm or boiling and will flow upstream.

EDDY LINE. The boundary at the edge of an eddy between two currents of different velocity and direction.

EDDY OUT. See **EDDY TURN.**

EDDY TURN. Maneuver used to move into an eddy from the downstream current.

ESKIMO ROLL. The technique used to upright an overturned decked canoe or kayak, by the occupant, while remaining in the craft. This is done by coordinated body motion and usually facilitated by the proper use of the paddle.

EXPERT BOATER. A person with extensive experience and good judgment who is familiar with up-to-date boating techniques, practical hydrology, and proper safety practices. An expert boater never paddles alone and always uses the proper equipment.

FALLS. A portion of river where the water falls freely over a drop. This designation has nothing to do with hazard rating or difficulty. See **RAPIDS.**

FERRY. Moving sideways to the current facing either up- or downstream.

FLOTATION. Additional buoyant materials (air bags, styrofoam, inner tubes, etc.) placed in a boat to provide displacement of water and extra buoyancy in case of upset.

GRAB LOOPS. Loops (about 6 inches in diameter) of nylon rope or similar material attached to the bow and stern of a boat to facilitate rescue.

GRADIENT. The geographical drop of the river expressed in feet per mile.

HAYSTACK. A pyramid-shaped standing wave caused by deceleration of current from underwater resistance.

HEADWARD EROSION. The wearing away of the rock strata forming the base of ledges or waterfalls by the current.

HEAVY WATER. Fast current, large waves, usually associated with holes and boulders.

HYDRAULIC. General term for souse holes and backrollers, where there is a hydraulic jump (powerful current differential), and strong reversal current.

K-1. One-person, decked kayak equipped with spray skirt. In this guidebook, this category does not include nondecked kayaks. The kayaker sits in the boat with both feet extended forward. A double-bladed paddle is used.

KEEPER. A souse hole or hydraulic with sufficient vacuum in its trough to hold an object (paddler, boat, log, etc.) that floats into it for an undetermined time. Extremely dangerous and to be avoided.

LATERAL EROSION. The wearing away of the sides or banks of a stream by the current.

LEDGE. The exposed edge of a rock stratum that acts as a low, natural dam or as a series of such dams.

LEFT BANK. Left side of river when facing downstream.

LINING. A compromise between portaging and running a rapids. By the use of a rope (line), a boat can be worked downstream from the shore.

LOGJAM. A jumbled tangle of fallen trees, branches, and sometimes debris that totally or partially obstructs a stream.

LOW-WATER BRIDGE. A bridge across the river that barely clears the surface of the water or may even be awash; very dangerous for the paddler if in a fast current.

POOL. A section of water that is usually deep and quiet; frequently found below rapids and falls.

RAPIDS. Portion of a river where there is appreciable turbulence usually accompanied by obstacles. *See* **FALLS.**

RIFFLES. Slight turbulence with or without a few rocks tossed in; usually Class I on the International Scale of River Difficulty.

RIGHT SIDE. The right bank of the river as you progress downstream.

ROCK GARDEN. Rapids that have many exposed or partially submerged rocks necessitating intricate maneuvering or an occasional carry over shallow places.

ROLLER. Also **CURLER** or **BACKROLLER;** it is a wave that falls back on itself.

SCOUT. To look at a rapids from the shore to decide whether or not to run it, or to facilitate selection of a suitable route through the rapids.

SECTION. A portion of river located between two points. *See* **STRETCH.**

SHUTTLE. Movement of at least two vehicles to the take-out and one back to the put-in. Used to avoid having to paddle back upstream at the end of a run.

SLIDE RAPIDS. An elongated ledge that descends or slopes gently rather than abruptly, and is covered usually with only shallow water.

SOUSE HOLE. A wave at the bottom of a ledge that curls back on itself. Water enters the trough of the wave from the upstream and downstream sides with reversal (upstream) current present downstream of the trough.

SPRAY SKIRT. A hemmed piece of waterproof material resembling a short skirt, having an elastic hem fitting around the boater's waist and an elastic hem fitting around the cockpit rim of a decked boat.

STANDING WAVE. A regular wave downstream of submerged rocks that does not move in relation to the riverbed (as opposed to a moving one such as an ocean wave).

STERN. The back end of a boat.

STOPPER. Any very heavy wave or turbulence that quickly impedes the downriver progress of a rapidly paddled boat.

STRETCH. A portion of river located between two points. *See* **SECTION**.

SURFING. The technique of sitting on the upstream face of a wave or traveling back and forth across the wave when ferrying.

SURFING WAVE. A very wide wave that is fairly steep. A good paddler can slide into it and either stay balanced on its upstream face or else travel back and forth across it much in the same manner as a surfer in the ocean.

TECHNICAL WHITEWATER. Whitewater where the route is often less than obvious and where manuevering in the rapids is frequently required.

THWART. Cross pieces used to reinforce the gunwales of an open canoe.

TRIM. The balance of a boat in the water. Paddlers and duffel should be positioned so the waterline is even from bow to stern and the boat does not list to either side.

UNDERCUT ROCK. A potentially dangerous situation where a large boulder has been eroded or undercut by water flow and could trap a paddler accidentally swept under it.

UPSTREAM FERRY. Similar to **DOWNSTREAM FERRY** except the paddler faces upstream. *See also* **SURFING**.

INDEX

Alphabetical Listing of Streams

CANOE—CAMPING STREAMS

WHITEWATER STREAMS